MAW RU... REVIEW

VOLUME 2   2011

The *Mawlana Rumi Review* is an annual academic review devoted to the life, thought, poetry and legacy of Mawlana (an honorific meaning 'Our master') Jalal al-Din Rumi (d.1273). It is a publication of the Rumi Institute, Near East University, Cyprus, and the Rumi Studies Group at the Centre for Persian and Iranian Studies, Institute of Arab and Islamic Studies, University of Exeter, UK. *Website* http://www.mawlanarumireview.com

The *Mawlana Rumi Review* publishes articles, reports, poems, review articles and book reviews in English and French. The editor welcomes articles on Rumi's art of story-telling, poetic imagery, theology, spiritual psychology, ecumenism, erotic spirituality, pedagogy, hermeneutics, ethics, epistemology, prophetology, metaphysics, cosmology, the heritage of Rumi's thought in modern and medieval literary history, interpretation and commentary of his works such as the *Mathnawi* and *Divan-i Shams-i Tabrizi*, and literary translations of his poetry.

Submissions
Address all corrrespondence to the Editor:
Dr Leonard Lewisohn
Institute of Arab and Islamic Studies, University of Exeter,
Stocker Road, Exeter, EX4 4ND, UK
Email: l.lewisohn@exeter.ac.uk

General enquiries concerning subscription and distribution address to:
Mr Yasin Salazar, Managing Editor,
Mawlana Rumi Review
119 Charterhouse Street, London, EC1M 6AA, UK
Email: info@mawlanarumireview.com

Subscription rates
Institutional rate: US$23/UK£15/€17
Personal rate: US$20/UK£13/€14
Postage to UK and Europe, add: £2/€2
Postage to the rest of the world, add: US$4/UK£3/€3

Payment can be made by accessing this link to the publisher and distributor (Archetype): www.archetypebooks.com

MAWLANA RUMI REVIEW

VOLUME 2   2011

Editor
LEONARD LEWISOHN
University of Exeter, UK

Managing and Book Review Editor
YASIN SALAZAR
Matmedia Productions, London, UK

Assistant Editors
LEILI ANVAR-CHENDEROFF – INALCO, Paris, France
RODERICK GRIERSON
Near East University, Nicosia, Cyprus
FRANKLIN LEWIS – University of Chicago, USA
JAMES MORRIS – Boston College, USA
SHAHRAM PAZOUKI
Iranian Institute of Philosophy, Tehran, Iran
MUHAMMAD ISA WALEY – British Library, UK

Poetry Editor
PAUL LOSENSKY
Indiana University, USA

First published in 2011 by Archetype
on behalf of the Rumi Institute (Founding Director, Gökalp Kâmil),
Near East University, Cyprus,
and the Rumi Studies Group at the Centre for Persian and Iranian Studies,
Institute of Arab and Islamic Studies, University of Exeter, UK

Title calligraphy by Tom Perkins
Figural calligraphy on back cover by Jila Peacock
Typeset by Agnesi Text, Hadleigh, Suffolk
Printed by Imprint Digital, Exeter

ISSN   2042–3357
ISBN   978–1–901383–42–3

Mawlana Rumi Review
ADVISORY COUNCIL

Contents

Cover Illustration: 'Derviches Tourneurs' or 'Turning Dervishes'

Roderick Grierson

The title appears in both French and English on a folio chromolithograph first published in 1858 as part of the album *Stamboul: Recollections of Eastern Life*. Printed by Lemercier & Cie. in Paris, the lithograph was based upon a watercolour that Amadeo Preziosi had painted in 1857.

Aloysius Rosarius Amadeus Raymondus Andreas Preziosi was the fifth Count Preziosi, and was born in 1816 on the island of Malta to a family ennobled almost a century earlier by the Duke of Savoy and King of Sicily. Despite his father's opposition, Preziosi became fascinated by painting as a child and was eventually trained in Paris. As Malta was a British colony, he travelled on a British passport when he made his way through Italy and toward the Ottoman capital in 1842. Forty years later, he would be buried in a village nearby after dying in a shooting accident. A prolific artist, his studio was conveniently located opposite the British Embassy in Pera, and much of his work was commissioned by the diplomatic community. During a visit to the city in 1869, the Prince of Wales purchased a number of his paintings.

The lithograph reproduced on the cover, which I purchased from Eren Kitabevi in Istanbul, depicts a *sema* in the Galata Mevlevihanesi, not far from Preziosi's studio, after it was rebuilt by Mahmud II in 1834. It is typical of a style that is rightly described as 'romantic or picturesque' but nevertheless 'generally accurate'. Although the composition is foreshortened, and suggests a more confined space than the artist would actually have seen, the *semahane* and the *semazen*s have been depicted with an attention to detail that modern scholars of the Mevlevi will find intriguing. While it is noticeable that the short jacket or *destegül* should be tied on the right rather than on the left, it would appear to have been reversed when the design was transferred to a lithographic plate. It is also noticeable that the semazens are dressed in a variety of colours, rather than the uniform white that is usually seen today, and that they are not wearing *başmak* (*paşmak*) on their feet. A preliminary watercolour depicting only the central figure is preserved at the Victoria and Albert Museum in London (SD.834). The *destegül* in the watercolour is tied correctly. A second watercolour in the same collection (SD.835) includes the entire composition with minor variations, the most notable being the *semazenbaşı* who stands on the right of the semazens rather than the left.[1]

---

1 Two catalogues of Preziosi's work are of particular interest: B. Llewellyn and C. Newton, *The People and Places of Constantinople: Watercolours by Amadeo Count Preziosi*, Victoria and Albert Museum exhibition catalogue (London 1985); and B. Kovulmaz, ed., *Amadeo Preziosi*, Yapı Kredi Kazım Taşkent Sanat Galerisi exhibition catalogue (Istanbul 2007). The opinion of Preziosi's style cited above is that of N. Micklewright ('Dervish Images in Photographs and Paintings', in R. Lifchez, ed., *The Dervish Lodge* (Berkeley, Los Angeles, and Oxford: University of California Press 1992), pp. 269–83).

A *Ghazal* from Rumi's *Divan-i Shams-i Tabrizi*

The Uses of Adversity

Translated by Franklin Lewis

To be intimate with Love. What is it?
To be cut off from heart's desire! Not else.
To be bloodied and swallow one's own blood.
To be doggedly at fidelity's door.

They'll sacrifice their life; it's all the same –
To be, to die and to 'move on' – to them.
Go, Muslim, be shielded by faith's peace, but
to be saintly, spotless, always strive. Strive!
Saints, the true witnesses, long for true death:
To be self-effaced – with this they're in love.
You flee from tribulation, fate's decree;
To be tribulation-free, that's what they fear.

Fast. Past Ramadan. And on Ashura.
To be at Karbala, you are unable.[1]

---

1 Rūmī, *Kulliyāt-i Shams yā Dīvān-i kabīr*, ed. B. Furūzānfar (Tehran: Amīr Kabīr 1355
A.Hsh./1976), V, p. 290; *ghazal* 2102, vv. 22198–204.

The Sword of *Lā* and the Fire of Love

WILLIAM C. CHITTICK

Numerous commentaries have been written on Rūmī's *Mathnawī* over the centuries trying to explain his teachings, but exposition of his thought nonetheless remains a daunting task, to put it mildly.[1] Among twentieth-century authors, few have paid more attention to this topic than the great Iranian scholar Jalāl al-Dīn Humā'ī, who died in the early 1980s. I had the pleasure of studying with him at Tehran University when he was persuaded to take a year off from retirement during the academic year 1968–69. One day in class he was bemoaning the fact that, as he put it, the new generation of scholars knew everything there was to know about a text: the life of its author, historical context, sources, literary techniques, textual variants of the manuscripts. However, they had no idea *what* the texts were saying. A few years later he published a book called 'The Rūmī Book' (*Mawlawī-nāma*) whose subtitle was, 'What is Rūmī Saying?' (*Mawlawī chih mīgūyad*). Clearly, he wanted to remedy what he saw as the gaping holes in contemporary Iranian scholarship on Rūmī. Professor Humā'ī was himself magnificently learned, even if he did not always find it possible to get right to the point – if, indeed, that be possible with Rūmī – and his book eventually came to fill two hefty volumes in 1100 pages. Although my discussion here is comparatively brief, in fact, less than one per cent the length of his grand study, I will endeavour to focus on what appears to me as Rūmī's core message.

Everyone knows that the appearance of Shams-i Tabrīzī acted as a catalyst in Rūmī's life. Before Shams, Rūmī was recognized as a man of learning and respected by other scholars. He was well versed in the

---

1 This essay was originally presented as a lecture at 'A Conference in Celebration of Molana Jalal ad-Din Mohammad Molavi Rumi' in November 2007 at the College of the Humanities, Carleton University, Ottawa.

Islamic sciences, including the Qur'ān, the Prophet's traditions (*Ḥadīth*), jurisprudence, scholastic theology (*Kalām*), and philosophy. He was probably trained best in Sufism, which was a standard part of the advanced curriculum. In its various theoretical forms, it provided a science of the human soul in relation both to God and the universe at large. This issue was important to every thoughtful person, but the only other stream of Islamic learning that addressed it was philosophy. Most Muslims, however, found philosophy too abstract and theoretical, and they did not appreciate the fact that the philosophers tended to keep the Qur'ān and the *Ḥadīth* at arm's length.

So, when people wanted to understand the secret of human embodiment and the nature of the human soul, most of them sought answers from the Sufis. Moreover, Sufism had an extremely broad appeal, because its teachers spoke to everyone, not just to scholars, and they offered the means to intensify one's personal engagement with God. In contrast, jurisprudence and *Kalām* were scholarly pursuits. Jurists, to the extent that they did address the common people, instructed them how to act in accordance with God's commandments. Experts in *Kalām* had nothing to do with non-experts other than to tell them in rather dogmatic terms what they should think about God. As for Sufi teachers, they explained to both the elite and the commoners how to find God's presence in everyday life.

According to the usual accounts, Rūmī was an erudite scholar with only a superficial understanding of Sufism, and Shams was an illiterate vagabond, intoxicated by love for God. Shams proceeded to convert Rūmī from the sober religion of scholarship to the drunken religion of love, enamoured of music and dance. This is a good story, and as a rough and ready picture of what happened, it is fine, but it can hardly be considered historically accurate. We know that Shams was far from illiterate, nor was he an easy-going and likeable guy, as we might imagine from all the talk of intoxication and love. In fact, he was a professional Qur'ān teacher and was familiar with Qur'ān commentary, jurisprudence, and philosophy; on a personal level, he was a terror, an extremely exacting taskmaster who held in contempt the meagre attempts at spiritual guidance that he saw in the teachers of Konya. Moreover, Shams recognized that Rūmī was already an accomplished Sufi master. He himself put it this way:

When I came to Mawlānā, the first stipulation was that I was not coming to be a shaykh. God has not yet brought to the face of the earth someone who could be Mawlānā's shaykh. That would not be a mortal. And I am not such that I could be a disciple. Nothing of that remains for me.[2]

My purpose is not to try to explain the role of Shams in Rūmī's transformation. Rather, I bring him up simply because the standard picture of his role highlights the core emphasis of Rūmī's teachings: Neither Shams nor the mature Rūmī had much patience with the pre-occupations of scholars. Both held that the true purpose of knowledge was to guide people on the path of self-realization, that is, the path of coming to know and love God and to achieve spiritual transformation. Scholarship, even in their time, was too caught up with the outward appearance of knowledge rather than its essence and purpose. More often than not it was considered a means to acquire respect from the community and to earn a nice stipend from a school or a university. As Shams says,

The reason these people study in the madrasahs is, they think, 'We'll become tutors, we'll run madrasahs.' They say, 'Good deeds – one must act beautifully!' They talk of such things in these assemblies so that they can get positions.

Why do you study knowledge for the sake of worldly mouthfuls? This rope is for people to come out of the well, not for them go from this well into that well.

You must bind yourself to knowing this: 'Who am I? What substance am I? Why have I come? Where am I going? From whence is my root? At this time what am I doing? Toward what have I turned my face?'[3]

It is often difficult for us moderns to understand that for the Sufi tradition, education was a means to prepare oneself for self-awareness, enlightenment and re-unification with the source of all being and all knowledge. Rūmī refers to this point when he says in his *Fīhi mā fīh*,

---

2 W. C. Chittick (trans.), *Me & Rumi: The Autobiography of Shams-i Tabrizi* (Louisville: Fons Vitae 2004), p. 212.   3 Ibid., pp. 50–51.

These people who have studied or are now studying imagine that if they attend faithfully here they will forget and abandon all their knowledge. On the contrary, when they come here their sciences all acquire a spirit. The sciences are all paintings. When they gain spirits, it is as if a lifeless body receives a spirit. The root of all these sciences is up yonder, but they have been transported from the world without sounds and letters into the world of sounds and letters.[4]

In this way of looking at things, all knowledge points toward the Supreme Reality that gave rise to the universe and the human soul. Seekers of knowledge should be striving to travel from the paintings and pictures to the divine spirit that dwells up yonder and animates themselves and the entire universe.

Two Sorts of Knowing

If we take a broad view of the quest for knowledge, it is not too difficult to see that most religious traditions acknowledge two basic sorts of knowing. Muslim sources have often differentiated them by speaking of the knowers or scholars ('ulamā'), and the recognizers, realizers or gnostics ('urafā'). The 'ulamā' are those who have learned everything they know from books and teachers. The 'urafā' are those who have followed the prophets on the path to self-realization and have found the spirit that animates the paintings and pictures. In a typical passage, Rūmī calls the gnostics 'Sufis' and explains the difference like this:

> The Sufi's book is not composed of ink and letters:
>   It is nothing but a heart white as snow.
> The scholar's provisions are the marks of the pen.
>   What are the Sufi's provisions? The footprints of the saints.[5]

Many Sufis and philosophers, including both Shams and Rūmī, distinguished between book learning and real knowledge by employ-

---

4 *Fīhi mā fīh*, ed. Badīʿ al-Zamān Furūzānfar (Tehran: Amīr Kabīr 1348 A.Hsh./1969), p. 156.
5 Rūmī, *Mathnawī-yi maʿnawī*, ed. R. A. Nicholson (Tehran: Amīr Kabīr 1357 A.Hsh./1978), II: 159–60.

ing the terms *taqlīd* or 'imitation' and *taḥqīq* or 'realization'. *Taqlīd* comes from the same root as *qalāda*, necklace or collar, and it means to follow someone else's opinion. *Taḥqīq* comes from the same root as *ḥaqq*, a Qur'ānic name of God that means truth, reality, rightness and appropriateness. Literally, realization (*taḥqīq*) means to actualize the truth (*ḥaqq*) of something. In the technical language of the Islamic intellectual tradition, it means to recognize God as the Supreme Reality and Absolute Truth and to act accordingly.

Another important term deriving from the same root as *taḥqīq* and *ḥaqq* is *ḥaqīqat*, which also means reality and truth. In one of the most common ways of explaining the totality of the Islamic tradition, *ḥaqīqat* is used to designate the ultimate goal of the religion, the Divine Reality that all seekers are striving to reach. In order to do so, people must follow the *Sharīʿat*, that is, the revealed law of Islam, and the *Ṭarīqat*, that is, the path of spiritual discipline that is taught by the Sufi shaykhs. In the introduction to Book Five of the *Mathnawī*, Rūmī explains how *Sharīʿat*, *Ṭarīqat*, and *Ḥaqīqat* are interrelated:

> The *Sharīʿat* is like a candle that shows the road. Without bringing a candle to hand, you will not be able to go forward on the road. When you walk on the road, your walking is the *Ṭarīqat*. When you reach the goal, that is the *Ḥaqīqat*. . . . The *Sharīʿat* is like learning the science of medicine. The *Ṭarīqat* is to avoid certain foods and take certain remedies according to this science. The *Ḥaqīqat* is to find everlasting health and to have no more need for the science and the remedies. . . . The *Sharīʿat* is knowledge, the *Ṭarīqat* is works, and the *Ḥaqīqat* is reaching God.

Reaching God then, is the goal of the spiritual quest, and it is commonly called realization, *taḥqīq*. No one can achieve realization without passing beyond imitation, *taqlīd*, which is ordinary, everyday knowledge, derived from ink and letters, that is, from hearsay. After all, what we know – or rather, what we think we know – is simply what we have heard and what we have read. We are not sure about any of it, even if it happens to be our deepest assumptions and our most cherished beliefs. We do not know that these are true, we simply trust that they are. In contrast, achieving realization means not simply knowing in a cognitive way, but rather undergoing a profound spiritual transformation by attaining oneness with the *Ḥaqīqat*, the

Source of all being and all knowing. At this stage of human development, there is no distinction to be drawn between knower and known.
The knowing self is none other than the reality that is known. Parallels
to this way of explaining the goal of knowledge are to be found in
most traditions and are especially obvious in the Indian religions (with
concepts like *Moksha* and *Nirvana*).

Attaining the *Ḥaqīqat* and realizing the Real is often discussed in
terms of degrees of certainty (*yaqīn*), based on expressions employed
in the Qur'ān. Then it is said that knowing has three stages. The first is
'the knowledge of certainty' (*ʿilm al-yaqīn*), which is knowledge
received by hearsay and confirmed by logical arguments. The second
is 'the eye of certainty' (*ʿayn al-yaqīn*), which is seeing what one has
come to know. The third is 'the truth (or reality) of certainty' (*ḥaqq al-
yaqīn*), which is to be united with the *Ḥaqīqat* that is known.

The usual analogy for the three stages is knowledge of fire. When
the evidence of heat convinces us that there is such a thing as fire, we
have the knowledge of certainty. When we see a burning blaze, we
have the eye of certainty. When we are consumed by fire, we have
reached the truth of certainty. A famous line attributed to Rūmī
alludes to the three stages:

> The sum of my life is no more than three words—
> I was raw, I was cooked, I was burnt.

The point of all such discussions is that our usual, everyday sort of
knowledge – which includes our academic learning and professional
expertise – is rooted in imitation, not realization. In Rūmī's view,
people should never be satisfied with explanations of the universe,
the human soul and God that they have read in books or heard from
teachers. Rather, they should be striving to reach the *Ḥaqīqat,* where
knower and known are one and the individual ego has been burned
away by the Everlasting Truth. In order to reach this stage, people
must follow the *Sharīʿat* and the *Ṭarīqat,* the revealed law and the
Sufi Path.

Before going further, it is necessary to forestall a possible misunder-
standing. For the past century, there has been a great deal of criticism
of blind imitation (*taqlīd*). Orientalists have suggested that blind
imitation has stultified the progress and development of Muslim
countries, and numerous Muslims have criticized *taqlīd* as the bane

of their societies. When Shams and Rūmī criticize imitation, we should not jump to the conclusion that they were centuries ahead of their times. In modern discussions, the conceptual opposite of *taqlīd* is not *tahqīq* but *ijtihād*, literally, 'striving'. In its technical sense *ijtihād* means sufficient mastery of the juridical teachings of Islam – the *Sharīʿat* – that one may re-interpret these teachings to fit new situations. Modern-day authors have often claimed that 'the gate of *ijtihād*' was closed in medieval times and that, if Muslims are to enter the modern world, they must re-open the gate.

For Rūmī, Shams, and many other Sufis and philosophers, the discussion of *taqlīd* versus *tahqīq* has nothing to do with that of *taqlīd* versus *ijtihād*.[6] They accepted that imitation in the realm of *Sharīʿat* is necessary for the vast majority of Muslims, for the simple reason that only a tiny fraction of the *ʿulamāʾ*, and none of the common people, can achieve the level of *ijtihād*. Nor is it desirable for everyone to try to do so, for mastery of this science brings no benefit to the soul. This is why it is classified by the jurists as being merely incumbent upon the community (*fard al-kifāya*), rather than incumbent in itself, that is, on the individual (*fard al-ʿayn*). It is sufficient for the community that there be scholars who master the science of jurisprudence. As for individuals, they should know enough of the Law to follow it and to ask for advice when they need it, but their goal should be to reach God, not expertise.

In short, in the view of the Sufi teachers, practically all Muslims should be, and will in fact be, imitators in the realm of the *Sharīʿat*. Moreover, they should also be imitators in the *Tarīqat*, which is to say that they should follow the instructions of a qualified shaykh. None the less, imitation itself is simply a means, not an end. The goal is to reach the *Haqīqat*, and reaching this goal is to be undertaken by the method of realization (*tahqīq*). By contrast, the issue in modern discussions of *taqlīd* is to make use of *ijtihād* to modify Islamic law so that it fits nicely into the contemporary world. The notion of *tahqīq* is utterly foreign to the proponents of *ijtihād*, whose goals always remain on the social, legal, and political levels.

---

6 For example, *tahqīq* lies at the very heart of the teachings of Ibn al-ʿArabī. This is obvious both from his own writings and from statements of his followers, such as his step-son Ṣadr al-Dīn Qūnawī, who calls the approach of his master *mashrab al-tahqīq*.

Rūmī never refers to *taqlīd* in the juridical sense of the word, and he almost never uses the word *ijtihād* and its cognates in anything other than their literal meaning, that of striving and struggling.[7] He constantly urges his readers to increase their efforts in following the prophets and saints on the path of the *Sharīʿat* and the *Ṭarīqat*. The aim of their quest should always be to see and know the Truth and Reality for themselves. They must strive to become recognizers and gnostics (*ʿurafāʾ*), not simply learned imitators. This is what he is getting at in these verses:

> You have eyes, look with your own eyes.
>   Don't look with the eyes of an uninformed fool.
> You have ears, listen with your own ears.
>   Why be in pawn to the ears of blockheads?
> Make vision your practice, not imitation –
>   think in accordance with your own intellect.[8]

When Rūmī criticizes *taqlīd*, he is not criticizing the observance of the *Sharīʿat* and the *Ṭarīqat*, but rather the claims of jurists, the experts in scholastic theology (*Kalām*) and philosophers to know the final truth of things. In fact, what they know is simply what they have heard from others or, in the case of the more sophisticated, what they have concluded through their own rational processes, but always on the basis of hearsay. They have not reached the ultimate reality or *Ḥaqīqat* themselves, so the best they can do is quote words from those who have. They are, in effect, children trying to talk like adults.

> How can children on the path have the thoughts of Men?
> How can their imaginings be compared with true realization?
> Children think of nurses and milk,
>   raisins and walnuts, crying and weeping.
> Imitators are like sick children,
>   even if they offer subtle arguments and proofs.[9]

---

7 Rūmī employs the terms *ijtihād* and *mujtahid* about thirty times in the *Mathnawī*, but only once in a technical sense (III: 3581). He typically uses *ijtihād* as a synonym for *jahd*, *mujāhada*, and *kūshish* – effort and struggle on the path to God – and he does not contrast it with *taqlīd*.
8 *Mathnawī*, VI: 3342–44.   9 *Mathnawī*, V: 1287–89.

In short, the knowledge of scholars, theologians, philosophers, scientists, and other learned people is grounded in hearsay, not vision. They do not use their own eyes, they do not see for themselves, and they have not undergone the fiery transformation that is demanded by self-realization.

> There are many differences between the realizer and the imitator –
>   the first is like David, the second an echo.
> The source of the realizer's words is burning –
>   the imitator has learned some old sayings.[10]

THE SWORD OF *LĀ*

Realization embraces the realms of both epistemology and ontology. The word *ḥaqq*, from which *taḥqīq* derives, means both truth and reality. God as *ḥaqq* is both the Ultimate Truth and the Supreme Reality. Realization is to recognize the absolutely True and to reach the supremely Real. It demands both discernment and transformation of the soul.

Insofar as the *Sharī'at* and the *Ṭarīqat* require imitation, the model is always the Prophet, and, secondly, 'the prophets and saints', as Rūmī commonly expresses it. The *Ḥaqīqat*, however, cannot be known by imitation – one must see with one's own eyes, not with the eyes of others. The theoretical basis for all knowledge of the absolutely True and the truly Real is *tawḥīd*, the assertion of divine unity, whose meaning is epitomized by the first testimony of faith, the words 'No god but God' (*Lā ilāha illā Allāh*).

The formula of unity is built of two elements, which are called the negation (*nafy*) and the affirmation (*ithbāt*). 'No god' negates all illusion and unreality, and 'but God' affirms the unique reality of the Real. Together, negation and affirmation establish a dialectic that reverberates throughout Sufi teachings. The formula denies the independent reality of all 'others' (*ghayr*) and affirms the sole reality of the One. Everything other than God is evanescent, fading, disappearing; God alone is permanent, everlasting, appearing. 'Everything in the earth is undergoing annihilation,' says the Qur'ān, 'and there subsists the face of your Lord, the possessor of majesty and generosity' (55:26). This

---

10 *Mathnawī*, II: 493–94.

verse provides one of the more common conceptual pairs used in the dialectic of negation and affirmation, that is, annihilation (*fanā'*) and subsistence (*baqā'*). Another common pair is existence or being (*wujūd, hastī*) and nonexistence or nonbeing (*ʿadam, nīstī*). As Rūmī says,

> We and our existences are nonexistent things –
> You are Absolute Existence showing Yourself as evanescent.
> All of us are lions, but lions on a banner –
> we attack moment by moment because of the wind.
> Our wind and our being is Your gift,
> All of our existence is Your bestowal.[11]

The formula of *tawḥīd* provides not only the theory behind realization, but also a good deal of the practice. It is, for example, one of the most common formulae of remembrance, *dhikr*, employed by the Sufi orders, and it provides much of the framework for meditation on God and his bounty. Sufi texts compare the first word of the formula, *Lā* or 'no', to a sword, partly because of the way it is written in Arabic (ﻻ). Seekers must use this sword to cut away all 'others' until only the Real remains. The 'others' to be negated are the world and its creatures, the nonexistent things that appear to us as existent. Rūmī uses the image of the sword in a passage that, to my mind, sums up his teachings as well as anything else in his writings. The verses tell us that the soul must be consumed by the fire of love, which is none other than the sword of negation or *lā* as it slices away all non-existent things.

> Love is that flame which, when it blazes up,
> burns away everything except the Subsistent Beloved.
> It drives home the sword of *lā* in order to slay other than God.
> Look closely – after *lā* what remains?
> What remains is 'but God', the rest has gone.
> Bravo, O great, idol-burning Love![12]

To come back to the role that Shams-i Tabrīzī played in the transformation of Rūmī, the sayings of Shams make clear that his core teaching was precisely the necessity of passing beyond non-existence

11 *Mathnawī*, I: 602–04.   12 *Mathnawī*, V: 588–90.

in order to reach Absolute Being, or, leaving imitation behind and achieving realization. Before the coming of Shams, Rūmī was certainly immersed in the *Sharī'at* and the *Ṭarīqat,* but he was not yet consumed by the flames of the *Ḥaqīqat.* The *Mathnawī* and the *Dīwān-i Shams-i Tabrīzī* are both hymns to the burning that he underwent, a process which brought about the dissolution of all phenomenal appearances, all 'the paintings and pictures', and the realization of the Real.

THE FIRE OF LOVE

To speak of the path to realization in terms of stages of knowledge is to describe it from the outside. Such an approach runs the risk of turning it into another theoretical discussion, to be bandied about by scholars and dilettantes. This is one reason why Rūmī seldom talks in these terms. He has recourse rather to love, which, as most everyone understands, cannot be explained.

> Love cannot be found in erudition, science, books, and pages.
> The path that people talk about is not the path of lovers.[13]

There is no way to understand love without being a lover. All those who want to pass beyond imitation and reach the *Ḥaqīqat* must embrace it with their whole being.

> Love makes the wine of realization boil –
> Love is the hidden cupbearer of the truly sincere.[14]

In short, although Rūmī frequently uses the technical language of theoretical Sufism, he focuses rather on the inner transformation that the language is meant to express. One of the many ways he does so is to describe the soul's burning in the process of eliminating every desire and longing except love for the *Ḥaqīqat* itself. So much does Rūmī stress the importance of love that one can readily agree with those who have said that love, or rather the call to love, is the core of his message. Precisely here, however, many people miss the point,

---

13 *Kulliyāt-i Shams yā Dīwān-i kabīr,* ed. Badī' al-Zamān Furūzānfar (Tehran: Dānish-gāh 1957–67), *ghazal* 395, v. 4182. 14 *Mathnawī,* III: 4742.

because they think of love as they experience it in everyday life and as it has been portrayed in modern culture, which is alienated from every sort of transcendent vision. If we want to recover what Rūmī is talking about, we need to clarify the traditional Islamic understanding of love.

I will try to sum up the background for Rūmī's call to love in terms of the most often cited Qur'ānic verse on the topic: 'He loves them, and they love Him' (5:54). According to this verse, God and human beings share in the attribute of love, so each side is the lover and beloved of the other. Rūmī sometimes makes this point in terms that echo a famous Zen koan, as in this passage from the *Mathnawī*:

> Never does a lover seek union
>   unless his beloved is seeking him. . . .
> When love for the Real has grown up in your heart,
>   without doubt the Real has love for you.
> You will never hear the sound of one hand
>   clapping without the other.
> The thirsty man laments, 'O sweet water!'
>   The water laments, 'Where is the drinker!'
> Our souls' thirst is the attraction of the Water –
>   we belong to It and It belongs to us.[15]

We belong to the Water because 'He loves us.' The Water belongs to us because 'We love Him.'

To understand some of the implications of the verse of mutual love, we can look at the notions of lover and beloved employing the sword of *lā*. The formula of *tawhīd* tells us that there is no god but God, there is nothing real but the Real. It negates nonexistent things and affirms True Being; it erases false lovers and beloveds and affirms the true Lover and the true Beloved. It is saying, in other words, 'There is no lover but God' and 'There is no beloved but God.'

To say that God alone is lover has two basic implications. The first is that all love in the universe is a trace of divine love; the second that, in the last analysis, God alone is the one who loves. Thus we see Rūmī echoing the Qur'ānic verse that God created everything in pairs (51:49) and affirming, like Avicenna and many others, that all movement in the universe is God's love reflected in the seeking and yearning of creation.

15 *Mathnawī*, III: 4393–99.

The wisdom of the Real in His destiny and decree
　　made us lovers one of another.
That foreordainment has taken all parts of the world
　　and made them pairs, each in love with its mate.[16]

When Rūmī applies the sword of *lā* with even more rigour, he tells us
that in truth there is no lover but God:

Lovers themselves do not seek –
　　in the whole world, there is no seeker but He.[17]

　　To say that 'There is no beloved but God' also has two basic implications. The first is that everyone loves God and only God. Anything else
that people think they love is in fact a sign or a showing of God, a
theophany, a display of the divine names and attributes.

Whenever you love something that exists,
　　it has been gold-plated by the attributes of the Real.
When the gold goes back to its root and the copper remains,
　　you become disgusted with it and you divorce it.
Pull yourself back from things gold-plated with God's attributes,
　　stop foolishly calling the counterfeit 'beautiful'.
The counterfeit coin has borrowed its beauty –
　　beneath its decoration lies nakedness.
The gold goes back from the counterfeit to its source –
　　you also, go to the source where the gold is going!
The light goes back from the wall to the sun –
　　you also, go to the sun, which always moves in harmony!
From now on take water from heaven –
　　you've never seen faithfulness from drainpipes![18]

　　The second implication of 'There is no beloved but God' is that,
when God says in the verse of mutual love, 'He loves them', he is
saying that he loves them only inasmuch as they have been trans-
muted into real gold by his names and attributes, because only he
himself can be the true object of love. One of the corollaries of this
discussion is that, although 'He loves them' refers to all human beings,

16 *Mathnawī*, III: 4400–01.　17 *Kulliyāt, ghazal* 425, v. 4471.　18 *Mathnawī*, III: 554–60.

he loves some of them more than others. To understand why this should be so, we need to look at the ancient question, 'Why did God create the universe?' For Rūmī and the Sufi tradition generally, the answer is that without the universe, there would be no 'them' to love.

This answer is typically explained in terms of the famous sacred tradition of the Prophet Muḥammad (ḥadīth qudsī), 'I was a Hidden Treasure, and I loved[19] to be recognized, so I created the creatures that I might be recognized.' To be recognized, God's love demands difference, otherness, multiplicity, and distance, because recognition and knowledge depend upon differentiation and distinction. In other words, God's love is the cause of the separation (firāq, judā'ī) from God that defines our existential plight, the separation that is mentioned in the first line of the Mathnawī and sets the tone for it and much of the Dīwān.

In this view of the human situation, all hunger, thirst, longing, need, pain, and suffering are rooted in our sense of separation, which is the fruit of God's 'love to be recognized'. If 'He loves *them*', that is, human beings and not other creatures, it is precisely because they alone have the capacity to recognize and love *him*, for they alone were created in his form and taught all the divine Names (Qur'ān, 2:30).

Typically, Rūmī discusses the human role as the unique beloved of God in terms of God's love for the most perfect human being, that is, Muḥammad, who was addressed by God in the ḥadīth qudsī, 'But for thee, I would not have created the spheres.'[20] But Rūmī also generalizes the discussion, making the object of God's love all the prophets and saints.

> The heavens are slave to the saint's moon,
> The east and the west beg bread from him.
> 'But for thee' is written on his diploma:
> He bestows and distributes all things.

19 See Badīʿ al-Zamān Furūzānfar, Aḥādīth-i Mathnawī (Tehran: Danishgāh-i Tehran, 1335 A.Hsh./1956; reprinted Amīr Kabīr, 1361 A.Hsh./1982), p. 29, no. 70. In the several versions of this ḥadīth, the verb is either aḥbabtu, 'I loved', or aradtu, 'I desired'. In the latter case, the ḥadīth ties in with the Qur'ānic discussion of God's desire as the root of creation, as in the verse, 'Our only word to a thing when We desire it is to say to it "Be!", and it comes to be' (16:40). In either case, the basic argument stays the same: God loves or desires specific objects, namely, those who can recognize him for who he is; only those made in his own form – i.e., human beings – can do so.

20 See Furūzānfar, Aḥādīth-i Mathnawī, p. 172, no. 546; p. 203, no. 655.

If he did not exist, the heavens would not revolve,
    nor would they be the place of light and the station of the angels.
If he did not exist, the seas would not have acquired
    splendour, fish, and royal pearls.
If he did not exist, the earth would not contain
    treasures inside and jasmine outside.[21]

To appreciate fully what is going on in God's love for human beings, we need to remember the essential role of beauty. In the Islamic ethos generally, the object of love – true love, at least – is always beauty. The Prophet points to the connection in the famous *Ḥadīth*, 'God is beautiful, and He loves beauty.'[22] Applying the sword of *lā* to this *Ḥadīth*, we see that the first clause: 'God is beautiful' means that there is nothing beautiful but God. In other words, all beautiful things other than God are gold-plated by his beauty. The second clause: 'He loves beauty' means that God's only object of love is the beautiful. If he loves human beings, he does so because and inasmuch as they are beautiful. Their beauty stems from the divine form in which he created them. The proper way to speak about God's 'form', that is, the guise in which God appears to us, is in the context of 'the most beautiful names' (*al-asmā' al-ḥusnā*) of God mentioned in the Qur'ān (17: 110). It is these names that help us understand what is meant by the saying, 'There is none beautiful but God.' And it is Adam's gold-plating by these names that bestows upon him any beauty that he may have. The Qur'ān says, 'He formed you, and He made your forms beautiful' (40:64). Having created human beings because of love, God then loves each and every one of them to the extent that he or she lives up to the innate beauty of their forms, which is what the tradition calls their primordial nature (*fiṭra*).

But human beings do not typically pay heed to their own beauty. They have forgotten who they are, and they are free to say 'no' to beauty, to God, to the prophets, to wisdom, to love. To the extent that they say 'no' instead of 'yes', they will be ugly. And God does not love the ugly. The Qur'ān makes this point explicitly in a number of verses, saying that God does *not* love the unbelievers, the wrongdoers, the workers of corruption, the transgressors, the immoderate, the proud, and the boastful.

---

21 *Mathnawī*, VI: 2102–06.   22 Furūzānfar, *Aḥādīth-i Mathnawī*, p. 42, no. 106.

So, although the verse does attest that 'God loves them', he does not love everyone with equal love. He only loves people to the extent that they reflect his beauty, for 'There is none beautiful but God' and 'There is none beloved but God.' Everyone does indeed reflect God's beauty, because all are created in his form. But to be truly beautiful, people must employ their freedom in striving to conform to the Supremely Beautiful, other than whom there is none beautiful. They can do so only inasmuch as they follow the prophets and the saints, those who have reached the ultimate reality (*Ḥaqīqat*) and achieved realization. The path to the *Ḥaqīqat* is defined by the *Sharīʿat* and the *Ṭarīqat*, which in turn are expressions of the Prophet's Sunnah, in both the outer realm of activity and the inner realm of transformation. The Qurʾān highlights the Prophet's role in the path of love in the verse, 'Say [O Muḥammad!]: "If you love God, follow me, and God will love you".' (3:31).

So, in brief, when God loves human beings, this means first that he creates the universe and establishes separation so that people may be aware of themselves as individuals and come to recognize the Hidden Treasure as the source of all; second, it means that he calls people to love him in return by following the prophets. Their created separation is compulsory, and it forces them to recognize their hunger and thirst, their love and need, their nothingness and God's Being. It turns them into lovers, who suffer the pain of hunger and longing, but it does not force them to recognize that it is God alone who is the object of their love. Only if they recognize this and strive to achieve nearness to him will his love for them be intensified.

In Sufi texts, the most often cited scriptural reference to the fruit of following the Prophet and achieving God's love is the authentic *ḥadīth qudsī* in which God speaks of the servant who is striving to achieve nearness (*taqarrub*) to him by performing both obligatory religious duties and voluntary good works. When he does this, God says, 'I love him, and when I love My servant, I am the hearing with which he hears, the seeing with which he sees, the hand with which he grasps, and the foot with which he walks.' This *ḥadīth* is understood as referring to the ultimate goal of creation. By displaying the Hidden Treasure, God brings about separative existence – he cuts the reeds from the reed bed. The reeds complain of their separation, which is to say that they express their longing to return to him. In response to their longing, God sends the prophets, who provide the path of return,

the path that leads to overcoming separation and establishing nearness and union, which is the joy of living forever with the true object
of their love.

In short, Rūmī applies the sword of *lā* to everything but the true
Beloved. He calls his listeners to experience the burning of love so that
they may reach the *Ḥaqīqat* and swim in the ocean of union. He tells
them that the goal of their human embodiment is to recover their
original identity with their Beloved and to realize in their own souls
that 'There is no lover but God, there is no beloved but God.'

Rūmī tells the story of lover and beloved, loss and gain, separation
and union, pain and joy, in many ways and in many contexts, always
coming back to the Ocean of Love, the Hidden Treasure that made
itself manifest out of love for human beings and that calls them to
rejoin the primordial realm. Lest it be imagined, however, that this is a
call for 'the drop to return to the ocean' and the annihilation of all that
bestows identity and reality on the human soul, one should recall this
little story from Rūmī's *Majālis-i sabʿa* ('Seven Sermons'), which can
also serve as fitting summary of his basic teachings:

> Like fish we say to the Ocean of Life, 'Why did You strike us with
> waves and throw us up on the dry land of water and clay? You
> have so much mercy – how could You give us such torment? . . .
>
> The Ocean replies, '"I was a Hidden Treasure, so I loved to be
> recognized." I was a treasure, hidden by the curtain of the Unseen,
> in the private cell of No-place. From behind the veils of existence I
> wanted My beauty and majesty to be known. I wanted it to be
> seen what sort of water of life and alchemy of happiness I am.'
>
> The fish say, 'We, who are the fish in the ocean, were in this
> Ocean of Life from the first. We knew its magnificence and gentle-
> ness, for we are the copper that receives the elixir of this infinite
> alchemy. We knew the exaltedness of this elixir of Life. As much
> as we spoke of it to those who were not at first fish of the ocean,
> they did not listen, or see, or understand. From the first we were
> the recognizers of this Treasure, and at the last we will be its
> recognizers. At whom did You direct this long exile for the sake of
> "I loved to be recognized."'
>
> The answer comes, 'O fish! Although fish know the water's
> worth and are lovers, and although they cling to union with it,
> their love is not of the same description, with such burning and

heat, with such self-abandonment, with such lamentation and weeping of blood, and with such roasting of the liver, as the love of that fish whom the waves throw up on dry land and who tosses for a long time on the hot earth and burning sand. "He neither dies there, nor lives" [Qur'ān 87:13]. Separation from the ocean allows him no taste of life's sweetness – after all, that is separation from the Ocean of Life. How can someone who has seen that Ocean find joy in this life?' . . .

God says, 'Just as I wanted to manifest My Treasure, so I wanted to manifest your ability to recognize that Treasure. Just as I wanted to display the purity and gentleness of this Ocean, so I wanted to display the high aspirations and the nurturing gentleness of the fish and creatures of the Ocean. Thus they may see their own faithfulness and show their own aspirations. 'Do people think they will be left to say "We have faith" and that they will not be tried?'" [Qur'ān 19:2].[23]

BIBLIOGRAPHY

Chittick, W. C. (trans.). *Me & Rumi: The Autobiography of Shams-i Tabrizi*. Louisville: Fons Vitae, 2004.

Furūzānfar, Badīʿ al-Zamān. *Aḥādīth-i Mathnawī*. Tehran: Dānishgāh-i Tehrān 1335 A.Hsh./1956; reprinted Amīr Kabīr, 1361 A.Hsh./1982.

Rūmī, Jalāl al-Dīn. *Fīhi mā fīh*, ed. Badīʿ al-Zamān Furūzānfar, Tehran: Amīr Kabīr, 1348 A.Hsh./1969.

—. *Kulliyāt-i Shams yā Dīwān-i kabīr*, ed. Badīʿ al-Zamān Furūzānfar, Tehran: Dānishgāh, 1957–67.

—. *Majālis-i sabʿa*, ed. Tawfīq Subḥānī, Tehran: Intishārāt-i Kayhān, 1379 A.Hsh./2000.

—. *Mathnawī-yi maʿnawī*, ed. R. A. Nicholson, Tehran: Amīr Kabīr, 1357 A.Hsh./1978.

23 *Majālis-i sabʿa*, ed. Tawfīq Subḥānī (Tehran: Intishārāt-i Kayhān 1379 A.Hsh./2000), pp. 121–22.

Society and Economy in the Teachings of Mawlana Jalal al-Din Rumi

ADEM ESEN

Translated by Roderick Grierson[1]

INTRODUCTION

There has invariably been a marked difference between the evaluations of economic life made by Sufi mystics and by those whose interpretations are based on other premises. On one side are those who view the teaching that we need very little in life as by definition a rejection of labour. On the other side are those who believe that we should support ourselves through labour. By examining the works of Mawlana Jalal al-Din Rumi, which have inspired individuals and entire communities for some seven hundred years, we shall try to offer a careful assessment of his own views on economic and social issues. Two points should be made at the outset. Although Mawlana lived at a time of political upheaval caused in large part by the extension of Mongol hegemony to Anatolia, economic life was not entirely disrupted in the Sultanate of Rum and social welfare appears to have

---

1   *Translator's Note.* It is a great pleasure to offer readers of the *Mawlana Rumi Review* a translation of the following essay by Prof. Dr Adem Esen, who has recently been appointed Rector of Istanbul Sabahattin Zaim University. For many years, Prof. Dr Esen has been a distinguished scholar at Seljuk University in Konya, having acquired a wide expertise in political science, administrative science, law, and economics, as well as in religious studies. He is not only an experienced university administrator, he has also served as the elected mayor of one of the largest municipalities in Konya. While he has devoted much of his career to academic work, he has not been limited to it, and he has a keen awareness that most of the students whom he teaches will not spend the rest of their lives in lectures or seminars. The present essay was delivered in Turkish to a large hall filled with undergraduates at Near East University in Nicosia, and is based on previous books and articles that Prof. Dr Esen has written, notably *Mevlana Celaleddin Rumi'nin İktisat Anlayışı* (Mevlana Jalal al-Din Rumi's Understanding of Economics), which was published at Konya in 2007.

been maintained at a high level. It is also essential to remember that however important Rumi's statements about economic issues might be, he was not directly involved in economic activity himself. His primary concerns and responsibilities lay elsewhere. The task on which we are embarking is therefore not always straightforward.

THE APPROACH TO ECONOMIC QUESTIONS IN THE WRITINGS OF RUMI

The writings of Mawlana Jalal al-Din Rumi comprise the *Mathnawi, Divan-i kabir, Maktubat, Majalis-i sab'ah, Ruba'iyyat,* and *Fihi ma fihi.* The *Mathnawi*, which was written in the form of an epic poem, is undoubtedly his most famous work. It contains a great many observations about our nature as individuals and about our social life. In the collection of letters known as the *Maktubat*, which was written in an informal Persian similar in style to his discourses or *Fihi ma fihi*, Mawlana sets out the principles by which we should live and provides examples for us to follow. *Inter alia,* some of his letters record that he appealed to the state authorities on behalf of those who owed debts to the state. The *Majalis-i sab'ah* is a collection of seven sermons in which Mawlana addresses the causes of social collapse, the power of belief, the value of knowledge, and questions such as irresponsibility and wisdom. In addition to their value for students of Sufism or of Persian literature, these books by Mawlana are among the most important sources for the study of economic and commercial life during the period in which he lived.[2] In them, Mawlana takes examples from daily life at the time, examining events by addressing the concerns of the people among whom he lived. Although he wrote in several genres, the views that he expresses in the metre and rhyme of poetry are also examined in his sermons and his letters.

In addition, a record of Mawlana's views about economic life can be found in books such as the *Manaqib al-'arifin* of Ahmad Aflaki, the *Risala-yi Sipahsalar* and the *Ibtida-nama* of Sultan Walad, which were written shortly after Rumi's death. In the *Manaqib al-'arifin*, which provides a great deal of valuable information about the time and the circumstances in which Rumi lived, Ahmad Aflaki describes the miracles that Mawlana was believed to have performed, including a

---

2 Erdoğan Merçil, *Türkiye Selçukluları'nda Meslekler* (Ankara 2000), p. 7.

miraculous gift of coins that had just been minted for circulation.[3] Although Mawlana himself does not mention such miracles in his own writings, Aflaki often refers to events such as the occasion on which Mawlana produced new silver coins from his pocket. Mawlana expressed his attitude to these events by remarking that 'miracles and those who perform them are known only to God.' Even the 'friends of God' who are given the name *Abdal* do not hear their names and do not know them.[4]

As Mawlana was not directly concerned with economic affairs in the way that a state official or a merchant would have been, he makes no attempt to offer an economic analysis. Instead, he tries to offer advice about human life as a whole. For this reason, we should avoid making exaggerated or excessive claims when we discuss his views about material objects or the material world in the context of an economic analysis of his writings. In any case, it is important to emphasize that Mawlana relied to a large extent on the Qur'an and on *hadith*. For this reason, it is impossible to consider his views on economic matters in isolation from the basic sources of Islamic teaching. During the period in which he lived, however, institutions of learning offered instruction not only in religious subjects such as jurisprudence and the details of individual and institutional charity, but also in disciplines such as mathematics, logic, physics, metaphysics, politics, and psychology.[5] During this period, in other words, religious sciences and other sciences were taught together. While Mawlana himself taught jurisprudence, the science of law, and came from a family well versed in the Hanafi school of law, he does not assign a paramount importance to this in his writings. His interests are much wider.

---

3 As an example, a dervish said on one occasion to Mawlana, 'It is so many days since I have been able to bring home any food, I wonder about the state of my family.' Even though they were in the midst of *sama*, Mawlana is said to have reached into his robe and brought out a handful of new silver money consisting of 900 coins, which he poured into the tambourine. See Ahmed Eflâkî, *Âriflerin Menkıbeleri (Mevlânâ ve Etrafındakiler)*, tr. Tahsin Yazıcı, vol. 1 (Istanbul 1964), p. 339 (§ 459).

4 *The Mathnawí of Jalálu'ddín Rúmi*, ed. Reynold A. Nicholson (London 1925–1940), III: 3106.

5 Afzal Iqbal, *The Life and Work of Jalaluddin Rumi* (London 1983), p. 63.

ECONOMY AND SOCIETY DURING THE LIFE OF MAWLANA

Under the Seljuks of Anatolia, both local and international trade improved and the general level of prosperity increased. During the twelfth century, commercial activity expanded because the Seljuk sultans pursued policies specifically intended to develop Anatolia.[6] During the second half of the thirteenth century, overseas trade began to flourish as well, with Anatolia opening at the port of Sinop in the north, and at Alanya in the south.[7]

I would argue that the Seljuk period was of critical importance for the development of European as well as Islamic civilization. In particular, I would suggest that the Muslims of the Seljuk period had a more pronounced impact than the Byzantine Empire on the Renaissance and the Reformation in Europe. The Islamic example contributed to the removal of ecclesiastical obstacles and the development of transactions based on currency. In this sense in particular, the Seljuk period did not represent a decline from the achievements of the Abbasid caliphate, but an advance. Nevertheless, the Mongol invasion did have a major impact in retarding the advance of Muslim civilization throughout the region.[8]

As the Turks who migrated into Anatolia represented a new consumer market for indigenous Christians, commercial activity increased. The Christian population tended to be involved in industry and local commerce, while Turks were more likely to be landowners or involved in international trade. In such a diverse society, village life was conducted according to regulations that were very different from those of the urban centres in which Seljuk administration was based.[9]

The Seljuk sultan ʿAla al-Din Kaykubad invited many Muslim scholars to Konya, including the father of Mawlana. Although the city had not previously been a centre of religious scholarship, it now became a centre of mystical activity as well, and this mystical activity was expressed in Persian. However, Mawlana was also exposed to an

---

6 Aydın Taneri, *Türkiye Selçukluları Kültür Hayatı (Menâkibü'l-Arifin'in Değerlendirilmesi)*, (Konya 1977), p. 92.

7 Aydın Yalçın, *Türkiye Tarihi* (Ankara 1979), p. 25.

8 Osman Turan, *Selçuklular Tarihi ve Türk-İslam Medeniyeti* (Ankara 1965), pp. 428–32, 439, 481, 485.

9 Mustafa Akdağ, *Türkiye'nin İktisadi ve İçtimai Tarihi*, 2 vols. (Ankara 1995), vol. 1, pp. 13, 14, 23.

Arabic cultural milieu in Damascus and Aleppo.[10] For these reasons, Anatolia has been described as a society founded upon a synthesis of Islamic elements of Turkish, Persian, and Arab origin.[11] In such a milieu, the mosque was obviously an important venue through which certain individuals were able to enhance their prestige.[12]

During the period in which Mawlana lived, slavery had not yet been abolished. The economic implications of slavery were obviously considerable. Although slaves and concubines undoubtedly existed, it is known that for a variety of reasons some were freed and allowed to marry. On one occasion, Rumi became angry with his daughter Maleke Khâtun, because she had been scolding a slave. As a result, he freed the woman and allowed her to take as her own all the clothes that she was wearing.[13]

THE WORLD AND THE MATERIAL ORDER

The *Malamatiyya*, who emerged during the second century of the Muslim era and were highly influential in Khurasan and Turkestan, influenced Mawlana as well.[14] According to the *malamati* view of the world, the material realm has been entrusted to believers so that they can work with it and give it shape and order.[15] In the *malamati* view

---

10 Franklin D. Lewis, *Rumi: Past and Present, East and West* (Oxford 2001), p. 397; A. Reza Arasteh, *Rumi the Persian, the Sufi: Rebirth in Creativity and Love* (London 1974), p. 156; Bediüzzaman Fürûzanfer (Badiʿ al-Zaman Furuzanfar), *Mevlânâ Celâleddin*, tr. Feridun Nafiz Uzluk (Ankara 1962), p. 82; Abdülbâki Gölpınarlı, *Mevlânâ: Hayatı, Sanatı, Yapıtlarından Seçmeler* (Istanbul 1951), p. 82.

11 Mustafa Akdağ, *Türkiye'nin İktisadi ve İçtimai Tarihi*, vol. 1, p. 11.

12 Franklin D. Lewis, *Rumi: Past and Present*, p. 398.

13 Ahmed Eflâkî, *Ariflerin Menkıbeleri (Mevlânâ ve Etrafındakiler)*, tr. Tahsin Yazıcı, vol. 1 (Istanbul 1964), pp. 282, 297 (§ 302).

14 The *Malamatiyya* were a group who took an extreme view of the need to preserve sincerity of devotion. They took the view that their spiritual condition and the validity of their actions would be diminished if they were not kept secret. If their actions were witnessed by anyone, they would attempt to hide themselves wherever they could, as if they thought that the recognition of good deeds was worse than the exposing of evil deeds. See İsmail Ankaravî, *Hadislerle Tasavvuf ve Mevlevi Erkanı: Mesnevi Beyitlerle Kırk Hadis Şerhi*, ed. Semih Ceyhan (Istanbul 2001), p. 77. The *Malamatiyya* rejected practices such as additional prayers, asceticism, distinctive costume, and *tekke*s. Their path was one of love and ecstasy. The *malamati* path was not dependant upon shaykh and dervish but upon lover and beloved. See Abdülbâki Gölpınarlı, *Melâmîlik ve Melâmîler* (Istanbul 1931), p. 12.

15 Ibid., pp. 9, 25, 168.

that was transmitted to the Mevlevi through Mawlana's life and through his writings, there was no *chilla* or contemplative retreat, no *zuhd* or asceticism, and no renunciation of the world. Labour was an activity that was regarded as close to worship. Work during the day and worship in the evening were not seen as separate activities, but as complementary and indeed essential. This attitude is given an eloquent expression in a Persian proverb: 'The hand is at work, but the heart is with the Beloved (*dast bih kar, dil bih yar*).' Some famous Sufis regarded labour simply as a means to accumulate profit, motivated by a desire for the financial resources that would allow them to perform meritorious works.[16] Mawlana himself was not inclined towards an exclusively esoteric (*batini*) version of Sufism and preferred a more ascetic approach. He taught that by working constantly for the benefit of other people, and by using the power of the human will, his disciples could help to shape economic conditions in Anatolia during the difficult circumstances of the thirteenth century. At the same time, however, he warned them against the love of money that can lurk within any of us.[17]

By accepting the relationship between individuals and their possessions, Mawlana saw money as a means of attaining the status of human perfection (*insan al-kamil*). As always, he addressed human nature and made it the basis of his approach. People are always drawn toward possessions. When a trade caravan came to Medina, for example, people gathered around the caravan even though the Prophet was delivering a sermon at the same time. The event is mentioned between verses 422 and 431 in the third book of the *Mathnawi*. Mawlana offers the explanation that individuals struggle to meet their needs. But later, when these needs have been satisfied and the burden has been removed, they become rebellious, like a donkey that kicks when its load is untied.[18]

Human nature is full of contradictions. When people are tested by God, they struggle with war and peace, with poverty and abundance. Mawlana explains that greed and ambition within us will destroy us. However, a cure for ambition can be found in patience and com-

16 Sabri Fehmi Ülgener, *Zihniyet ve Din: İslam, Tasavvuf ve Çözülme Devri İktisat Ahlakı* (Istanbul 1981), p. 85.
17 Ahmet Güner Sayar, *Gönül Pazarı: İnsanlar, Olaylar ve Mekanlara Dair Yazılar* (Istanbul 2007), p. 33.
18 Rumi, *Mathnawi*, ed. Nicholson, IV: 3620–26.

posure. The world draws near, as it were, to those who act with *zuhd* or asceticism and contentment. This means that they can live with peace and tranquillity in the world.

In his books, Mawlana develops a symbolism based upon animals such as cattle, oxen, birds of various sorts, and monkeys. Cattle and oxen are used as symbols of concupiscence. The monkey or horse symbolizes our inner nature. Different types of birds serve as symbols of different types of human character. Mawlana notes the four types of birds that appear in verse 260 of Surah II ('The Cow'),[19] and explains that these four birds – the gander, the peacock, the crow, and the rooster – refer to four types of behaviour. The gander corresponds to greed, the peacock to pride, the crow to worldly ambition, and the rooster to concupiscence.[20]

According to Mawlana, life in the present world leads us to forget God. Nevertheless, possessions, property, business, or family do not in themselves constitute the world. Mawlana compares the relationship between our selves and the world to the relationship between a ship and the sea. Just as water is necessary to support the ship, the world is necessary to sustain life. However, if a ship takes water into its hold, it will sink. If we take the world into our hearts, we too will lose our way. In other words, the real world is not outside us; it must be sought within. Wealth in the present world should therefore be desired for others, but our own desire should be for God. For this reason, the Unseen is the ground from which the world emerges. People cannot attain the Unseen simply by renouncing the world, and success in this world depends upon diligence and on knowledge. 'What is the world?' Mawlana asks. 'It is being forgetful of God. It does not consist of external things such as fine clothes or money or children or a wife. While water inside a ship will cause its destruction, water beneath a ship helps to keep it afloat.'[21] In this way, Mawlana makes the point

---

19 According to the Quran, Surah II, 260: 'Abraham once said, "O Lord, show me how you raise the dead." "Do you not believe?" He replied. "I do believe," Abraham answered, "but I ask so that my heart will rest assured." "Catch four birds and tame them, and put each of them on the top of a hill, and call them. They will come flying to you. Know that God is great and wise."' According to tradition, these birds are the peacock, the crow, the pigeon, and the vulture. See Elmalılı Hamdi Yazır, *Hak Dini Kur'an Dili* (Istanbul 1936), vol. 2, p. 889.

20 Rumi, *Mathnawi*, ed. Nicholson, v: 43–44; Annemarie Schimmel, *The Triumphal Sun: A Study of the Works of Jalāloddin Rumi*, 2nd ed. (Albany 1993), pp. 96–113.

21 Rumi, *Mathnawi*, ed. Nicholson, I: 983–85. In the next verses (986–90), Mawlana

that the world, like water, is necessary if the ship of life is to remain afloat, but it must not enter the heart. 'Because he banished possessions and property from his heart, the prophet Solomon called himself poor . . . Even though the entire world belonged to him, property and wealth were as nothing in the eyes of his heart.'[22] Therefore, the world is not to be found outside us; it must be found within us.

Although the world appears to be vast, it is narrow and constricting to our souls. For this reason, our souls find an escape from our predicament in sleep.[23] Mawlana clarifies the point by adducing several examples. He compares the world to a *hamam* or Turkish bath. Because it is difficult to breathe within a *hamam*, people become stupefied and dull. The width and the height of the *hamam* makes no difference because of the oppressive heat that fills it. Mawlana also describes a man who wears narrow shoes in a large field. Despite its size, the field seems to be narrow and constricted to him, as if it were actually a prison. The reason is that his shoes are pinching his feet. In this way, the body resembles a cramped and miserable house. Within it, the soul is sick and in pain, disabled as if it were bent in two.

Mawlana compares life in the present world to a dream. We must not allow ourselves to be imprisoned through our belief that the dream is reality. Those who have knowledge understand the reality. However, most people do not have this knowledge, because greed is blind to the blessings of the world and imposes a thick curtain that hides reality from them. When people become greedy, they reach a state in which they are no longer willing to listen. Mawlana advises people that they should not be greedy in their desire for the life of the world, but should admire instead the beauties of the world of reality. The present world may seem vast to the eyes of those who are greedy, but it is nothing when compared to the immense power of God.

---

continues to discuss the topic in the following manner. A vessel filled with air whose mouth is stopped stays floating on the surface of deep, endless, and limitless water. The dervish ethos of detachment (*darvishi*) is rather like air, so that man does not sink into the ocean of the world but stays on the surface. If the entire world is his possession, in his eyes this possession is nothing. In this state, due to his awareness of God, he fills his heart with the air of the sublime, he fastens his mouth, and seals it. See also Tahirü'l Mevlevi, *Şerh-i Mesnevi* (Istanbul 2007), vol. 2, p. 566.

22 Rumi, *Mathnawi*, ed. Nicholson, I: 986, 989.

23 Şefik Can, *Mesnevi'den Seçmeler: Cevâhir-i Mesneviyye*, 2 vols. (Istanbul 2001), vol. 1, p. 270.

According to Mawlana, the unseen world is our real home, and not this world. Those of us who are spiritually dead see this world as bright and shining. But while it appears to be vast on the outside, it is decidedly narrow on the inside. The pleasures of this world may appear to be beautiful, but they are fleeting. In fact, the delights of this world will merely deceive us.

Rumi advises us to profit from the blessings of the world but to remain close to God in the following way:

> Make good use of the kindness that God has shown to you. But do not allow this kindness to spoil you by taking too much pleasure in it, because God does not love those who take pride in their good fortune. Make good use of the blessings of the world that come to you and enjoy a portion of them. But also know that the blessings of the world – wealth, money, position, fame – will all take you farther from your Lord if you take an excessive interest in them. O companion of God, rejoice in God. Find joy in God, and in nothing other than God. Because He is like the season of spring, and anything else is like a harsh month in winter. If you are a sultan and are preoccupied with your riches, your property, your armies, your crown, and your throne, you should be very aware that anything other than God is something that will lead you slowly but nevertheless directly to death.[24]

I wonder if these ideas of Mawlana can be understood as suggesting that we detach ourselves from the world and turn our backs upon it. Max Weber claimed that an inverse relationship usually exists between religion and work, and that the combination of business discipline and a sense of being a chosen people of God was only seen in the ascetic strand of Protestantism in the West. However, is this true? The goal is surely not to renounce the world, but to remain inside the world, and at the same time to remain detached from the distractions of sensual indulgence. Sabri Ülgener argues that an Islamic perspective has been removed from modern history because Weber emphasized Christianity, and one version of Christianity in

---

24 Ibid., vol. 1, 285. This teaching is reiterated by Rumi in verse as well; see *Mathnawi*, ed. Nicholson, III: 507–09.

particular, namely Calvinism.[25] Ülgener explains Rumi's view of the world as involving a series of fluctuations in one direction and then another, reflecting the turbulence of a society struggling to make decisions as it attempted to find its way between the values of two views of life that were in opposition to each other.

> It can be said that Rumi, like many others, preferred a view that emphasized the role of struggle and of the will. The attitude toward the world that we see in Islam in a pure and genuine form at its beginning continued among those who took such a view and was not diminished. The only connection between the two views of life is found in their rejection of pride, vanity, arrogance, and ostentation. After paying due attention to this point, there is no reason not to establish an honest but detached relationship with material things and possessions. Obvious examples of this can be found in Rumi.[26]

Furthermore, unlike in Christianity, the principle that there is no monasticism in Islam is accepted by all Muslim scholars. With this in mind, Feridun Nafiz Uzluk states that Mawlana did not condone the practice of *çile* or *chilla*, a solitary retreat lasting for either forty days or a thousand and one days. The reason was that a religion requiring its adherents to work cannot also include a religious elite detached from the community as a whole. Furuzanfar offers his own opinion in the following terms:

> Rumi did not approve of *chilla* or other similar customs. Regarding them as activities that were not legitimate, he instructed his disciples not to practise them. Although he emphasizes the importance of working, he also emphasizes the importance of detachment from the business of the world. Nevertheless, he does not go as far as requiring his disciples to abandon physical labour altogether. Severing this attachment, and thereby achieving a spiritual equilibrium in relation to the

25 Sabri Fehmi Ülgener, *Zihniyet ve Din: İslam, Tasavvuf ve Çözülme Devri İktisat Ahlakı* (Istanbul 1981), pp. 33, 44, 51.
26 Ibid., pp. 70, 79.

body through physical labour, is considered one of the roads to perfection.[27]

Rumi explains the subject of monasticism in these verses: 'The bird has said, "Do not sit alone; monasticism has no place in the religion of Ahmad."'[28] 'The path of Jesus is solitary struggle and renunciation of desire; the path of Muhammad is to endure the suffering and sorrow of man and woman.'[29] The reason for this is that Islam depends upon engaging with the world and resisting its temptations rather than fleeing from it. Ülgener remarks that the rejection of monasticism meant that there was no distinction within the community of believers in its earliest years, although a distinction between a spiritual elite and the majority of the population would certainly arise in later Islamic mysticism.[30]

It is worth noting that Mawlana offers the following advice in the *Divan-i kabir*: 'The person who is lazy in the world destroys his own shop.'[31]

QUIETISM, ACTIVISM, AND SOME ECONOMIC QUESTIONS

Quietism (*tawakkul*) and activism in earning a living (*kasb*) are among the most debated questions where Sufism is concerned. According to Mawlana, the path of the saint and the prophet involves work. Indeed, the prophets were known to have been craftsmen.[32] Mawlana believed that unearned income was illicit, and remarked that the prophet

---

27 Bediüzzaman Fürûzanfer (Badiᶜ al-Zaman Furuzanfar), *Mevlânâ Celâleddin*, tr. Uzluk, p. 178.

28 Rumi, *Mathnawi*, ed. Nicholson, VI: 478.

29 Jalal al-Din Rumi, *Fihi ma fihi*, ed. Badiᶜ al-Zaman Furuzanfar (Tehran 1348 A.Hsh./ 1969), chap. 20, p. 87.

30 Sabri Fehmi Ülgener, *Zihniyet ve Din: İslam, Tasavvuf ve Çözülme Devri İktisat Ahlakı* (Istanbul 1981), p. 37.

31 Jalal al-Din Rumi, *Divan-i kabir* (*Kulliyat-i Shams ya Diwan-i kabir az guftar-i Mawlana Jalal al-Din Muhammad mashhur bih-Mawlavi, ba tashihat wa havashi*), ed. Badiᶜ al-Zaman Furuzanfar, 3 ed., 10 vols. in 9 (Tehran 1363 A.Hsh./1984), vol. 1, ghazal 1023: 10790.

32 There is a tradition that Şis, the son of Adam, took no interest in the business of the world but learned weaving through divine inspiration. When he made clothes for the first time and wore them, his brothers liked them and bought them. In this way, the cloth that Şis had woven passed to Moses and from him to Abu Bakr. See Eflâkî, *Ariflerin Menkıbeleri (Mevlânâ ve Etrafındakiler)*, vol. 2, p. 343 (§ 467).

Solomon regarded manual work as better than receiving the tribute due to a king. Mawlana did not despise any work or trade.[33] He saw earned income as in accordance with the path of the Sunna.[34]

In Mawlana's view, God provides us with what we need, and there is a reason for everything. The purpose of work and labour is to earn our sustenance, and God prefers exertion to resignation. Mawlana offered the following explanation of the proverb 'the hero's place is at the edge of the oven'. A man who works during the summer months, and only then sets his flour aside at the edge of the oven so that he can rest during the winter months, is behaving as he should. A man who is lazy and sits down without first attending to his work becomes indolent and incapable of achieving his goal in the difficulties of winter. He is therefore unable to sit at the edge of the oven. This comparison is a parable of the present world and the future life.[35]

The characteristic that guides people to success is patience. An individual must value the moment that is actually lived and must not waste time. We should offer thanks for the blessings that we receive, because gratitude will lead to even more blessings.[36] Mawlana explained that offering financial support to other people is essentially distributing the wealth of God. For this reason, he called upon those who were rich to support others who were not.

Mawlana recommended generosity. It seems that those around him often appealed to him for help. It is important to remember that in centuries when there was no social insurance in the modern sense, the distribution of funds in the form of obligatory alms (*zakat*) and voluntary almsgiving (*sadaqa*) fulfilled this function. Mawlana suggested that unsecured loans known as (*qars-i hasan*) should also be given.

In this world, Mawlana argued, we are dependent upon one another. The rich need the poor so that they will have a way in which they can display generosity. For this reason as well, the poor must behave in the manner appropriate to them:

> Those of you who are in need, come! Generosity depends upon the poor just as the poor depend upon generosity. Generosity

33 Ibid., vol. 1, 214.   34 Iqbal, *The Life and Work of Jalaluddin Rumi*, p. 230.
35 Eflâkî, *Ariflerin Menkıbeleri (Mevlânâ ve Etrafındakiler)*, vol. 1, p. 230 (§ 188).
36 Rumi, *Mathnawi*, ed. Nicholson, III: 2895–9.

needs the poor and the weak just as the beautiful need a clean and polished mirror. The face of beauty is revealed to be beautiful in the mirror. Benefaction and benevolence are revealed among the beautiful poor . . . While the poor are a mirror for generosity, however, it is important to remember that breathing on the mirror will distort the reflection.[37]

In addition to applying the word poverty to a shortage of property and wealth, a person who sees himself and all his possessions as literally nothing is in Sufism described as poor, even if he is in fact wealthy. Mawlana saw himself as related to the family of the Prophet, whom he called 'the Sultan of the Poor' and not to the Egyptian Pharaoh. Poverty in a strictly material sense, he believed, could result from an excessive number of children. He explained the *hadith* 'I take pride in poverty' as meaning that nothing belongs to us and everything belongs to God. He adduced this *hadith* again by asking: 'Is the *hadith* that tells us "poverty is my pride" meaningless? No, there are thousands of wonderful and enticing things hidden in it.'[38] For this reason, the *hadith* that poverty is a reason for pride is a splendid precept, offering a way for wealth to pass to God from the avaricious, from those who might hide riches and treasure in ruins to protect them from the desire of those who live in towns or cities.[39]

If the resources that are essential for production remain idle, there is obviously no production. One of the essential resources for production is knowledge. Although Mawlana sees production as a benefit to society, he never took the position that it was the basis for social structure in a political and especially in a feudal sense, as was the case with spoils seized during military campaigns. For this reason, we can say that he does not regard it as determinative.

Mawlana sees the division of labour in society as dependent upon the differences in human character: 'A task becomes easy for someone in accordance with his nature.'[40] The point is important because life in this world is based upon activity. Indeed, our sustenance depends upon activity, and the world in which we live is *dar al-masaʿi* (a place of work). Prophets who were able to perform miracles nevertheless supported themselves by manual labour. Mawlana preferred earning

---

37 Ibid., I: 2744–50. 38 Ibid., I: 2357–62. 39 Ibid., V: 715–16.
40 Jalal al-Din Rumi, *Maktubat*, ed. Tawfiq Subhani (Tehran 1371 A.Hsh./1992), p. 112, letter 40; tr. Abdülbâki Gölpınarlı, *Mevlânâ Celâleddin Mektuplar* (Istanbul 1963), p. 62.

money and donating it as a way of achieving the real goal of labour. He reminds us that if no one had any desire or inclination, there would be no sense in prohibiting either of them. After all, no one fights against the dead. Mawlana therefore teaches that if God has given us a general command that is not expressed in a specific instruction about feeding the poor, we should understand that our responsibility is to earn money first and then feed the poor. God has set a trap for desire by urging us to eat and after that not to waste what we have.[41]

Despite his obvious concern with spiritual and ethical matters, Mawlana does provide some specific information about commercial life. An examination of incidents described in his works will show that commerce was flourishing while he was alive. When he explains the administration of bazaars, Mawlana mentions the superintendent of markets and the warden of bazaars among those who were authorized to direct such activities. When he addresses the limits placed on the profit generated by bazaars, he mentions the highest rate of profit.

Rumi also devotes space in his books to those who do not rely on conventional means to support themselves, embarking instead on schemes for enrichment such as alchemy, astrology, searching for treasure, and praying for miracles. Rumi does not forbid inheritance where money has been acquired by such methods, but disapproves of these methods because they are inherently unreliable, because the heir cannot assess the real value of the property, because deceitful conduct will invariably cause regret, and because hunting for treasure is not an activity that actually requires knowledge, even though the treasure hunters might well possess it. He did not allow his disciples to beg, and advised them to support themselves through trade, writing or physical labour: 'We closed the door to begging for our own disciples. Let them ensure their livelihood through trade, writing, or any kind of manual work or physical labour. We have carried out the command of the Prophet: "Your strength is sufficient; be careful about being in need."[42] If any of our disciples does not keep to this path, he is worthless.'[43]

41 Rumi, *Mathnawi*, ed. Nicholson, v: 574, 582.

42 Our Prophet spoke in this way in one of his *hadith:* 'Begging blackens the face. People stain their faces by the manner of begging. The only exceptions are if one asks for justice from the head of the state or begs in order to procure the essentials of life.' Tirmizi, *Zekât* 38; Nesai, *Zekât* 93.

43 Eflâkî, *Ariflerin Menkıbeleri (Mevlânâ ve Etrafındakiler)*, vol. 1, p. 213 (§155); Fürûzanfer (Badiʿ al-Zaman Furuzanfar), *Mevlânâ Celâleddin*, tr. Uzluk, p. 177.

When Rumi discusses his views about society and about our know-ledge of our selves, in other words about human psychology,[44] he explains that the state is essential to ensure order in society.[45] He also addresses the fiscal measures necessary to ensure the management of life and property. His views do not advocate market intervention. In other words, we can assume that he preferred the independence of markets where supply and demand was concerned.

Just as there is a balance in nature, social peace and progress depend upon accommodation and cooperation. In this sense, society resembles an orchestra. Order in society depends upon justice, which means that everything should be in its proper place. The reason why measure-ments and weights were created for commercial transactions was to ensure social justice.

In his books, Mawlana primarily used descriptions of an urban society. The size of the houses built in Konya during this period provides evidence of affluent social conditions. However, Mawlana explained that his path was the path of the Prophet, and that he therefore had no desire for worldly wealth or for a lavish mansion.[46] Just as he advised a son that the sky was far loftier than any house or palace, he explained that an inheritance from the radiance of the Prophet would be more splendid than any other.[47]

CONCLUSIONS

Mawlana Jalal al-Din Rumi addressed social and economic topics con-nected with human behaviour in his works, especially in the *Math-nawi*. Although in some later accounts, Mawlana is said to perform astonishing miracles such as 'putting his hand in his pocket and pulling out a new silver coin', he does not mention the subject in his own books.

---

44 Mustafa Tekin, 'Mevlana Celaleddin Rumi'de Din ve Toplum', Selçuk Üniversitesi Sosyal Bilimler Enstitüsü unpublished master's thesis (Konya 1995), p. 42.

45 Adem Esen, 'Mevlana'nın Eserlerinde Sosyal İlişkiler ve Toplum Düzeni', *Uluslar-arası Düşünce ve Sanatta Mevlana'nin Sempozyum Bildirileri*, Çanakkale Onsekiz Mart Üniversitesi İlahiyat Fakültesi (25–28 Mart, 2006), pp. 9–20.

46 Eflâkî, *Ariflerin Menkıbeleri (Mevlânâ ve Etrafındakiler)*, vol. 1, p. 208 (§ 148).

47 Ülgener holds views of this sort about Sufism having made the greatest contribution to social order. In this way, a religious and spiritual aristocracy was revealed to be above the princes of the world. See Sabri Fehmi Ülgener, *Zihniyet ve Din: İslam, Tasavvuf ve Çözülme Devri İktisat Ahlakı* (Istanbul 1981), p. 100.

Mawlana did not assess economic questions directly. However, because he was examining human behaviour, he discussed our views of the world and our attitude to material possessions. He based his thoughts on the Qur'an and on the *hadith*. Although the years in which he lived were a time of political turmoil, it was nevertheless a period during which production and trade flourished in Anatolia.

Mawlana believed in the value of work and ascetic discipline, and therefore considered labour as part of service to God. He advocated the use of human will to give shape to economic development, and at the same time warned against the materialism that can lurk within us. The following metaphor which was cited above gives an excellent illustration of his view of the world. The buoyancy of a ship depends upon the existence of water. The world needs it for life. If a ship takes on water, it sinks; if we take the world into our hearts, we lose our purpose. In other words, the world is not outside us. It must be sought within us.[48]

Mawlana referred to a famous *hadith:* 'There is no monasticism in Islam.'[49] In this way, he demonstrated a fundamental difference between Christianity and Islam: the religion of Jesus involves the renunciation of desire, as well as a spiritual battle conducted in solitude; the religion of Ahmad, or Muhammad, requires us to work.

Mawlana placed activity above passivity, and saw the fact that every prophet had a profession as a lesson for all of us. For this reason, we too must have a profession. He connects the division of labour with the differences in human nature.

It is essential for us to be generous, according to Mawlana. In a period when a system of social security was not provided by the state, in any modern sense, the institutions of *zakat* and *sadaqa* performed this essential function. Mawlana therefore advised the rich to fulfil their duty. He stood as a patron of the poor. In fact, he lived the life of a poor man and endured poverty himself. But he did not identify himself with poverty in the literal sense. When he discussed poverty, he explained the *hadith:* 'I am proud of poverty' as meaning that nothing belongs to us because everything belongs to God.

---

48 Rumi, *Mathnawi*, ed. Nicholson, I: 985–90.
49 Badiʿ al-Zaman Furuzanfar, *Ahadith-i Mathnawi* (Tehran 1335 A.Hsh./1966; reprinted 1361 A.Hsh./1982), p. 189, no. 598.

The world in which we live depends upon activity. Mawlana's view of material objects and of the physical world is derived from this conviction: 'There is blessing in activity.'

In his books, Mawlana also observed various deficiencies that arise in the operation of the markets – in other words, in economic life – from an imbalance of information. Alongside more conventional ways of accumulating wealth, Mawlana discusses techniques of searching for treasure and activities such as astrology, as well as the essential characteristics of each of them. He assigned importance to knowledge and to production. He does not examine the question of wealth acquired as plunder during military campaigns.

Although Mawlana does not make any direct statement about intervention in the markets, what we would describe as a liberal approach to the question was characteristic of the period in which he lived.

Mawlana assumed that he was addressing an urban society. The various sizes of house in Konya at the time indicate the stratification of this society. Nevertheless, rather than offering an economic or political critique of the society in which he lived, Mawlana examined these fundamental questions in spiritual and ethical terms.

BIBLIOGRAPHY

Aflaki, Shams al-Din Ahmad. *Manaqib al-ᶜarifin*, ed. Tahsin Yazıcı as Aḥmed al-Aflākī al-ᶜArifī, *Manāqib al-ᶜārifīn*. 2 vols., Ankara, 1959 and 1961. Tr. Tahsin Yazıcı as Ahmed Eflâkî, *Ariflerin Menkıbeleri (Mevlânâ ve Etrafındakiler)*. 2 vols., Istanbul, 1964.

Akdağ, Mustafa. *Türkiye'nin İktisadi ve İçtimai Tarihi*. 2 vols., Ankara, 1995.

Ankaravî, İsmail. *Hadislerle Tasavvuf ve Mevlevi Erkanı*. Ed. Semih Ceyhan, Istanbul, 2001.

Arasteh, A. Reza. *Rumi the Persian, the Sufi: Rebirth in Creativity and Love*. London, 1974.

Can, Şefik. *Mesnevi'den Seçmeler: Cevâhir-i Mesneviyye*, 2 vols., Istanbul, 2001.

Esen, Adem. *Mevlana Celaleddin Rumi'nin İktisat Anlayışı*. Konya, 2007.

—. 'Mevlana'nın Eserlerinde Sosyal İlişkiler ve Toplum Düzeni', *Uluslararası Düşünce ve Sanatta Mevlana Sempozyum Bildirileri*. Çanakkale Onsekiz Mart Üniversitesi İlahiyat Fakültesi, 25–28 Mart, 2006, pp. 9–20.

Furuzanfar, Badiᶜ al-Zaman. *Risala dar ahwal va zindigani-yi Mawlana*

Jalal al-Din Muhammad. Tehran, 1315 A.Hsh./1936. Tr. Feridun Nafiz Uzluk as Bediüzzaman Fürûzanfer, *Mevlânâ Celâleddin*. Ankara, 1962.

—. *Ahadith-i Mathnawi*. Tehran, 1335 A.Hsh./1966; reprinted 1361 A.Hsh./1982.

Gölpınarlı, Abdülbâki. *Mevlânâ: Hayatı, Sanatı, Yapıtlarından Seçmeler*. Istanbul, 1951.

—. *Melâmîlik ve Melâmîler*. Istanbul, 1931.

Iqbal, Afzal. *The Life and Work of Jalaluddin Rumi*. London, 1983.

Lewis, Franklin D. *Rumi: Past and Present, East and West*. Oxford, 2001.

Merçil, Erdoğan. *Türkiye Selçukluları'nda Meslekler*. Ankara, 2000.

Mevlevi, Tahirü'l (Tahir Olgun) and Şefik Can. *Şerh-i Mesnevi*. 18 vols., Istanbul, 2007.

Nicholson, R. A. *Rumi: Poet and Mystic*. London, 1950. Tr. Ayten Lermioğlu as *Mevlâna Celâleddin Rûmî*. Istanbul, 1973.

Rumi, Jalal al-Din. *Kitab-i Fihi ma fihi*. Ed. Badi° al-Zaman Furuzanfar, Tehran, 1348 A.Hsh./1969

—. *Mathnawi*. Ed. and tr. Reynold A. Nicholson as *The Mathnawi of Jalálu'ddín Rúmí*. 8 vols., London 1925–40.

—. *Maktubat*. Ed. Tawfiq Subhani as *Maktubat-i Mawlana Jalal al-Din Rumi*. Tehran, 1371 A.Hsh./1992.

—. *Divan-i kabir*. Ed. Badi° al-Zaman Furuzanfar as *Kulliyat-i Shams ya Diwan-i kabir az guftar-i Mawlana Jalal al-Din Muhammad mashhur bih-Mawlavi, ba tashihat wa havashi*. Tehran, 1363 A.Hsh./1984, 10 vols. in 9.

Sayar, Ahmet Güner. *Gönül Pazarı: İnsanlar, Olaylar ve Mekanlara Dair Yazılar*. Istanbul, 2007.

Schimmel, Annemarie. *The Triumphal Sun: A Study of the Works of Jalâloddin Rumi*. 2nd ed., Albany, 1993.

Taneri, Aydın. *Türkiye Selçukluları Kültür Hayatı (Menâkibü'l-Arifin'in Değerlendirilmesi)*. Konya, 1977.

Tekin, Mustafa. 'Mevlana Celaleddin Rumi'de Din ve Toplum'. Selçuk Üniversitesi Sosyal Bilimler Enstitüsü. Unpublished master's thesis, Konya, 1995.

Turan, Osman. *Selçuklular Tarihi ve Türk-İslam Medeniyeti*. Ankara, 1965.

Ülgener, Sabri Fehmi. *Zihniyet ve Din: İslam, Tasavvuf ve Çözülme Devri İktisat Ahlakı*. Istanbul, 1981.

Yalçın, Aydın. *Türkiye Tarihi*. Ankara, 1979.

Yazır, Elmalılı Hamdi. *Hak Dini Kur'an Dili*. 9 vols., Istanbul, 1936.

From Rumi's *Mathnawi*

The Touchstone

Translated by Leonard Lewisohn

The stone of death acts as touchstone for all
Who'd stake a claim to elegance and grace.
Now that touchstone is gone it's time to boast –
Watch how the fakes boast and swagger and brag
Now the touchstone's gone and lost to woman and man
Around the land, they fete and celebrate
You from place to place. Look how the counterfeit
Coin scoffs with scorn – 'What? – *Pure gold*!? –
When were you ever any better than me?'
'You're honourable indeed,' the gold replies,
'But beware, my touchstone is on the way!'
The body's death is a welcome gift to adepts:
What loss does pure gold suffer from a secateurs' blade?

The benevolent pass away but their benevolence
Remains behind – one who rides this steed knows the joy.
The doers of iniquity perish but injustice from them
Remains – wretched the soul that cheats and wreaks
Duplicity and deceit! Hence it was the Prophet said,
'Delighted are they who've left the world behind
And from them their good deeds alone remained.'[1]

1 *The Mathnawi of Jalálu'ddín Rúmí*, ed. Reynold A. Nicholson (London: Luzac & Co.
1925–40), IV: 1674, 1677–81; 1201–03

Rūmī on Tolerance: A Philosophical Analysis

Mehdi Aminrazavi[1]

Ever since the very inception of Islam, there have been two distinct approaches and interpretations of what constitutes 'religion'. The first interpretation is that of the Muslim jurists (*fuqahā*), according to whom Islam is a collection of Divine laws that must be followed unconditionally.[2] The second interpretation belongs to the Muslim philosophers and sages (*ḥukamā*), who understand Islam as a dynamic and multi-layered sacred doctrine subject to a variety of interpretations. The latter group includes not only Muslim philosophers and theologians, but also the Sufis and the gnostic theosophers (*ʿurafā*) of Islam.

The jurists, who have traditionally advocated an orthodox and legalistic version of Islam, rest their claims on the following premises:

1 Islam is the divinely revealed Truth.
2 This Truth is none other than the *Sharīʿa*.
3 The jurists (*fuqahā*) are the experts in matters of *Sharīʿa*.
4 Therefore, the jurists are the only ones who know the *Truth* of Islam.

These simple but disingenuous propositions have proved extremely detrimental to Islamic civilization in general and have led to the closing of the Muslim mind in particular. One of the most important figures in the history of classical Islam who declared war on this epistemological viewpoint, the claim that one can know the absolute Truth in this fashion, was Jalāl al-Dīn Rūmī. He consistently struggled to combat the philistine authoritarianism of such an exclusivistic

1 I am grateful to the editor, Leonard Lewisohn, for his extensive suggestions and comments especially with regard to the translations of Rūmī's poems.
2 Basing themselves on the Qurʾānic passage (v: 59) which exhorts: 'O believers! Obey God, obey the messenger and those of you who are in authority.'

legalistic vision of religion. Throughout his *Mathnawī*[3] in particular, he utterly subverts the legitimacy and authority on the basis of which certain individuals or classes attempted to dictate their version of Islam as the only truth.

Traditionally, Rūmī has been perceived as a Sufi poet, the kind who not only was disinterested in discursive thought, but who scorned philosophy and ridiculed philosophers for walking on wobbly stilts:

> Rationalists' legs are just like stilts;
> How unfixed and stolid are feet of wood![4]

Although it is true that Rūmī had no direct interest in Greek philosophy, it would be a mistake to ignore the profound philosophical concepts that are deeply embedded in the ocean of his thought. Anyone who reads Rūmī's *Mathnawī* and the *Dīvān-i Shams* with the trained eye of a philosopher can easily find most of the philosophical themes and topics discussed among Peripatetic philosophers in Islam scattered throughout his poetry in a non-discursive manner.[5] Rūmī's critique counters the claims of those who adhere to an absolutist version of the Truth, and offers a kind of epistemological humility that opens the door to tolerance.

While traditionally there have been several epistemological theories on how truth can be obtained, four of the major theories are as follows:

1 Truth by correspondence;
2 Truth by authority;
3 Truth by reasoning;
4 Truth by intuition.

'Truth by correspondence' is the most common form of gaining cognition. This theory posits that by reflecting on the external reality of appearances through the use of the senses, one can claim to know the

---

3 Rūmī, *Mathnawī-yi maʿnawī*, ed. R. A. Nicholson (Tehran: Amīr Kabīr 1357 A.Hsh./1978).
4 Ibid., I: 2127.
5 See for instance Jalāl al-Dīn Humaʾī, *Mawlawī-nāma: Mawlawī chih mīgūyad* (Tehran: Nashr-i Humā 1385 A.Hsh./ 2006), 10th printing, 2 vols., which presents the full range of the philosophical themes in his *Mathnawī*.

object of one's cognition. In any act of cognition, there are three components: the knower, the known, and the epistemic relation between them. This view, initially elaborated upon by Aristotle, maintains that the soul/self is like a mirror which reflects the external world: I know there is an apple because there is an apple in the external world whose reflection in my mind allows me to make a truth claim in this regard. However, 'Truth by correspondence' relies on all the five senses, not just sight, and therefore their reliability and verifiability becomes a necessary condition for one's truth claim to be authentic.

Throughout his *Mathnawī* and *Dīvān-i Shams*, Rūmī criticizes the reliability of the senses, deconstructing the validity of the truth claims made on the basis of sensory perception:

> All the senses of man are impermanent
> For in the presence of the light of the Day of Resurrection
>   they're naught.
> The light of the senses and spirits of our fathers
> Is not totally evanescent and naught like plants.[6]

Even if the senses provide us with knowledge, it is not a type of knowledge that can lead to any serious spiritual and existential truth, since it is simply knowledge of the external world, which, although useful within its own domain of application, fails in attaining the ultimate Truth. Rūmī thus asserts:

> The animal man who by deceit and cunning knows . . .
> The intricacies of the science of geometry
> Or astronomy, medicine and philosophy
> Which are concerned with this world
> Is barred from finding the way to the seventh heaven.
> All those sciences are fit for is building a stable;
> They serve as columns for the abode of camels and cows.
> Their purpose is but to let the animal survive a day or two
> And yet these imbeciles call those sciences 'mysteries'.[7]

The above are a few of literally hundreds of verses in which Rūmī criticizes sense perception as a valid means of attaining knowledge.

---

6 Ibid., IV: 431–33.   7 Ibid., IV: 1516–19.

The theory of 'Truth by authority' is also assessed and appraised by Rūmī as a viable epistemological basis for accepting a truth claim. According to this theory, which was well known to traditional Islamic jurisprudence, people are to be divided into two categories; one is either a follower of authority (*muqallid*) or an independent legal authority (*mujtahid*) oneself. It is incumbent upon the former to follow the latter. 'Truth by authority' was widely accepted by Muslims in two ways: exoterically by Sunni Muslims in the form of absolute obedience to the religious law and the 'men of learning' (*ʿulamā*'), and both exoterically and esoterically by many Shi'ite Muslims with respect to obeying those who are learned in legal and spiritual matters. Among the Shi'ite Ismā'īlī Muslims, this theory led them to propound absolute obedience to their Imāms – considered to be infallible – as the only source of emulation and truth; thus the Ismā'īlīs became nicknamed 'the followers of authority' (*taʿlīmiyyūn*).

In the *Mathnawī*, Rūmī repeatedly rejects the idea that truth can be realized by following an authority alone and alludes to the dangerous nature of blindly following those who claim to know the truth. Needless to say, this theory remains particularly appealing, if not axiomatic, to the fundamentalist mindset, whether one be a jurist belonging to the Shāfi'ī school, a follower of the puritanical Wahhābī sect, or a desperado like Bin Laden and his al-Qā'ida affiliates. However, Rūmī contests this theory, protesting:

> A myriad of servile conformists who follow conjecture
> Are cast down into the lowest depths, struck by scruples.
> For the speculative following of precedent and logical supposition
> Is their foundation and the very feather and wing of their flight.
> Their inner devil arouses doubts and specious arguments in them
> Till benightedly they plummet headlong down like blind folk.[8]

Finally, Rūmī tells us that the intellect has a tendency to ascend and elevate consciousness, whereas following the doctrine of 'Truth by authority' with blind imitation (*taqlīd*) debases the intellect:

> Even though your intellect tends to fly aloft,
> The bird of your religious conformism descends to feed on what
>   is base.

8 Ibid., IV: 2125–27.

Knowledge based on blind imitation [of authority] is our souls' bane;
It is borrowed knowledge, yet we rest assured that it's truly ours.[9]

In what appears to be a commentary on the Qur'ānic verses which rebuke those who cast doubt on the Islamic eschatological doctrine and instead offer their personal opinions and conjecture (*al-ẓinn*), admonishing that 'conjuncture avails nothing regarding Truth',[10] Rūmī likens the truth to a bird with two wings. Followers of conjecture and personal opinion, that is, those who blindly follow the doctrine of 'Truth by authority' (*taqlīd*), are like birds that fly with only one wing.

> Knowledge has two wings; conjecture only one wing;
> Conjecture is deficient and so its flight is curtailed.
> The one-winged bird quickly falls down headlong,
> Then skips up a step or two or more;
> The bird of conjecture first soars up, then falls down,
> Dragging itself with its one wing, hoping to reach its nest.
> Once from conjecture it's delivered and knowledge to it revealed,
> The one-winged bird gains two wings and flitters away.
> . . . With two wings, she flies aloft like Gabriel
> Without supposition, without 'perhaps', 'maybe' and vain parley.[11]

Addressing the doctrine of 'Truth by reasoning', the noose around the neck of those who purport to know the Truth becomes tighter as Rūmī moves forward to offer his criticism of the most powerful tools in the arsenal of the learned: reason and rationality. His scathing attack upon them is relentless and systematic, but often misunderstood. First and foremost, Rūmī divides the intellect into two types: the universal intellect (ʿaql-i kullī) and particular intellect (ʿaql-i juzʾī).[12] For Rūmī, the universal intellect attends to the affairs of the Divine realm, whereas the particular intellect's scope is restricted to matters pertaining to this world. The difference between the two intellects is fundamental and central to his understanding of creation and human

---

9 Ibid., II: 2326–27.   10 Qur'ān, LIII: 27–28.

11 Rūmī, *Mathnawī*, ed. Nicholson, III: 1510–13; 1515.

12 For further discussion of this distinction, see William Chittick, *The Sufi Path of Love: The Spiritual Teachings of Rumi* (Albany, NY: State University of New York Press 1983), pp. 35–37.

nature. In his response to the Islamic rationalists (Mu'tazilites) Rūmī asserts:

> The difference among intellects was intrinsic in origin –
> You should hear the doctrine according to the Sunnis
> – Contrary to the opinion of the Mu'tazilites,
> Who maintain all intellects in their origin were basically equal
> But by experience and learning, minds increase or decrease
> So one is made more knowledgeable than the other one –
> Their doctrine is false because even a boy's counsel
> Who has no experience in any course of action
> – From that young child a thought will spring up
> Of which a wise old sage with manifold experience has no inkling.[13]

It is imperative to realize that Rūmī was not opposed to reason or rationality *per se* – as many have assumed. His views regarding the use and function of reason and rationality were similar to those of Ghazālī, who argued that within their own domain, reason and rational analysis do have validity and a proper use. Both types of intellect are needed for human beings to function; the problem, philosophers have argued, occurs when their functions are conflated. Rūmī's clear distinction between these two intellects is a serious critique of the claims of both sorts of absolutists: those who on the one hand advocate the blind following of 'Truth by authority', and those dogmatic intellectuals who inculcate the doctrine of the exclusive pursuit of 'Truth by reasoning' on the other hand:

> The intellect is of two kinds: the first acquired,
> Which you learn in school like a child –
> Through books and teachers, by reflection and repetition,
> From abstract ideas and the best and newest sciences,
> Your intelligence thus becomes superior to others,
> Though retention [of this knowledge] is burdensome and weighs
>   you down.[14]

---

13 Rūmī, *Mathnawī*, ed. Nicholson, III: 1539–43.   14 Ibid., IV: 1960–62.

As for the other intellect, the universal intellect (ʿaql-i kullī), Rūmī tells us:

> The other intellect is a gift from God,
> Whose source is like a spring within the soul.
> When the water of knowledge gushes forth from the heart,
> It neither becomes fetid, grows old nor wilts.
> If its path where it flows is blocked, why worry?
> For like a spring it gushes forth from the house constantly.
> The acquired intellect is like a water sluice
> Running down into houses from the hills;
> If the path of water is obstructed, it's undone:
> Seek the spring from within yourself.[15]

'Reason' as employed by philosophers, Rūmī tells us, is a stranger to revelation because of its reliance on rational demonstrations and proofs; this dependence on rational modes of cognition leads it to reject anything else that is not objectively verifiable by the five external senses or by its own limited powers of analysis. Philosophers thus reject the validity of both the intuitive knowledge of the Sufis and divine revelation:

> The philosopher through thought and surmise is in denial –
> Tell him go and smash his head against this wall.
> The language of water, of earth and mire
> Is comprehensible to the senses of the heart's adepts.
> The philosopher who is sceptical about the moaning pillar[16]
> Is himself estranged from the senses of the saints.
> Such things are, he says, but a reflection of melancholic passions
> Which generate these wild fantasies in people's heads.[17]

---

15 Ibid., IV: 1964–68.

16 This refers to a story about a palm-trunk used as a pillar in the Prophet's mosque in Medina, which the Prophet used to lean against when preaching. At a later date, when a pulpit (*minbar*) was built for him to sit on, the palm-trunk wailed aloud and moaned in agony from being separated from the Prophet. See Nicholson's Commentary on *Mathnawī*, Bk. 1, p. 141 (verse 2113).

17 Rūmī, *Mathnawī*, ed. Nicholson, I: 3278–81.

If neither sense-perception, nor external authorities, nor rationality, nor logic can provide us with truth and certainty, perhaps intuition will do so. The theory of 'Truth by intuition' has two aspects:

First, this theory posits, indeed insists on the idea, that there exists a faculty through which truth and reality can be apprehended with certitude. In the mystical sense of the word, this faculty has to be 'awakened' through the arduous process of following the mystical path.

The second aspect of the faculty of intuition, according to Muslim philosophers, relates to its more gnostic connotation. In this sense, intuition has traditionally been employed as the basis for an epistemological theory known as 'knowledge by presence' (*ʿilm al-ḥuḍūrī*).[18] Rationalists, from Plato to Descartes, and the majority of post-Avicennan Muslim philosophers, have supported some version or other of this theory. Despite its variations, elaborations and reformulations by masters of the School of Isfahan, such as Mullā Ṣadrā (d. 1050/1640), this theory remains the basis for the most common form of truth claims concerning our knowledge of the universals, the intelligible realities and particularly, knowledge of the 'self' in the Islamic intellectual tradition. The most important philosopher-sage in Islam to have based his philosophical paradigm on this theory was Shihāb al-Dīn Yaḥyā Suhrawardī (d. 587/1191), the founder of the Illuminationist (*ishrāqī*) school.[19] In this respect, the theory attempts to address and answer our knowledge of *a priori* and axiomatic concepts such as 'How do I know that part of something is smaller than the whole, or that the shortest distance between any two points is a straight line?' Similarly, as Plato tells us in his dialogue with the slave boy in his work *Meno*, much of the mathematical knowledge one possesses is innate and recollected intuitively, independent of the senses or any authority.

This rather complex issue is thoroughly treated by Rūmī in the following manner. First, he posits that there are five *internal spiritual senses* that complement the five external physical senses, which are capable of attaining a superior suprasensory type of knowledge. All of the ten senses, internal and external, are controlled by the 'heart',

---

18 See Mehdī Hāʾirī Yazdī, *The Principles of Epistemology in Islamic Philosophy: Knowledge by Presence*, (Albany: SUNY 1992).

19 See Mehdi Aminrazavi, *Suhrawardi and the School of Illumination* (Richmond, UK: Curzon 1997).

which is the organ of supersensory perception. These senses are described by Rūmī as follows:

> There are five [spiritual] senses besides these five [physical] senses.
> The former are like red gold and the latter like copper.
> In the marketplace where the expert connoisseurs are busy
> How should the copper and golden senses be priced the same?
> The physical senses' nutriment is murky and tenebrous;
> The spiritual sense sups and dines on the sun.[20]

And referring to the heart's control of the ten senses, he writes:

> Has not the heart indeed got Solomon's seal
> So that it has the five senses under control?
> The five external senses it easily manages,
> The five internal senses are subject to its sway.
> There are ten senses, seven bodily limbs. As for the rest,
> Reckon them up as being beyond discourse.[21]

In these verses he describes the transmutation of the physical senses into spiritual senses:

> Once one sense breaks its chain,
> Other senses were transformed as well;
> Once one sense perceives supersensory things,
> The invisible realm is revealed to all the other senses . . .
> Every sense of yours then becomes a messenger to the others,
> Leading all the senses into paradise.
> Those senses then will share their secrets with your sense
> Without language, transcending truth and abstraction . . .
> Once all those senses become subject to your sense,
> The heavenly spheres cannot avoid obeying your command.[22]

Here we see that although Rūmī tacitly endorses the superiority of knowledge by intuition over knowledge gained by sense perception,

---

20 Rūmī, *Mathnawī*, ed. Nicholson, II: 49–51.
21 Ibid., I: 3575–77.   22 Ibid., II: 3240–41; 3245–46; 3249.

ratiocination and logic, he acknowledges that this method has its limits too. Knowledge by intuition can transcend the sensible world and attain what is often called 'non-propositional truth claims' but ultimately the mode of thought that is needed to approach the truth must transcend thought itself.

> I'll derange word, sound and speech
> So without these three I can talk to you.[23]

As long as one relies on thought and thinking, one is operating conceptually within the limits of intellection. Even the arch-rationalist mathematician and astronomer, ʿUmar Khayyam, is said to have uttered the following shortly before his death, 'O God, I have come to know you in as much as it is possible for me. Forgive me, for my knowledge is from you and my journey is towards you.'[24] Human thought, no matter how profound and refined, is nevertheless a by-product of human intellection and thus ultimately always fails to know God completely.

With the recognition of the limitations of human ability to categorically obtain knowledge of the truth, Rūmī completely abandons the pursuit of knowing God through intuition for a more epistemologically experiential mode of cognition. Here, 'knowing' changes to 'becoming'. Information becomes transformation and the knower becomes a lover who is no longer interested in merely knowing some inconsequential niceties concerning his beloved; instead he becomes interested in experiencing her presence. Abandoning the domain of intellection, the object of which is the material realm and the knowledge thereof, Rūmī embraces the madness of love as ultimately the most authentic and veridical mode of both being and cognition. He asserts:

> Love is a stranger to the two worlds
> For in love there are seventy-two madnesses.[25]

---

23 Ibid., I: 1730.

24 ʿAllahuma inī ʿaraftaka ʿalā mablagh imkānī fā aghfirlī faʿn maʿrifatī iyāka wa sayyalatī alayka. Bayhaqī, Tatimah Ṣiwān al-ḥikmah, (Beirut: Dār al-Fikr al-Lubnānī 1994), pp. 116–17.

25 Rūmī, Mathnawī, ed. Nicholson, III: 4719.

I've tested enough reason's lengthy reveries;
From now on, I will embrace madness[26]

One must wallow in ignorance of this worldly intelligence,
And take insanity into one's embrace.[27]

Although the doctrine of 'Truth by Love' pervades Rūmī's *Mathnawī*, which is a work that contains a methodical commentary on a vast body of gnostic themes, it is the central and dominant theme throughout his collection of lyrics, the *Dīvān-i Shams-i Tabrīzī*.[28] To better appreciate this doctrine, it is to this work we should turn. Here, we witness a bewildered, tormented lover, lamenting separation and seeking unity with God, abandoning the desire to *know* about his beloved for the sake of experiencing love itself. One does not *know* the beloved, one *experiences* love; one does not *know* the truth, one *becomes* the truth; one does not *know* food, one *tastes* food. In this fashion, a mode of knowledge becomes replaced by a mode of being, using Søren Kierkegaard's memorable phrase; henceforth it is not *what* one knows that matters, but *how* one relates to the truth understood which becomes of primary importance to the knower.

Rūmī's emphasis on a personal, spiritual and existential mode of being is precisely the opposite of the orthodox mindset concerned with the piety and salvation of the 'Other'. Rūmī is too intoxicated with his own experience to be concerned with anyone else's, and encourages his reader to concentrate on the inner work of moral and spiritual self-purification, to resolve his own inner conflict within and ignore the vain 'wars' raging without.[29] His social relevance lies in precisely this focus on self-reformation since his philosophical programme is inwardly directed towards refinement of the heart of each individual, the heart being the key internal supersensory organ which is the quintessence of humanity itself.

In one of the most exquisite examples of his poetry, Rūmī alludes to the two distinct phases of his life, one as the early teacher of the

26 Ibid., II: 2332.   27 Ibid., II: 2328.
28 See ʿAlī Riḍā Mukhtārpūr Qahrūdī, ʿIshq dar manzūma-yi Shams: vāzha-yābī-yi ʿishq dar Dīvān-i kabīr-i Mawlānā Jalāl al-Dīn Muḥammad mashhūr bih Mawlavī (Tehran: Amīr Kabīr 1378 A.Hsh./1999)
29 See Rūmī, Mathnawī, ed. Nicholson, VI: 51–54.

Qur'an, jurisprudence and religious sciences and the other later as an intoxicated mystic, who abandoned 'knowing' and embraced 'becoming'. He describes his love affair as follows:

> My drunkenness today is not like my drunkenness yesterday.
> Do you not believe me? Take the goblet and drink this wine –
> I was drowned in wine, my intellect was washed away.
> Discursive wisdom said farewell; I will not find sobriety.
> In my madness, intellect and wisdom left the world
> Like a pot that boils over when it cooks too much,
> My drunken heart broke the chain and freed itself.
> Leave the drunkard alone, speak not, remain silent![30]

A glance at *Dīvān-i Shams* reveals an astonishing number of poems in which Rūmī advocates personal spiritual attainment as the ultimate goal of the spiritual odyssey. He asserts that neither the sciences of philosophy, theology nor the study of the Canon Law can lead one out of the bewilderment of our earthly maze. Only love can. The non-propositional nature of love, transformed into a profound experience which transcends language, is the antidote to all self-consciously 'orthodox' and sanctimonious doctrinal approaches to the question of truth.

In response to many questions, Rūmī simply maintains a pregnant apophatic silence; 'Go seek an explanation of this in the mirror of your deeds and actions, for it cannot be grasped by words and discourse,' he advises in one place.[31] From the viewpoint of comparative religion, this suspension of the claim to know the ultimate Truth is a humbling admission that paves the road for adopting different interpretations of religious Truth, one in which Divine sapience and sacred knowledge are expressed as a mode of being and experience and not as theories, beliefs and propositional truth claims. This metamorphosis, Rūmī tells us, requires spiritual death and rebirth, which the Prophet Muḥammad symbolically referred to in his injunction to 'Die before you die.'[32]

---

30 *Kulliyāt-i Shams yā Dīwān-i kabīr az guftār-i Mawlānā Jalāl al-Dīn Muḥammad mashhūr bih Mawlavī, bā taṣḥīḥāt wa ḥawwāshī*, ed. Badī' al-Zamān Furūzānfar, 3rd ed., (Tehran: Sipihr 1363 A.Hsh./1984), ghazal 1270; vv. 13432–35.

31 Rūmī, *Mathnawī*, ed. Nicholson, IV: 2768.

32 Badī' al-Zamān Furūzānfar, *Aḥādīth-i Mathnawī* (Tehran: Dānishgāh-i Tehrān 1335 A.Hsh./1956; reprinted Amīr Kabīr 1361 A.Hsh./1982), p. 116, no. 352.

Die, die and move above this cloud,
Once the cloud is removed, you are a luminous moon
Silence, silence, for silence is close to death
   It is to life that this silence guides.[33]

To be reborn in spirit is to divorce the exoteric sciences and embrace the kind of contemplatively reflective silence which allows a real dialogue to begin:

Be silent, be silent, drink silently.
Veil yourself, veil yourself for you are the hidden treasure.
Speak not, speak not of this exposition of my heart
So you be not bewildered, so you do not remain perplexed.[34]

So taking Rūmī's advice to heart, and bringing this discourse to a silent conclusion, we'll cite his final exhortation:

I will be silent, I will be silent,
So love may narrate its own story;
A soul-nourishing joyous description without finale.[35]

BIBLIOGRAPHY

Aminrazavi, Mehdi. *Suhrawardi and the School of Illumination.* Richmond, UK: Curzon, 1997.

Bayhaqī. *Tatimah Ṣiwān al-ḥikmah.* Beirut: Dār al-Fikr al-Lubnānī, 1994.

Chittick, William. *The Sufi Path of Love: The Spiritual Teachings of Rumi.* Albany, NY: State University of New York Press, 1983.

Furūzānfar, Badī' al-Zamān. *Aḥādīth-i Mathnawī.* Tehran: Dānishgāh-i Tehrān 1335 A.Hsh./1956; reprinted Amīr Kabīr, 1361 A.Hsh./1982.

Humā'ī, Jalāl al-Dīn. *Mawlawī-nāma: Mawlawī chih mīgūyad?* Tehran: Nashr-i Humā, 1385 A.Hsh./2006

---

33 Rūmī, *Kulliyāt-i Shams yā Dīwān-i kabīr,* vol. 2, *ghazal* 636, vv. 6633–34.
34 Ibid., vol. 2, *ghazal* 637, vv. 6649, 6653.   35 Ibid., vol. 5, *ghazal* 2442, v. 25782.

Qahrūdī, ʿAlī Riḍā Mukhtārpūr. *ʿIshq dar manẓūma-yi Shams: vāzha-yābī-yi ʿishq dar Dīvān-i kabīr-i Mawlānā Jalāl al-Dīn Muḥammad, mashhūr bih Mawlavī.* Tehran: Amīr Kabīr, 1378 A.Hsh./1999.

Rūmī, Jalālal-Dīn. *Mathnawī-yi maʿnawī.* Ed. R. A. Nicholson. Tehran: Amīr Kabīr, 1357 A.Hsh./1976.

—. *Kulliyāt-i Shams yā Dīwān-i kabīr az guftar-i Mawlānā Jalāl al-Dīn Muḥammad mashhūr bih Mawlavī, ba taṣḥīḥāt wa ḥawwashī.* Ed. Badīʾ al-Zamān Furūzānfar. 3rd edn, Tehran: Sipihr, 1363 A.Hsh./1984.

Safavi, Seyed Ghahreman. *Rumi's Teachings.* London: Iranian Studies Press, 2008.

Schimmel, Annemarie. *As Through a Veil: Mystical Poetry in Islam.* Oxford: Oneworld, 1982.

—. *Mystical Dimension of Islam.* Malaysia: Islamic Book Trust, 2008.

Yazdī, Mehdī Hāʾirī. *The Principles of Epistemology in Islamic Philosophy: Knowledge by Presence.* Albany: SUNY, 1992.

Rumi and the Abyss of Longing

ROKUS DE GROOT

> Longing is the core of mystery.
> Longing itself brings the cure.
> The only rule is, suffer the pain.
>
> Your desire must be disciplined,
> And what you want to happen
> in time, sacrificed.[1]
>
> (Rumi)

THE METAMORPHOSIS OF THE HUNTER

In his *Metamorphoses,* Ovid recounts the story of Syrinx and Pan. The horns and goat's hindquarters betray Pan's instinctive nature. He is

---

1 John Moyne and Coleman Barks, *Say I Am You* (Athens: Maypop 1994), p. 72. I am grateful to Donca Vianu for bringing this *ruba'i* to my attention, and to Sipko den Boer for providing the reference to its source and other translations. The quatrain is found in B. Furuzanfar, *Kulliyat-i Shams ya Diwan-i kabir az guftar-i Mawlana Jalal al-Din Muhammad mashhur bih-Mawlavi, ba tashihat wa havashi* (Tehran: Sipihr 1363 A.Hsh./1984), vol. 8, Quatrain 311, p. 53. Other translations include that by Ibrahim Gamard and Rawan Farhadi, *The Quatrains of Rumi: Ruba'iyat-é Jalaluddin Muhammad Balkhi-Rumi* (San Rafael, CA: Sophia Perennis 2008), p. 366:

O heart, you must remain with longing pain for Him, for this is the remedy.
Endure longing and don't groan, for this is the command.
If you stamp your foot upon desire for a while,
You will kill the dog of ego. And this is the sacrifice.

– and in John O'Kane's translation of Shams al-Dīn Aḥmad-i Aflākī's *The Feats of the Knowers of God* (*Manāqeb al-'arefin*), (Leiden: Brill 2002), p. 373:

Oh heart, you be in pain because of Him! This is the cure.
Feed on sorrow and speak not. This is the command.
If for a while you press your foot on your desires,
You've killed that dog the carnal soul. This is sacrifice.

quite eager for females. If he espies the beautiful nymph Syrinx he is sure of one thing, he has to get her:

> Descending from Lycaeus, Pan admires
> The matchless nymph, and burns with new desires.
> A crown of pine upon his head he wore;
> And thus began her pity to implore.
> But e'er he thus began, she took her flight
> So swift, she was already out of sight.
> Nor stay'd to hear the courtship of the God;
> But bent her course to Ladon's gentle flood:
> There by the river stopt, and tir'd before;
> Relief from water nymphs her pray'rs implore.
> Now while the lustful God, with speedy pace,
> Just thought to strain her in a strict embrace,
> He fill'd his arms with reeds, new rising on the place.
> And while he sighs, his ill success to find,
> The tender canes were shaken by the wind;
> And breath'd a mournful air, unheard before;
> That much surprizing Pan, yet pleas'd him more.
> Admiring this new musick, Thou, he said,
> Who canst not be the partner of my bed,
> At least shall be the comfort of my mind:
> And often, often to my lips be joyn'd.[2]

As for the last lines, the original Latin has:

> *arte nova vocisque deum dulcedine captum*
> *'hoc mihi colloquium tecum' dixisse 'manebit'*

So Pan says that the 'new art' of the new instrument's 'sweetness of voice' will remain to him like a 'conference' with his beloved in her physical absence.

Comments on this story usually concentrate on the metamorphosis of the nymph Syrinx, the object of longing. She is transformed from a desired woman into a musical instrument in the hands of the one who

---

2 Ovid, *Metamorphoses*, Book I, vv. 698–710. Translation by John Dryden in 1717, available at: http://www.sacred-texts.com/cla/ovid/meta/meta01.htm

desires her: the 'Pan-pipe' which in many languages still carries her name 'Syrinx'.

However, Pan also experiences a transformation. A metamorphosis befalls him because he happens upon what we may call 'the abyss of longing'. It is the experience of many: at the very last moment the object of longing escapes from our intention to catch it. One may describe 'the abyss of longing' as the beloved's sudden disappearance at the very moment when the longing of the lover is fully ignited. Expressed differently, the beloved refuses categorically to serve as the object of the lover's longing, and recedes. Being confronted with this has profound consequences for the lover.[3] In the case of Pan, the abysmal experience transforms him from someone who blindly follows his instincts to one who refines himself into a musician. Significantly this transformation is heralded by his meeting with an *ars nova*, the 'new art' of intimate music.

Music makes the pain of 'the abyss of longing' audible, and helps Pan to temporarily bear the pain and, to some degree, alleviate it. It even seems as if the musician has contact with the object of his longing: it is as if the sound of the 'syrinx' evokes Syrinx herself into presence. That is why Ovid calls the sound of the Pan-pipe a 'conference' (*colloquium*) with the beloved. Ultimately however, all musical tones do die out, down to the very last one.

The melancholy of loss and the semblance of temporary fulfilment has been made audible in a striking way by Claude Debussy's composition devoted to this myth. Listening to his *Syrinx*, a composition for flute solo, is a musical exercise to deal with the abyss of longing. Having to release the object of love, the ensuing pain, the temporary relief realized through expressing that pain, the apparent contact through a musical 'conference' with the beloved, followed by the seeming dissolution of the longing subject into the longing itself while vicariously immersing oneself into the music: Debussy's music touches on all these aspects of the lover's transformative experience in a truly unforgettable fashion.

---

3 For further discussion of the issue of longing, see Mark Epstein, *Open to Desire* (New York: Gotham Books 2004).

THE SUFI SCHOOL OF LOVE

In this essay devoted to the theme of longing in Rumi's poetry, I will first and foremost focus on the phenomenon of the metamorphosis of the subject. In Rumi's texts one encounters many cases similar to that of Pan, in which the one who is taken as an object of longing turns out to have a very powerful transformative effect on the one who longs. The beloved brings about an unexpected metamorphosis in the lover.

Rumi has investigated longing (*shawq*) at various levels. In one verse he expresses in a lucid way that longing, as long as it is a kind of lust to grasp something, only creates duality since it causes a division into subject and object. In his *Divan-i Shams-i Tabriz* we read:

> Those drunk with God, tho' they be thousands, are yet one;
> Those drunk with lust – tho' it be a single one, he is double.[4]

Unlike mere lust, true love transcends the desire for objects, which is why if a lover would even imagine that he might subdue the object of his love, he will be conquered himself. To illustrate this switch, similar to Ovid's myth of Pan and Syrinx, Rumi tells a striking story about a hunt which ends in the metamorphosis of the hunter. The story concerns an episode from the life of the Sufi saint Ibrahim Adham, who before his conversion was the king of Balkh:

> While he was still a king, Ibrahim Adham went on a hunt. Charging after a gazelle, he became utterly separated from his army. Although his horse was drenched in sweat, he galloped on. After passing the end of the plain, the gazelle turned around and said: 'You were not created for this! You were not brought out of non-existence into being in order to hunt me down. Suppose you catch me. Then what?' Hearing this, Ibrahim cried out and threw himself down from his horse. There was no one in that wilderness but a shepherd whom he begged to take his regal, jewel-studded garments, his arms, and his horse. 'Take these,' he said, 'and give me your felt cloak. But tell no one, and give no one any sign of me.' Putting on the felt cloak, he set off on his way.[5]

4 Reynold A. Nicholson, ed. and trans., *Selected Poems from the Divani Shamsi Tabriz* (Richmond: Curzon Press 1994), ghazal xv, pp. 60–61.
5 Wheeler M. Thackston, trans., *Signs of the Unseen: The Discourses of Jalaluddin Rumi*

Rumi unveils the metaphor of the story by mentioning its climax that 'Ibrahim wanted to make the gazelle his prey, but God made him the prey of the gazelle in order that you might realize that things happen in the world as He wills.'[6]

Both the myth of Pan and the tale of Adham point to the same necessary course of inner transformation. Rumi emphasizes this necessity later on in the same discourse by turning to the story of ʿUmar's conversion. ʿUmar was a contemporary of Muhammad, initially an adamant adversary of Islam.

Once, before he became a Muslim, ʿUmar went to his sister's house. She was reciting aloud from Chapter *Taha* of the Koran, but when she saw her brother, she fell silent and hid the book. ʿUmar drew his sword and said, 'Tell me what you were reciting and why you have hidden it away, or I will cut your head off this very instant with my sword and give no quarter!'

Knowing the intensity of his wrath and ferocity and fearing for her life, his sister confessed, 'I was reciting from the words that God has sent down in these latter times to Muhammad.'

'Recite them, then, that I may hear,' said ʿUmar. So she recited Chapter *Taha*. ʿUmar grew a hundred times more wrathful and said, 'If I were to kill you now, it would be an undignified slaying. First I shall go and cut his head off and then I shall see you!' And so, full of wrath and brandishing his naked sword, he set out for the Prophet's mosque.[7]

However, the course of events would take a radically different turn.

The moment ʿUmar entered the mosque he saw plainly a shaft of light fly from the Prophet and pierce his heart. He let out a cry and fell unconscious. Affection and love were born in his soul and, in this great love, he wanted to be obliterated and consumed in the Prophet.[8]

[*Fihi ma fihi*], (Boston & London: Shambhala 1999), Discourse 43, p. 169. See also Coleman Barks, *The Essential Rumi* (Edison: Castle Books 1997), p. 286.

6 *Fihi ma fihi*, in *Signs of the Unseen*, Discourse 43, p. 169.

7 Ibid., p. 169.   8 Ibid., p. 170.

In India we hear similar tales, in which a *guru* or *pir* is made into the target of extreme fury or intense longing, which is the onset of the eventual fundamental change of the subject.[9] Likewise, the New Testament presents a radical story of the same nature: Saul hates Christ to such an extent that he wishes to destroy the entire early Christian community. Wherever he goes he threatens Christians with death.

> And as he journeyed, he came near Damascus: and suddenly there shined round about him a light from heaven: And he fell to the earth, and heard a voice saying unto him, Saul, Saul, why persecutest thou me?[10]

At the height of his campaign of terror against the Christians, on the road to Damacus, Saul undergoes a complete metamorphosis. From then on, with the new name of Paul (derived from Greek *paulos*, meaning 'poor'), he would become one of the main apostles of Christianity.[11]

Common to all these stories is that total concentration on an object – which turns out to be a non-object – brings about a metamorphosis of the subject – who will turn out, as we will see, to be a non-subject. It does not really matter whether love or hate is involved. What counts is the complete one-pointedness of the lover or hater. This is what is emphasized by all the various schools of love and wisdom in these different religious traditions.

Intense longing also plays an important role in the 'School of Love' to which Rumi belongs. This school, the origins of which in Islam are traced back to Rabi'a al-Adawiyya of Basra (d. ca. 172–76/788–92), Dhu'l-Nun al-Misri (d. 245/860), Bayazid al-Bastami (d. 261/875) and later Mansur al-Hallaj (d. 309/922) among many others, views human longing as ultimately a trace of a yearning for God.[12] In fact *all* longing

---

9 See e.g. H.W.L. Poonja, *Wake Up and Roar* (Kula, Maui, Hawaii: Pacific Center Publishing 1993), vol. 2, pp. 12–13.
10 *Bible*, Acts of the Apostles 9: 3–4; King James Version.
11 'Poor' implies the same turn as in 'Umar's desire for obliteration (becoming 'nothing'). I will elaborate on this subject in relation to the concept of *fana'* below. A striking image of this epiphanic event may be seen in a painting by Cornelis Cornelisz of Haarlem, exhibited in the Hrad Gallery, Prague, in which Saul/Paul, surrounded by his retinue, almost has lost his shape in the light radiated on him/ from him.
12 See Ahmet T. Karamustafa, *Sufism: The Formative Period* (Cairo: The American Uni-

is conceived of as being derived from one Longing. Ultimately, it is the origin and destination of all other longings, which it will eventually absorb. This seems to be the message of Rabi'a's song: 'The heart can love none other but Thee.'[13]

These stories described above also share the characteristic that the object of love or hate turns out to evade all attempts by the subject to grasp it. It is exactly this which sets the metamorphosis into motion. Another shared feature is that the object of total love, hate or desire is considered to be something exceptional, an embodiment or messenger of the divine. This is what makes the transformation so irresistibly powerful. Rumi's life is especially exemplary in this respect.

READING RUMI'S TEXTS

One of the main admonitions which Rumi conveys through the voice of the reed flute is that one should not read his words for one's own personal interests and ends, be those emotional needs, personal identity or social constraints. That is one of the meanings of his oft-cited verse-maxim: 'Every one became my friend from his own opinion; none sought out my secrets from within me.'[14] The source of this admonition is divine Unity or *tawhid* (*La ilaha illa Allah*, the main part of the Muslim confession of faith in which the believer declares 'There is no other god save God'), the root of Islam, which informs all of Rumi's words. We find similar expressions of the same root belief espoused in other mystic traditions as well. The school of *Advaita Vedanta* is a case in point. These Sanskrit words mean 'non-duality' and 'the end of knowing', respectively. The latter follows from the former: if there are not two, there cannot be a knower of knowledge, that is, both a subject and an object of knowing. The *Advaita Vedanta*-master Ramana Maharshi has expressed this concisely in his work, *Upadesa saram*:

versity of Cairo Press 2007), and Leonard Lewisohn on 'Shawk', in *Encyclopaedia of Islam*, 2nd ed., ed. P. Bearman, Th. Bianquis, C. E. Bosworth, E. van Donzel and W. P. Heinrichs (Leiden: Brill 2000), IX, pp. 376–77.

13 Margaret Smith, *Muslim Women Mystics. The Life and Work of Rabi'a and Other Women Mystics in Islam* (Oxford: Oneworld 2001), p. 79. Translated from Shu'ayb ibn 'Abdu'llah Hurayfish, *Al-Rawd al-fa'iq* (Cairo: Bulaq 1289 A.Hsh./1872 or 1873), p. 213.

14 Reynold A. Nicholson, ed. and trans. *The Mathnawi of Jalálu'ddín Rúmí* (Warminster, Wiltshire: E.J.W. Gibb Memorial Trust 1926), I: 6.

sattvabhâsikâ cit kvavetarâ   sattayâ hi cicittayâhyaham

Illuminating that which exists Awareness, where is any other?
Awareness is only as existence, as Awareness alone I am.[15]

Neither the Muslim confession of *tawhid,* nor the *Advaita* teaching
of *Upadesa saram* speak of 'union' or advocate the 'unification' of
lover and Beloved. In their absoluteness they do not touch the expression 'one', since that in turn implies 'two', etc. The main emphasis of
both is that 'there is no other'. Ramana Maharshi's verse ends with 'as
Awareness alone I am'. Put in the context of orthodox Islam these
words sound outrageous. Yet there are voices in the Sufi School of
Love which have given testimony to a similar intuition. The most
famous of those voices is that of Hallaj's famous adage: *Ana al-Haqq,* 'I
am the Truth.' Instead of ostracizing Hallaj's alleged saying as being
the summit of arrogance, Rumi explained it as being the ultimate
consequence of *tawhid.* To him, the 'I' of Hallaj did not show a trace of
an individual human 'I.' It is the 'I' of which also Abu Saʿid al-Kharraz
(d. 286/899) has stated in his *Kitab al-faragh* (Book of Surrender) that it
is the only true subject of human history, God; whoever speaks of 'I'
in another way, remains shielded from true knowledge.[16] Just as the 'I'
in Ramana's words is completely surrendered to the '*a-dvaita*', the
'not-two' of Awareness, so is Hallaj's 'I' absolutely surrendered to the
One 'Truth,' 'no other than'.

There are also countervoices among Sufis which reject the elocution
of 'I' by a human being, even when in the enraptured state of Hallaj,
and certainly when uttered in public to ears which have not acquired
the adequate receptivity. It suits man to keep quiet here.

RUMI AND LONGING

Although in his poetry Rumi describes longing in all its various
aspects: ephemeral and eternal, mundane and divine, his own longing
was directed towards God. To him the principal representative of God

---

15 Bhagavan Sri Ramana Maharshi, *Upadesa saram* (Essence of Teaching), trans. A. R.
Natarajan; word by word rendering by Viswanatha Swami (Bangalore: Ramana
Maharshi Centre for Learning, 4th edition, 1997), verse 23, p. 61.
16 See Karamustafa, *Sufism,* pp. 9–10.

in human form was Shams al-Din Tabrizi, whose name, Shams, means 'Sun'. Their meeting in Konya, in 1244, profoundly changed Rumi's existence, making him totally concentrated on the sun of his existence – Shams – around whom he circled like a particle of dust, Shams who would conduce him into the metamorphosis of divine intoxication. It is in this sense that Rumi's life story fits into the chain of stories that opened the present study.

Within the absolute perspective of orthodox Islam it may seem strange that Rumi directed his total attention towards a human being. To understand this further, we may look at schools of love and wisdom, like *Advaita Vedanta* in India, which hold that, as long as a human being thinks he is an individual, the divine will appear in the guise of an individual in order to take away in due course – or suddenly – the idea of separate individuality. This could be called the homeopathy of the school of love. Ultimately, it is believed, the divine shape will cause a definitive metamorphosis within the lover, as it is utterly impossible to make that shape into an object of love or hate. The shape bounces off all projections. This is what happened in the stories of Ibrahim, ʿUmar and Saul. Their projections found no point of attachment whatsoever, and this destroyed their endeavour to love or hate, to understand or deny. This is what also Rumi would learn with Shams.

Rumi has left us many clues about longing. His *Mathnawi* opens with the intimation: 'My secret is not far from my plaint . . .'[17] The essence of longing has rarely been expressed so succinctly in words as it is in this poem by Rumi:

> Longing is the core of mystery.
> Longing itself brings the cure.
> The only rule is, suffer the pain.
>
> Your desire must be disciplined,
> And what you want to happen
> in time, sacrificed.[18]

---

17 Nicholson, *The Mathnawi of Jalálu'ddín Rúmí*, I:7.
18 J. John Moyne and Coleman Barks, *Say I Am You*, p. 72. See also note 1 above for other translations of this quatrain.

Here, Rumi indicates that one cannot arrive at an understanding of longing or its object by trying to grasp it. To him there is nothing else than the Beloved. The Beloved precedes all words and understanding. Because there is nothing else than the Beloved, everyone who enters into the endeavour to develop a separate individuality will suffer pain, and will constantly aspire to remove the separateness. Thus, 'Longing itself brings the cure' when one traces longing back to its source. Ultimately this will bring the destruction of the cause of longing, the source of which lies in the assumption of an independent existence apart from the Beloved as a separate 'I'. Longing cannot be satisfied or alleviated by externalizing it by means of objectivation and consequent projection of longing upon external objects. The story of Pan and Syrinx taught us that the object of longing will always escape from one's grasp, for just as one attempts to seize it, one finds one's hands clutching a bundle of dry reeds. One does not honour longing by acting in this way, as Rumi points out; one does not 'suffer the pain', but instead wishes fulfilment 'to happen in time', and be content with a surrogate ('desire').

The poem teaches that when one systematically rejects temporary fulfilment through objects, longing becomes sublimated and ever more pure and intense. Rumi gives an indication of this process of purification in *Fihi ma fihi*, where he reflects that: 'One needs love and yearning to distinguish wine from the cup.'[19] The wine lives, the cup is dead. All objects of love are lifeless, there is only love itself. Rumi sings in *Divan-i Shams-i Tabriz*:

> 'Tis love and the lover that live to all eternity;
> Set not thy heart on aught else: 'tis only borrowed.
> How long wilt thou embrace a dead beloved?
> Embrace the soul which is embraced by nothing.
> What was born of spring dies in autumn,
> Love's rose-plot hath no aiding from the early spring.[20]

Rumi's poem shows that he was well aware of the human inclination to run away from the abyss of longing. This abyss seems to lead to unbearable solitude. Though the solitude essentially heralds the con-

---

19 *Signs of the Unseen*, Discourse 16, p. 75.
20 Nicholson, *Selected Poems from the Divani Shamsi Tabriz*, XIII, p. 51.

sciousness that there is no one else than the Beloved, this is still veiled. The lover does not yet know that it is not he who is solitary: it is the Beloved who is without a second. The rest is a specious reflection, a remnant of the distance caused by the illusion of subject-object division.

Rather than confronting the abyss and tracing longing back to its source, one tries to quench longing by resorting to external means. If these are indeed used as means of avoiding the Beloved, we are only engaged in moribund and mechanical play. Should a sense of unity arise here, then this would not be real, according to Rumi, but only a transitory state of mind. Duality still remains. Such surrogates for the Beloved are unsatisfactory, and by hankering after repetition of what is merely temporary fulfilment, due to the ever imminent boredom of the mind, one tends to pursue more and more of such surrogates. Any kind of means may act as surrogates, especially those that seem to temporarily obliterate the divide between inside and outside, subject and object, such as music, dance, sex, alcohol, drugs.

Rumi certainly was not against dance and music. On the contrary, he often felt compelled to answer the call to dance ecstatically. However, this was not a case of finding a surrogate for the Beloved. He did not try to abolish the abyss of longing so as to realize a kind of experience of union; to him music and dance were not a means to evoke the Beloved's nearness or oneness, but rather a mode of expressing it.[21] Simply put, if one does not trace back longing to its source, does not probe into the core of mystery, one becomes a slave of surrogates. Rumi is intent on liberation, not addiction.

DANCE, MUSIC, EROTICISM, WINE

At the same time it is striking that Rumi's poetry constantly refers precisely to such alleged surrogates as wine, eroticism, music and dance. Since man's metamorphosis for Rumi starts *within* the human sphere of experience, unveiling its divine origin therein, one must read and approach these passages in a way similar to the figure of

---

21 Rumi reportedly renounced dancing if he did not sense in it the presence of the Beloved. See Annemarie Schimmel, *The Triumphal Sun* (Albany: State University of New York Press 1978), p. 218. See also *Divan-i Shams-i Tabriz*, 1760:18457; 1295:13681; 1296:13691.

God's representation by the Beloved in human guise: Shams' appari-
tion to Rumi. Rumi understood well that dance, music, eroticism and
alcohol enable the mystic to shatter conventional routines of habit
and drive man out of, and make him 'beside himself'. Such means in
fact subvert the dominance of the intellect, and thus make the adept
more receptive to love. The following quatrain in praise of *Sama*ᶜ, the
Sufi's spiritual 'audition' to music and practice of mystical dance,
celebrates this experience, the quatrain's rhythmic form inspiring its
content:

> *Imruz sama°ast u sama°ast u sama°*
> *Nurast u shu°ast u shu°ast u shu°a°*
> *In °ishq, musha°ast u musha°ast u musha°*
> *Az °aql vada°ast u vada°ast u vada°*

> Today it's time for *Sama*ᶜ, for *Sama*ᶜ, for *Sama*ᶜ.
> Today is bright and illuminating, illuminating, illuminating.
> This love is unifying, unifying, unifying.
> And it's bidding the intellect farewell, farewell, farewell.[22]

Those who do not understand the transformative language of Rumi's
School of Love will take such words literally, yet Rumi makes his
audience constantly aware of the necessity of penetrating behind the
veil, of descending from the vehicle of metaphorical language in order
to understand the tenor of his verse, complaining, for instance, that
'ear and eye lack the light' or 'only to the senseless is this sense
confided . . .'[23]

Lest from his frequent references to wine and intoxication, one draw
the conclusion that the poet was drunk on wine most of the time, we
need only to listen to this verse: 'We are drunk, but not drunk on
grape's wine (*Mastim, nah mast-i bada-yi angurim . . .*)',[24] whilst if one

---

22 Adapted from Shahram T. Shiva, *Rending the Veil. Literal and Poetic Translations of
Rumi* (Prescott: Hohm 1995), p. 140. See also Rumi, *Kulliyat-i Shams*, ed. B. Furuzanfar, vol. 8, no. 1046, p. 177. The author of the present study has written a composition for 12-voice choir in which the difference between alcoholic and divine
intoxication has been thematised: *Bee Bade Mast! Drunk Without Wine!* (Amsterdam: Donemus/Muziekcentrum Nederland 2009). It is based on quatrains by Omar
Khayyam/Edward FitzGerald in English and quatrains by Rumi in Persian.
23 *Mathnawi*, trans. Nicholson, I: 7, 14.
24 Shiva, *Rending the Veil*, p. 177.

were to imagine that Rumi's references to music are to its usual powers of intoxication, disillusionment quickly ensues. He admonishes:

> Go ahead and break our harp, for there are thousands of harps more still here. Since we have fallen into the grip (*chang*) of love, how can we ever suffer loss of harp and oboe? If all the robabs and harps in the world were burnt to a crisp, many more hidden harps would still exist. Their resonance and strumming would still rise to heaven although they would not penetrate the adamant human ear.[25]

Likewise, for those who would interpret Rumi's poetical abundance as a mystic's aesthetic self-indulgence or else mere addiction to the beauties of poetry, he has this observation in store:

> I am loved by those who come to see me, and so I compose poetry to entertain them lest they grow weary. Otherwise, why on earth would I be spouting poetry? I am vexed by poetry. I don't think there is anything worse.[26]

This does not mean that the imagery of dance, music, eroticism and wine are just metaphorical. This is clear from Rumi's quatrain on *sama*. In order to bring about a metamorphosis, spiritual masters mobilise vital powers.[27] Yet, if one does not read Rumi's imagery in a

---

25 Rumi, *Kulliyat-i Shams*, vol. 1, ghazal 110: 1240–44. Prose translation by Leonard Lewisohn. For a possibly more poetic but actually less accurate rendition of these verses, see Coleman Barks, *The Essential Rumi*, pp. 34–35.

26 *Fihi ma fihi*, in *Signs of the Unseen*, Discourse 16, p. 77. I have discussed elsewhere the complex relationship between art and mysticism; see Rokus de Groot, 'Music, Religion and Power: Qawwali as Empowering Disempowerment', in M. B. ter Borg and J. W. van Henten (eds.), *Powers: Religion as a Social and Spiritual Force* (New York: Fordham University Press 2010), pp. 243–64.

27 Irina Tweedie offers an extensive report on this, relating to her own experience in the 1960s, when her Sufi master from Kanpur (Northern India) is constantly engaged in arousing her love energy, sexual drives included. He turns her into a *Daughter of Fire* – the title of her book – in all senses of human existence. However, the master does not allow any physical fulfilment of the sexual and erotic longings, and keeps directing her concentration on the one Beloved only. The master of Kanpur sings: 'The love is from both sides: from the side of the Beloved all currents are absorbed and love is not shown. From the side of the lover, his love cannot be hidden. To be loved is an easy thing; but to love requires a supreme self-sacrifice.' See Tweedie, *Daughter of Fire. A Diary of a Spiritual Training with a Sufi Master* (Nevada City: Blue Dolphin 1986), *ghazal* on p. 187, originally in Persian.

transformative sense, one may miss its point. Literal reading may make one a prisoner of concepts of *becoming* (longing as striving, completing, surviving), numb to the irresistible attraction of what *Is*. With him eroticism turns into the homeopathy of the 'emptiness of love', which allows neither projections nor any point of attachment.

THE SONG OF THE REED

We opened our discourse with the metamorphosis of Syrinx into a musical instrument: the reed-pipe. This beloved one has disappeared as the object of longing, but the sound of the flute still preserves the memory of her existence. In his own way, Rumi in the 'Song of the Reed' (*Nay-nama*) beginning his *Mathnawi* versifies the mournful plaint of the flute as follows:

> Listen to the reed how it tells a tale, complaining of separations –
> Saying, 'Ever since I was parted from the reed-bed, my lament hath caused man and woman to moan.
> I want a bosom torn by severance, that I may unfold the pain of love-desire.
> Every one who is left far from his source wishes back the time when he was united with it.
> In every company I uttered my wailful notes, I consorted with the unhappy and with them that rejoice.
> Every one became my friend from his own opinion; none sought out my secrets from within me.
> My secret is not far from my plaint, but ear and eye lack the light.
> Body is not veiled from soul, nor soul from body, yet none is permitted to see the soul.'
> This noise of the reed is fire, it is not wind: whoso hath not this fire, may he be naught!
> 'Tis the fire of Love that is in the reed, 'Tis the fervour of Love that is in the wine.
> The reed is the comrade of every one who has been parted from a friend: its strains pierced our hearts.
> Who ever saw a poison and antidote like the reed? Who ever saw a sympathiser and a longing lover like the reed?
> The reed tells of the Way full of blood and recounts stories of the passion of Majnún.

Only to the senseless is this sense confided: the tongue hath no
    customer save the ear [. . .]
The Beloved is all and the lover but a veil; the Beloved is living and
    the lover a dead thing.[28]

As we can see, the delight in music which a skilful player evokes out
of the 'air' on a wind-instrument is hardly the theme which Rumi's
'Song of the Reed' celebrates. His verse has little to do with art or
aesthetics *per se*; on the contrary, Rumi's emphasis on the fire in the
flute's lament alludes to the depths of spiritual longing, a longing
which must be very strong if it is to survive the attraction of addic-
tions and to face the abyss of the absence of any object. This is only
possible by one-pointed concentration on the Beloved.

THE BELOVED

It is an exceptional beloved to whom Rumi's song is dedicated. In fact,
it is the only Beloved, which is Love itself, requiring everything from
the lover. It is the Beloved who at first arouses longing and then takes
away all ways of fulfilment by means of surrogates. As the abyss of
longing, the Beloved cannot brook any objects. The Beloved is truly
simple. Single.

    We just witnessed the absolute way in which Rumi spoke about the
Beloved: 'The Beloved is all and the lover a veil; the Beloved is living
and the lover a dead thing . . .' Rumi's verse is essentially the traditional *tawhid* of Islam but phrased in the language of love. 'There is no
other god than God' may be understood as 'There is no other beloved
than the Beloved.' What does it require to meet the Beloved? Meeting
is impossible here, as it presupposes two persons, while the presence
of the Beloved implies the absence of duality. This dissolution of
duality and separative identity is described by Rumi in the *Mathnawi*
in the following parable:

    A certain man came and knocked at a friend's door: his friend
        asked him, 'Who art thou, O trusty one?'
    He answered, 'I.' The friend said, 'Begone, 'tis not the time: at a
        table like this there is no place for the raw.'

28 *Mathnawi*, trans. Nicholson, I:1–14; 30.

> Save the fire of absence and separation, who will cook the raw
>   one? Who will deliver him from hypocrisy?
> The wretched man went away, and for a year in travel in
>   separation from his friend he was burned with sparks of fire.
> That burned one was cooked: then he returned and again paced
>   to and fro beside the house of his comrade.
> He knocked at the door with a hundred fears and respects, lest
>   any disrespectful word might escape from his lips.
> His friend called him, 'Who is at the door?' He answered, ''Tis thou
>   art at the door, O charmer of hearts.'
> 'Now,' said the friend, 'since thou art I, come in, O myself: there is
>   not room in the house for two I's.'[29]

Hallaj, too, expresses the singleness of the Beloved in a radical way.
The story goes that just before his execution he exclaimed: 'All that
matters to the ecstatic is the increasing solitude of his Only One, in
Himself.'[30] In *Fihi ma fihi* Rumi underlines that the Beloved is the only
one for whom one longs for his own sake alone, the only one to whom
no other reason is acceptable.[31] This is quite different from the stories
with which we started: there the longing was entwined with explicit
aims, usually several ones at the same time. Ibrahim wanted to kill the
gazelle for sport, to shine among his fellow hunters, or to have a good
meal of it; ʿUmar wanted to undo Muhammad in order to keep authority over his sister and strengthen his power in society; Pan wanted
Syrinx to partake of her beauty and satisfy his lust; Saul wanted to
gain the respect of the Jewish religious establishment of his day. The
dramatis personae in these stories through their metamorphosis were
made to renounce all these aims. The essence of Rumi's words is that
all longing serves only self-interest unless it is concerned with the
Beloved.

> So long as you have an iota of self-love left within you, no beloved
> would pay any attention to you. Neither would you be worthy of
> union nor would any beloved grant you admittance.[32]

29 Nicholson, *The Mathnawi of Jalálu'ddín Rúmí*, I, 3056–63.
30 Testimony of ʿIsa Qassar Dinawari, cited in Louis Massignon, *Hallaj: Mystic and
   Martyr*, trans. and ed. H. Mason (Princeton: Princeton University Press 1982;
   abbreviated edition), p. 289.
31 *Fihi ma fihi*, in *Signs of the Unseen*, Discourse 23, pp. 105–06.
32 Ibid., Discourse 26, p. 120.

The School of Love cures self-interest through the absorption of the lover in the Beloved. The School's female founder, Rabiʿa of Basra, thus showed in a very vivid manner that the Beloved should be sought for his own sake only. Recasting a story originally told by ʿAttar in his *Memoirs of the Saints*, Rumi's biographer Aflaki relates:

> One day a group with enlightened hearts saw that Rābeʿa had taken fire in one hand and a jug of water in the other, and was running in haste. They asked: 'O Lady of the world to come, where are you running and what are you doing?' She said: 'I am going to set fire to Paradise and to pour water over Hell so that both these veils which bar the way are removed and the goal becomes clear and God's bondsmen serve God without the motive of hope and the incentive of fear. For were it not for hope of Paradise and fear of Hell, no one would worship God and be obedient.'[33]

According to Rabiʿa total love is not the lover's merit but the Beloved's grace. This is the theme of her famous poem about the two loves:

> I have loved Thee with two loves, a selfish love
> and a love that is worthy (of Thee),
> As for the love which is selfish, I occupy myself therein with
> remembrance of Thee to the exclusion of all others,
> As for that which is worthy of Thee, therein Thou raisest the veil
> That I may see Thee.
> Yet is there no praise to me in this or that,
> But the praise is to Thee, whether in that or this.[34]

Ramana Maharshi has pointed to the same idea in stating that God cannot be searched for by the lover as if he were an object (of 'selfish love'); rather God is the Subject itself (who 'raises the veil'). In other words, the Beloved is not the *Object* but the *Subject* of the lover. Conversely the lover turns out to be an object to be annihilated by the Subjectness of the Beloved. Again, as Rumi has it: 'The Beloved is all and the lover a veil; the Beloved is living and the lover a dead thing.'[35]

33 *The Feats of the Knowers of God* (*Manâqeb al-ʿarefîn*), trans. O'Kane, p. 274.
34 M. Smith, *Muslim Women Mystics* (Oxford: Oneworld 2001), p. 126.
35 *Mathnawi*, trans. Nicholson, Bk. 1:30.

The metamorphosis of the School of Love amounts to a reversal of roles. The hunter becomes the prey of the hunted.

ACTIVE AND PASSIVE, MALE AND FEMALE IMAGERY IN THE MYSTICAL LANGUAGE OF LOVE

Until now we have encountered an imagery of lover and Beloved, hunter and hunted, that is, of seemingly active and seemingly passive roles. Those to whom 'lover' in relation to 'Beloved' would imply a too actively male connotation may be interested in inversions, in which the roles are qualified as (male) 'beloved' and (female) 'lover'. Certain schools of bridal mysticism inspired by the Biblical *Song of Songs* like those of Hadewijch (thirteenth century) and Teresa of Avila (1515–1582), as well as the Radha-Krishna lore show this tendency.[36] However, it does not make a difference whether one orients oneself toward an active or passive, or male or female pattern (which pairs are not always synonymous – certainly not in Hinduism). In the course of Rumi's School of Love, any trace of gender difference, including identification with femininity or masculinity, in relation to the One, whether experienced as Lover or Beloved, will ultimately vanish.[37]

The schools of love have chosen as a reference one of the strongest biological forces: sexual attraction. Originally this attraction serves the temporal physical unification of male and female organisms in the service of procreation. During such physical unification human beings may experience moments of ecstasy while the limits of the individual recede. The individual as a separate entity temporarily yields to a more encompassing mode of existence. Mystical references to sexuality and eroticism can be misleading if we view 'lover' and 'beloved' only in the modern sense of equal partners. Rumi does not have in mind love between human partners, with the incessant alternation of duality and unification. To him the Beloved is love itself, to which nothing separate exists, including the lover. Ibn ʿArabi spoke of the 'love of Love', *hubb al-hubb*, in which not only the lover but

---

36 Hadewijch, *Visioenen*, trans. Imme Dros, intro. and ed. Frank Willaert (Amsterdam: Prometheus/Bert Bakker 1996); Teresa of Avila, *Sobre los Cantares*; Jayadeva, *Gîta-govinda*. Juan de la Cruz uses extraordinary language in his poem *En una noche oscura*, by applying the passive grammatical form for both 'roles': *amada* and *amado*, 'beloved'.

37 Cf. *Mathnawi*, trans. Nicholson I: 1785–88. – Ed.

even the Beloved is forgotten.[38] Similarly Hadewijch sang about '*min de Minne*'. The lover cannot even become unified with the Beloved, as only the Beloved truly is. There is no procreation, but the disappearance of the lover into the 'not two', 'none other than'.

Gender references may engender confusion in still another way. The imagery of 'lover' and 'Beloved' may get tied up with gender identification with its complementarity and almost inevitable partiality. This may lead to the idolatry of the one for whom one longs, as the complement of one's own assumed identity, or, conversely, to the idolatry of one's own identity, by means of (super) human or divine role models. However, to Rumi the Beloved is not in need of a complement, being already complete, knowing 'no other'.

FANA': ANNIHILATION IN THE BELOVED

In the face of the Beloved no lover can maintain his own identity. Entertaining any identity would impede love and count as idolatry.[39] The disappearance of the lover's identity in order to be totally available to the Beloved, is called *fana'*, 'annihilation', in the Sufi School of Love. European schools of love mysticism have alluded to the 'becoming nothing' of the aspirant as well. The key notion is *kenosis*. Eloquent examples are Marguerite Porete (d. 1310) with her treatise *Le Miroir des âmes simples et anéanties*,[40] and Meister Eckhart (1260–1328), who in his sermon *Beati pauperes spiritu* states that one should ultimately be empty of even the last concept of anything, including one's own identity and any image of God up to any idea of emptiness: *er soll quit sîn alles des bekennendes, daz in im lebende ist.*[41]

Although the notion of annihilation is found in most mystical traditions of the world's religions,[42] it makes little sense to the modern

---

38 Ibn 'Arabi, *Kitab al-Futûhat al-Makkiya*, chapters III and XII, section 33. Maurice Gloton, ed. and trans., *Traité de l'Amour* (Paris: Albin Michel 1986), pp. 53, 250.

39 That is another meaning of 'The Beloved is all and the lover a veil.' (Nicholson, *Mathnawi*, Bk. I:30).

40 Marguerite Porete, *Le Miroir des âmes simples et anéanties*, ed. Max Huot de Long-champs (Paris: Albin Michel 1984).

41 Meister Eckhart, *Deutsche Predigten*, ed. and trans. Uta Störmer-Caysa (Stuttgart: Reclam 2001), p. 114. In the apostle's name of Paul, referred to above (Greek 'paulos', cf. Latin 'pauper'), the required poorness of mind is implied.

42 For an overview of various concepts of annihilation in the world's faiths, see Whitehall Perry, *A Treasury of Traditional Wisdom* (Cambridge, U.K.: Quinta Essentia 1991), 'The Destruction of I-Consciousness,' pp. 220ff.; 'Identity,' pp. 887ff. – Ed.

rationalist mentality based on post-Enlightenment ideals of self-emancipation and self-empowerment. Neither does *fana'* suit post-modern ideas about the subject. Postmodernism, itself a philosophy in flux, perplexed about all notions of religious and secular authenticity, is still caught up in negotiating fleeting multiple identities, however empty these identities may seem. *Fana'* is the release of the idea of 'I' as an acting instance. Ultimately *fana'* is the liberation from the idea of a chronic lack connected with the individual, and consequently from the root of longing. Rumi views *fana'* as the essential issue of the *tawhid*: 'There is no other god than God' (*La ilaha illa Allah*) and in several poems sounds out the *la* – 'no' or 'none' – of this credo as a reference to annihilation in ultimate love.[43] In his *Divan-i Shams-i Tabriz*, he rephrases 'The lover is a dead thing' by playing with the Arabic letter for *la* which he takes as having the form of a broom:

> Clean this house from yourself, see that imperial beauty, go, take the broom No [*la*], for the No is good for sweeping the house.[44]

This *la* (*fana'*) is a preliminary stage. Ultimately only the Beloved remains: *illa Allah*. In *The Triumphal Sun,* referring to Rumi's *Divan,* Annemarie Schimmel presents an analysis of this process. The lover asks the Beloved to consider him as *la*, 'no', and to transform him into *illa*, '[No] other than [the Beloved]'. He does so because also the stage of *la* should be left behind in favour of the completeness of the Beloved itself. Rumi praises the Beloved Shams:

> Whoever found help from your hand,
> became an *illa'i* [a positive affirmant of God]
> without the vestige of *la*.[45]

What these lines express in the language of Islam, we meet every-where in schools of love and wisdom. Ramana Maharshi thus kept

---

43 For a comprehensive discussion of this theme in Rumi's poetry, see William Chittick's essay: 'The Sword of *La* and the Fire of Love' in the present volume of the *Mawlana Rumi Review*. – Ed.
44 *Divan*, 587/6204; 1876/19771. Cited and translated by Schimmel, *The Triumphal Sun,* p. 320.
45 *Divan*, 2725/28944, trans. Schimmel, *The Triumphal Sun*, p. 321.

emphasizing that the individual 'I' should be annihilated (that is, recognized as not real), so that the Sun of the One 'I' may become manifest unimpededly.[46]

MAJNUN AND LAYLI

Rumi mentions a person in his Song of the Reed who has won fame in the Sufi School of Love. He is Majnun, the supreme exemplar of annihilation in love. In his total love of Layli he gave up everything, home and family, name and fame. The Persian poet Nizami Ganjavi (d. 605/ 1209) has composed a beautiful epic about this lover and his beloved. This is how he characterizes Majnun:

> Because of this complete [gnostic] knowledge of love
> Majnun stands for the elevated name of love.
> As long as he lived, he carried the burden of love,
> Like a rose he was happy with the breeze of love.
> And now that his rose has wilted,
> The last drops of him are attar of roses.
> I, too, through this fragrant rose water
> Refresh my waters in this brook.[47]

---

46 Ramana Maharshi, *Talks with Sri Ramana Maharshi*, ed. Swami Ramananda Saraswati (Tiruvannamalai: Sri Ramanasramam 2000), *passim*. Similarly, when I asked the contemporary Flemish mystical poet Erik van Ruysbeek (1915–2004) what is necessary for enlightenment, he replied: 'Nothing'. And he continued: 'One should pass through nothing, lose everything, in order to be all.' (Conversation with the author in Brussels, 21 March 1999.) During another meeting (23 November 2001), Van Ruysbeek observed: 'Islam takes a step further than Christianity. In Islam there is no interlocutor between man and God. It insists on giving up all human projections of God.' As a non-theist, Van Ruysbeek took 'God' to be the last projection of man; he welcomed the high degree of abstraction from this in Islam as a preparation for an ultimate (what he conceived to be a 'post-Islamic') mystical insight, which involved the dissolution of all theism. See E. van Ruysbeek, *Zangen van Ongrond* (Haarlem: Altamira/Becht 2000) for examples of recent *fana'* poetry, e.g. p. 104, with lines like 'If Nothing were your present/It is your presence I love', 'By not being, I am truly you/Annihilate me so that I am/Not I but you/Not I but you . . .' (my translation).

47 English trans. in Ali Asghar Seyed-Gohrab, *Laylī and Majnūn: Love, Madness and Mystic Longing in Niẓamī's Epic Romance* (Leiden & Boston: Brill 2003), pp. 47, 86.

Like Pan, Majnun was prevented from enjoying consummation with his beloved. And just as Pan tried to bridge the abyss of longing by means of music, Majnun used poetry as a means to survive the fires of yearning. The reason that Sufis view Majnun as the ideal lover is that to him nothing else existed save his beloved. When her family violently excluded him from her world, he withdrew into the desert in order to concentrate on her even more. Stories mention that Layli came to see Majnun at the end of his life. As the *Advaita Vedanta* master H.W.L. Poonja, who learned the tales of the famous lovers during his youth in the Punjab (formerly in India, but now part of Pakistan), relates:

> Layli comes to Majnun in the desert. This man is dying the next moment. She goes in front of him, and shakes him at the shoulders, 'Here I am, wake up, look at me, here am I.' He says, 'Who are you?' And she replies, 'I am your beloved.' Then he says, 'There cannot be two beloveds. I have only one beloved. And it is me. It is me.' So much he has been thinking of her. So much, day and night, has he been thinking of her. And so he himself became her. He forgot this attachment [to her physical presence]. He forgot everything else. Even physical love was attachment to him, and [his longing of] meeting [her] was dropped. That person in front of him he did not recognise. 'I am that myself.'[48]

Rumi and Shams al-Din: from Scholar to Lover

Shams was to Rumi the representative of the divine Beloved. He even calls him *Shams al-Haqq*, the 'Sun of the Truth':

48 Recorded during *Satsang* with this master, 31 December 1992, Lucknow, India. Recording available at Avadhuta Foundation, P.O. Box 296, Boulder, Colorado 80306-0296, USA. See also Rokus de Groot, 'The Arabic-Persian story of Laila and Majnun and its Reception in Indian Arts', *Journal of the Indian Musicological Society*, Volume 36–37 (2006), Special Issue Indo-Iranian Music: Confluence of Cultures, with discussion, pp. 120–48. The present author has composed an opera on the epic, *Layla and Majnun, A Composition about the Night* (Amsterdam: Donemus/ Muziekcentrum Nederland 2006), connecting various traditions of love mysticism. It is based on texts by Qays b. Mulawwah (Arabic), Nizami Ganjavi (in English translation), Jalal al-Din Rumi (Persian), Juan de la Cruz (Spanish), and on Turkish folk and *ashik* songs (Turkish).

Save pure-souled Shamsi Tabriz
None ever was drunken and intoxicated and distraught.[49]

In Shams' presence Rumi underwent a metamorphosis from scholar to lover. Shams enables him to experience *fana'*. He ended up as nothing, a particle of dust circling like a planet around his *Shams*, his sun. In this context, it is significant to remember the way many of the *ghazals* in Rumi's *Divan* poems usually conclude. Traditionally their last line is the place where the *takhallus*, in which the poet 'signs off', is found, when he mentions his own name as a signature in the final couplet. However, in about a third of these poems, Rumi's own *nom de plume* is not given, but instead the name of his beloved Shams, which is the reason why he called his collection the *Divan of Shams of Tabriz*. Rumi is like Majnun, who says 'I have become Layli herself.'

Rumi does not only give up his identity as a poet, he renounces his identity as a dervish and seeker of God. He must have been aware that the 'I' can be a very subtle object, much harder to relinquish than other objects of adoration, such as idols. The 'I' may even assume the form of a dervish. Therefore he writes in his *Mathnawi* about *fana'*:

'There is no dervish in the world; and if there be a dervish, that dervish is non-existent.'[50]

If we assume that Shams himself had traversed the whole path of longing including *fana'*, this must have had an effect on his presence. When the lover becomes the Beloved this often results in a great concentration of spiritual power. In any case his impact on Rumi was literally upsetting. The extent to which this has been the case can be measured from the fact that Rumi had already devoted himself to great teachers in the past and was himself considered as a master.

It is fascinating that text fragments of Shams about Rumi have been handed down. They show that Shams longed to meet someone who could bear his presence. In the *Maqalat-i Shams* (Discourses of Shams) we read:

---

49 Nicholson, *Selected Poems from the Divani Shamsi Tabriz*, XVIII, pp. 72–73.
50 *Mathnavi* III: 3669, trans. Schimmel, *The Triumphal Sun*, p. 308; she refers to Kharaqani as the speaker.

I implored God's majesty for the friendship and the company of one of His saints. In my sleep I was told, 'I shall make you into a companion of a saint.' I said to myself, 'Where is this saint?' The following night I was told, 'He is in Anatolia (Rum).' When after some time I finally saw him, I was told, 'It is not yet time. All in due course.'[51]

Like Rumi, Shams was aware of the essential asymmetry in the School of Love between Beloved and lover, sun (*shams*) and moon:

Shall I speak plainly or with hypocrisy? This Mawlana [Rumi] is like the moonlight. The eyes can perceive the Moon, but not the Sun of my being. The eyes are not able to endure the Sun because of the intensity of its intense radiance and light. The Moon cannot attain the Sun, unless the Sun attains the Moon. 'No regard can reach Him, but He reaches everyone's regard.'[52]

The last words originate from the Surah *al-An'am* (Qur'an 6: 103), which continue with: 'and He is the Subtle, the Aware One.' This quotation suggests that Shams, referring to his name 'Sun', had surrendered to the One, and no longer spoke as the person called 'Shams', in the same vein as implied in the utterance *Ana al-Haqq* ascribed to Hallaj.

It is likely that Rumi knew the full scope of longing from his own experience. It is reported that after his first meeting with Shams, they were inseparable. For months they were each other's companions. Rumi seemed to have lost interest in his disciples. This is maybe first and foremost how they experienced the situation. Yet the disciples got the chance of their lives: they could witness first-hand what it means to completely surrender to the Beloved. It must have been evident that their master went through a metamorphosis. However, it seemed that they had a different opinion. They became jealous, maybe because they wanted to be the beloved themselves rather than lovers.

Suddenly Shams was gone. Rumi was desperate. The one on whom all his longing was concentrated had disappeared. He was confronted

51 Shams-i Tabrizi, *Maqalat-i Shams-i Tabrizi*, ed. Muhammad 'Ali Muvahhid (Tehran: Intisharat-i Khwarazmi 1377 A.Hsh./1998), II, 161: 24, 162: 1–3.
52 *Maqalat-i Shams*, I, 115:17–20.

with an abyss, just like Pan experienced when Syrinx vanished before his eyes, or Majnun when Layli became unattainable. Rumi tried everything he could to find Shams. There were rumours that he was staying in Damascus. One of Rumi's sons was sent. He brought Shams back.

THE APPARENT DISAPPEARANCE OF THE BELOVED

Again a period ensued in which Rumi was completely lost in Shams' presence. And again resentment arose among his disciples. Once more Shams disappeared, this time definitively. Stories recount that disciples and even one of Rumi's sons were involved. Rumi himself went in search after him. This search turned into a trauma as finally he had to admit that Shams was untraceable.

Rumi stays behind with a fully aroused longing; now, however, without the one who has ignited the fire of his longing, on whom he had totally concentrated that longing. The one who had set in motion the process of *fana'* is not present any more with Rumi to fill the remaining emptiness. This abyss of longing has to be suffered by Rumi. When no further hope of the Beloved's physical presence remains, the longing, which until then was bitter-sweet but endurable, turns into real torment. Rumi himself had to arrive at the awareness that all that one wishes to occur within the confines of space and time, however sublime, has to be sacrificed. He has intensely lived through what his own words express:

> The only rule is, suffer the pain.
>
> Your desire must be disciplined,
> And what you want to happen
> in time, sacrificed.

He had to put out of his mind the possibility of any further encounter with Shams in person. The composition of the *Divan-i Shams-i Tabriz,* which was to continue for the next thirty years until Rumi's death, became a reflection of this process.

We have started our reflections by recounting the story of Pan's metamorphosis at the moment the object of his longing disappeared in front of him. We have witnessed the much more profound transformation of Majnun when he was forcefully kept away from his beloved Layli. And now Rumi goes through an even more devastating ordeal. All these lovers try to deal with the abyss of longing by means of music, dance or poetry.

'hoc mihi colloquium tecum manebit'
This will remain to me the conference with you

All kinds of hypotheses have been postulated regarding Shams' disappearance. Murder is one of them. Virtually absent is the proposition that the sudden absence of Shams essentially pertains to the School of Love's teaching. It is quite common in this school for the master to allow the disciple to project his amorous longings on to him. During this period of projection the master feeds that longing to the extreme. Then, unexpectedly, the master creates the abyss of longing by disappearing, either physically or psychologically, by not conceding to the disciple's projection of love any more. The lover is radically left alone to his longing.

There are various examples of the transformation wrought in Rumi by Shams in other religious traditions. The Indian *Bhagavata Purana* relates that Krishna, with his seductive flute playing and elusive dance, completely enchants the *Gopis* (female cowherders of Braj). He steals their hearts. They are in his spell as he plays with them on the banks of the river Yamuna. All of a sudden, he disappears. The *Gopis* are inconsolable. They look for him everywhere. Then they experience a profound transformation. While they search for the shape of their Beloved known to them and do not find it, they start seeing him everywhere – in the flowers, the trees, the clouds, the animals, in each other.

The apostles, too, undergo a metamorphosis, after the physical departure of their master Jesus, who himself had gone through utter solitude, calling out with a loud voice to his Beloved: *Eli, Eli, lama sabachthani?* 'My God, my God, why hast thou forsaken me?'[53] As the Bible reports, the apostles gathered on the day of Pentacost, 'all with one accord in one place' –

And suddenly there came a sound from heaven as of a rushing mighty wind, and it filled all the house where they were sitting.

53 Bible, New Testament, St Matthew 27:46, St. Mark 15:34, King James Version.

And there appeared unto them cloven tongues like as of fire, and it sat upon each of them.

And they were all filled with the Holy Ghost, and began to speak with other tongues, as the Spirit gave them utterance.[54]

We may view this metamorphosis yet in another way. The disappearance of Shams is the necessary consequence of *fana'*. It is here that the core of mystery may reveal itself. After all, if the lover (the alleged subject of longing) surrenders to 'becoming nothing', then the Beloved (the alleged object of longing) effectively ceases to exist as well. What remains is solely love. This is the ultimate 'metamorphosis' that surpasses the transmutation of form into the formless. It is effected with the most powerful means: the apparent disappearance of the one Beloved who has become all.

The Beloved as All in All

Sought everywhere, and found nowhere, as the definitive disappearance of Shams turned into the abyss of Rumi's longing, he may have been drawn into this last metamorphosis. Shams dissolves into the one divine Beloved who has lost all traits of an object of longing. The Beloved is nowhere that one searches, and at the same time there is nowhere that he is not:

> Grasp the skirt of his favour, for on a sudden he will flee;
> But draw him not, as an arrow, for he will flee from the bow.
> What delusive form does he take, what tricks does he invent!
> If he is present in form, he will flee by the way of spirit.
> Seek him in the sky, he shines in water, like the moon;
> When you come into the water, he will flee to the sky.
> Seek him in the placeless, he will sign you to place;
> When you seek him in place, he will flee to the placeless.
> As an arrow speeds from the bow, like the bird of your imagination,
> Know that the Absolute will certainly flee from the Imaginary.
> I will flee from this and that, not for weariness, but for fear
> That my gracious Beauty will flee from this and that.

---

54 Bible, New Testament, The Acts 2:2–4, King James Version.

As the wind I am fleet of foot, from love of the rose I am like
    the zephyr;
The rose in dread of autumn will flee from the garden.
His name will flee, when it sees an attempt at speech,
So that you cannot even say, 'Such an one will flee.'
He will flee from you, so that if you limn his picture,
The picture will fly from the tablet, the impression will flee from
    the soul.[55]

RUMI AND RELIGION

The Sufi School of Love makes Rumi a Muslim in the original sense of
the word, that is, a devotee who is completely surrendered to the
Beloved. His metamorphosis leads him to the root of Islam, deeper
still, beyond the formulations of exoteric religion. Religion is not a
matter of identity to him, since, being a 'surrendered one', he is without identity. In his *Fihi ma fihi* Rumi advises his audience to fathom
their religious practice and look to what extent it is an affair of
human making:

> O man, so long as you are in this search, which is temporal and a
> human quality, you are far from your goal. When your own
> search passes away into God's search, when God's search gains
> dominion over your search, then you will be a seeker through
> God's seeking.[56]

Rumi postulates that ultimately it is not we who have been searching,
who have been longing; it is the Beloved from whom all has issued
and to whom all returns. This is the essence of the *hadith qudsi:* 'I was
a hidden treasure, and I wished to be known, so I created the world'
(*Kuntu kanzan makhfiyan*).[57]

---

55 *Divani Shamsi Tabriz*, trans. Nicholson, xx, pp. 80–83.
56 *Fihi ma fihi*, in *Signs of the Unseen*, Discourse 51, p. 198.
57 Annemarie Schimmel, *Mystical Dimensions of Islam* (Chapel Hill: University of North
    Carolina Press 1975), p. 189; William Chittick, *The Sufi Path of Love: The Spiritual
    Teachings of Rumi* (Albany, NY: State University of New York Press 1983), pp. 47–48.

BECOMING THE SUN

When all temporal fulfilment of longing has been rejected, when the lover has become nothing, when the Beloved has disappeared as a definite shape, when longing has been transformed into total solitude, only then the core of mystery may dawn:

> One, therefore, must pass beyond these pleasures and delights which are only shadows and reflections of the Real. One should not become content with this small amount, which, although is of God's grace and a shadow of His beauty, it is still not permanent. It is permanent in relation to God but not in relation to man. It is like a ray of sun shining into a house. Even though it is a ray of sunlight, it is still attached to the sun. And when the sun sets its light will cease. One must, therefore, become the sun in order for there to be no fear of separation.[58]

It is possible that something may become apparent here about which nothing can be stated and about which it is better to keep quiet. Yet Rumi and others have given pointers. When only the 'I' of the Beloved remains after the lover's *fana'*, we may hear 'One must become the sun' as Rumi declared, or 'As Awareness alone I am' (Ramana Maharshi), or the *Ana al-Haqq* ascribed to Hallaj, or, as an example of total love surrender between human beings, Majnun's claim that 'I am Layli.'

For those not acquainted with the School of Love, this may sound as the summit of arrogance and even as blasphemy. And indeed, if there is the slightest trace of egoism in the speaker, the consequences of such sayings are bound to be disastrous. Even when these utterances are sincere, if heard by ears lacking in spiritual aptitude, they can lead to life-threatening misunderstandings. After all, precisely because of misinterpretations of their words by the uninitiated, Jesus, Hallaj and Marguerite Porete suffered physical death in the most terrifying ways.

---

58 *Fihi ma fihi*, in *Signs of the Unseen*, Discourse 12, p. 62.

'BE QUIET'

Rumi has a radically different view on Hallaj's exclamation. To him it was not at all an expression of extreme arrogance, but of utter humility. The pious are rather the ones who often are arrogant:

> When Mansur's (Hallaj) friendship with God reached its logical end, he became an enemy of himself and annihilated himself [*fana'*]. He said, 'I am the Real' [*Ana al-Haqq*] – that is, I have passed away; only God remains. To say this, that only He exists, is extreme humility and servitude. It is pretentious to say, 'You are the Lord, and I am a servant,' for by saying so you will have affirmed your own existence, and duality necessarily follows. When you say, 'He is God', there is also duality because the use of the third-person 'he' is not possible unless there is a first-person 'I'. Therefore, since there is no existent thing other than God, only He can say, 'I am God.' Mansur had passed away, and so his words were God's.[59]

There are also those who maintain Hallaj's utterance was due to immaturity, both in respect to his audience evidently not attuned to its spiritual meaning and in regard to the speaker. No one less than Shams was one of his critics in this respect:

> The full beauty of the world of the spirit had not yet fully revealed itself to Hallaj. Otherwise how could he have ever said, 'I am Reality, Truth'? What has 'I' to do with Reality? What does this 'I' amount to? What do words amount to? If he were fully immersed in the world of spirit, how could any words be contained therein?[60]

Rumi himself has also given suggestions in the same direction, mentioning three states in human spiritual development:

> Man has three states. The first is not to focus on God but to adore and serve anyone and anything – woman, man, wealth, children, stones, land. Next, when he acquires a certain knowledge and

59 *Fihi ma fihi*, in *Signs of the Unseen*, Discourse 52, pp. 202–3; see also Discourse 11.
60 *Maqalat-i Shams*, I, p. 280: 9–12.

awareness, he does not serve other than God. Finally, when he progresses in this state, he falls silent: he says neither, 'I do not serve God,' nor, 'I do serve God' — that is, he leaves both states. In their world no sound comes from such people.[61]

This leads him to the observation that 'If the heart is totally absorbed, then everything else is obliterated by it, and there is no need for the tongue.'[62] Thus, Rumi was called the 'Silent one'. Indeed, 'silence' (*khamush*) was one of the pen-names Rumi used for himself in the *Divan-i Shams*. He may be considered to have been the embodiment of 'Keep quiet', like Ramana Maharshi, who said that speaking disturbs the unbroken eloquence of silence.[63] In this silence even confessing divine Unity, acknowledging *tawhid*, sounds like verbosity, for there is nobody left to enunciate it. In *Divan-i Shams-i Tabriz* Rumi prepares us for what happens after the disappearence of the 'I' of the lover into the 'I' of the Beloved, with the admonition to 'keep quiet' (*khamush kun*):

> At the moment the Beloved arrives, keep quiet.
> He knows without words, keep quiet.
> With a draught of silent and eloquent wine
> he puts you outside of yourself, keep quiet. [. . .]
> If you keep your breath in front of the mirror,
> he spares you the word, keep quiet. [. . .]
> Any thought you bury in your heart,
> one by one he reads them, keep quiet [. . .]
> Do not utter a word about the two worlds. He leads you
> to the only colour, keep quiet.[64]

To Rumi longing reveals its own fulfilment ultimately in silence.

BIBLIOGRAPHY

Aflaki, Shams al-Din Ahmad. *The Feats of the Knowers of God* (*Manāqeb al-ʿārefīn*), trans. John O'Kane. Leiden: Brill, 2002.

61 *Fihi ma fihi*, in *Signs of the Unseen*, Discourse 53, p. 207.
62 Ibid. Discourse 11, p. 44.
63 *Talks with Sri Ramana Maharshi* (Tiruvannamalai: Sri Ramanasramam 2000), *passim*.
64 Translation by the author after Mahin Tajadod, trans., *Mowlâna, Le Livre de Chams de Tabriz* (Paris: Gallimard 1997), p. 304.

Barks, Coleman, ed. and trans. *The Essential Rumi*. Edison: Castle Books, 1997.

Bearman, P., Bianquis Th., Bosworth C.E., van Donzel E. and Heinrichs W.P. *Encyclopaedia of Islam*, 2nd ed. Leiden: Brill, 2002.

Chittick, William. *The Sufi Path of Love: The Spiritual Teachings of Rumi*. Albany: State University of New York Press, 1983.

—. 'The Sword of *Lā* and the Fire of Love', *Mawlana Rumi Review*, Vol. 2, 2011: pp. 10–27.

Eckhart, Meister. *Deutsche Predigten*, ed. and trans. Uta Störmer-Caysa. Stuttgart: Reclam, 2001.

Epstein, Mark. *Open to Desire*. New York: Gotham Books, 2004.

Gamard, Ibrahim W. and Rawan Farhadi, A. G., ed. and trans. *The Quatrains of Rumi: Ruba'iyat-e Jalaluddin Muhammad Balkhi-Rumi*. San Rafael, CA: Sophia Perennis, 2008.

Gloton, Maurice, ed. and trans. *Traité de l'Amour* [Ibn Arabi, parts of *Kitab al-Futuhat al-Makkiya*]. Paris: Albin Michel, 1986.

de Groot, Rokus. *Bee Bade Mast! Drunk Without Wine!* Composition for 12-voice choir. Amsterdam: Donemus/Muziekcentrum Nederland, 2009.

—. *Layla and Majnun, A Composition about the Night*. Composition for music theatre. Amsterdam: Donemus/Muziekcentrum Nederland, 2006.

—. 'Music, Religion and Power: Qawwali as Empowering Disempowerment' in *Powers, Religion as a Social and Spiritual Force*, eds. Meerten B. ter Borg and Jan Willem van Henten. New York: Fordham University Press, 2010.

—. 'The Arabic-Persian story of Laila and Majnun and its Reception in Indian Arts.' *Journal of the Indian Musicological Society*, Vol. 36–37, Special Issue on Indo-Iranian Music: Confluence of Cultures, 2006.

Hadewijch. *Visioenen*, trans. Imme Dros, intro. and ed. Frank Willaert. Amsterdam: Prometheus/Bert Bakker, 1996.

Hurayfish, Shuʿayb ibn ʿAbd Allah. *Al-Rawd al-fa'iq*. Cairo: Bulaq, 1289 A.Hsh./1872 or 1873.

Karamustafa, Ahmet T. *Sufism: The Formative Period*. Cairo: The American University of Cairo Press, 2007.

Massignon, Louis. *Hallaj: Mystic and Martyr*, trans. and ed. Herbert Mason. Princeton: Princeton University Press, 1982.

Maharshi, Ramana. *Upadesa saram* (Essence of Teaching), trans. A. R. Natarajan; word by word rendering Viswanatha Swami. Bangalore: Ramana Maharshi Centre for Learning, 1997.

—. *Talks with Sri Ramana Maharshi*, ed. Swami Ramananda Saraswati. Tiruvannamalai: Sri Ramanasramam, 2000.

Moyne, John and Barks, Coleman, trans. *Say I Am You* [Rumi]. Athens: Maypop, 1994.

Nicholson, Reynold A. ed. and trans. *Selected Poems from the Divani Shamsi Tabriz*. Richmond: Curzon Press, 1994.

Ovid. *Metamorphoses*, trans. John Dryden. London: J. Tonson, 1717. Available at: http://www.sacred-texts.com/cla/ovid/meta/meta01.htm

Perry, Whitall. *A Treasury of Traditional Wisdom*. Cambridge: Quinta Essentia, 1991.

Poonja, H.W.L. *Wake Up and Roar*. Kula, Maui, Hawaii: Pacific Center Publishing, 1993.

Porete, Marguerite. *Le Miroir des âmes simples et anéanties*, ed. Max Huot de Longchamps. Paris: Albin Michel, 1984.

Rumi, Jalal al-Din. *Kulliyat-i Shams ya Diwan-i kabir az guftar-i Mawlana Jalal al-Din Muhammad mashhur bih-Mawlavi, ba tashihat wa havashi*, ed. B. Furuzanfar. Tehran: Danishgah-i Tehran, 1964. Reprinted Tehran: Sipihr, 1363 A.Hsh./1984. 10 vols.

—. *The Mathnawi of Jalálu'ddín Rúmí*, ed. and trans. Reynold A. Nicholson. Warminster, Wiltshire: E.J.W. Gibb Memorial Trust, 1926.

—. *Signs of the Unseen. The Discourses of Jalaluddin Rumi* [*Fihi ma fihi*], trans. Wheeler M. Thackston. Boston & London: Shambhala, 1999.

Ruysbeek, Erik van. *Zangen van Ongrond*. Haarlem: Altamira/Becht, 2000.

Schimmel, Annemarie. *Mystical Dimensions of Islam*. Chapel Hill: University of North Carolina Press, 1975.

—. *The Triumphal Sun*. Albany: State University of New York Press, 1978.

Seyed-Gohrab, Ali Asghar. *Laylī and Majnūn: Love, Madness and Mystic Longing in Niẓamī's Epic Romance*. Leiden: Brill, 2003.

Shiva, Shahram T. *Rending the Veil. Literal and Poetic Translations of Rumi*. Prescott: Hohm, 1995.

Smith, Margaret. *Muslim Women Mystics. The Life and Work of Rabiʿa and Other Women Mystics in Islam*. Oxford: Oneworld, 2001.

Tabrizi, Shams-i. *Maqalat-i Shams-i Tabrizi*, ed. Muhammad 'Ali Muvahhid. Tehran: Intisharat-i Khwarazmi, 1377 A.Hsh./1998.

Tajadod, Mahin, trans. *Mowlâna, Le Livre de Chams de Tabriz*. Paris: Gallimard, 1997.

Tweedie, Irina. *Daughter of Fire. A Diary of a Spiritual Training with a Sufi Master*. Nevada City: Blue Dolpin, 1986.

From Rumi's *Mathnawi*

Prayer's Synchronous Response

Translated by Jawid Mojaddedi

One night, '*Allah!*' a Muslim would repeat
   Until, through prayer, his pious lips grew sweet.
Satan said, 'That's too much! You've yet to hear
   To your *"Allah!"s* the answer "*I am here!*"
Not one response from His throne will come down,
   So why keep chanting "*Allah!*" with that frown?'
That Muslim's heart broke and he hung his head low,
   But then he dreamt he saw Khidr in a meadow:
Khidr asked him, 'Why don't you chant any more?
   Do you regret the prayers you sent before?'
He said, '"*Here I am!*" won't come as reply;
   I've been rejected.' Khidr said, 'That's a lie:
Your "*Allah!*" is the Lord's "*Here I am!*" too,
   Your need and pain God's messenger to you!
God says, "Your struggles were our moves to meet,
   Approaching you and setting free your feet.
The noose of Our Grace formed your fear and love;
   To your "*Allah!*", "*Here I am!*" rings above.'
The souls of stupid men are far from prayer
   Because to pray '*O Lord!*' is not their share.
Their mouths and hearts are closed up with a seal,
   So they can't moan to God of pain they feel:
God gave to Pharaoh riches, and then he
   Boasted about his might and majesty;
In his whole life that monster felt no pain,
   So that to God that wretch could not complain –
God gave to Pharaoh all of this world's wealth,
   But didn't grant him sorrow and ill-health.
Pain is much better than the wealth men horde
   Because it leads you to pray to your Lord.

Praying without pain means you are depressed,
　　But with pain it means that with love you're blest.
Such love's expressed when you hold your voice in,
　　Remembering your actual origin,
Which makes your voice pure when you finally pray:
　　'O God, to Whom we turn, send help our way!'
Even a dog's whine can have some attraction,
　　For everyone through love finds some distraction:
The dog of Sleepers in the Cave spurned carrion,
　　Then feasted as the emperor's companion;
Till Resurrection it drinks at that place,
　　Without a bowl, water of mystic grace.
Many look low as dogs and have no name –
　　In secret they down that drink all the same.
Submit your life for one cup's sake, my son!
　　Strive and be patient till the battle's won![1]

1　*Mathnawi*, ed. Muhammad Isti'lami (Tehran: Zawwar 1369–70 A. Hsh./1990–91, 2nd
　ed.), III: 189–211.

'We Believe in Your Prophet': Rumi, Palamas, and the Conversion of Anatolia

RODERICK GRIERSON

Pamyati I. F. Meyendorfa

A few weeks before a recent symposium organized by the Rumi Institute in Cyprus to commemorate the *Şeb-i Arus* of 17 December, I received a telephone call from the chairman of the institute, Gökalp Kâmil. He was rather tired, he explained, because he had been watching television until the early hours of the morning. The programme had consisted of a lengthy discussion between İlber Ortaylı, the director of Topkapı Sarayı Müzesi, and Halil İnalcık, who is generally recognized as the most eminent Ottoman historian of the past century, and perhaps of any century. During their conversation, Prof. İnalcık suggested that Gregory Palamas, the greatest of Hesychast mystics,[1] owed a considerable debt to Sufism, notably to Ibn al-ʿArabi and Jalal al-Din Rumi. After all, Palamas had been captured in 1354 and spent a year as an Ottoman prisoner while he waited to be ransomed.

---

1 The term Hesychasm, from the Greek word *hesychia*, meaning 'silence', has been applied in at least four senses to Orthodox Christianity during the Byzantine period: a technique of prayer, especially involving bodily postures and the control of breathing; a type of mystical experience, especially involving a vision of divine light; a theology to explain and justify the mystical experience, especially involving a distinction between the essence and the energies of God; and a political faction reflecting the concerns of monks who saw the technique, experience, and theology described above as the essence of Orthodoxy, and who refused to abandon Orthodox tradition in order to secure military assistance from the Catholic West against Turkish incursions. The literature on Hesychasm in general, and Palamas in particular, is vast. A brief introduction that is both recent and convenient is provided by Dirk Krausmüller, 'The Rise of Hesychasm', in *Eastern Christianity*, ed. Michael Angold, (Cambridge: Cambridge University Press 2006), pp. 101–26.

Especially while he was at the court of Orhan Gazi, the Ottoman Emir, he must have been influenced in some way by what he saw and heard of Turkish Sufism. This seemed a reasonable assumption, Mr Kâmil thought, but he wanted to know if it was anything more than a mere possibility. In other words, was there any convincing evidence for it?

The likelihood of a close relationship between Sufis and Hesychasts, or between Orthodox Christian mystics and Muslim mystics in general, has often been discussed by European and North American scholars, and the debate has tended to focus on several recurring themes. The case of Palamas, however, has been of particular interest to exponents of the Perennial Philosophy, especially among followers of the Traditionalist School associated with René Guénon and Frithjof Schuon.[2] Their concerns have been very different from those of the two Turkish historians, however, and for an intriguing reason. Traditionalists have argued that the startling similarity between certain aspects of the teachings of Palamas and of Ibn al-ʿArabi in particular should be taken as evidence for the fundamental unity of mystical experience at its most elevated level, especially when placed alongside mystics from other traditions such as Shankara or Meister Eckhardt.[3] If the teachings of one of these mystics were dependent on those of another, the similarity would obviously be of less value. Indeed, it might be of no value at all. Furthermore, according to this position, the similarity between Sufism and Hesychasm can be taken as an encouraging sign not only that a common ground exists between Christianity and Islam, but also that it can be rediscovered once doctrinal beliefs have been put aside. In other words, it possesses an ecumenical significance at a time when Christians and Muslims in particular have become obsessed with an imagined, or at least exaggerated, 'Clash of Civilizations'.[4]

---

2   The movement is usually assumed to have been founded by René Guénon. Several leading experts on Sufism and on Jalal al-Din Rumi in particular are often associated with it, including William Chittick and Seyyed Hossein Nasr. A useful introduction to its history and characteristics can be found in a review by Carl W. Ernst, 'Traditionalism, the Perennial Philosophy, and Islamic Studies', *Middle East Studies Association Bulletin* 28 (1994), pp. 176–81.
3   Although an enormous amount has been published, a characteristic study of the relationship between Hesychasm and Sufism whose value has not diminished with the passage of several decades, is Seyyed Hossein Nasr, 'The Prayer of the Heart in Hesychasm and Sufism', *Greek Orthodox Theological Review* 31, (1986), pp. 195–203.
4   The term 'Clash of Civilizations' is usually associated with Samuel Huntingdon's

I find these propositions stimulating and, indeed, indeed encouraging. The problem, however, is that the captivity of Palamas is often adduced in a way that can reasonably be described as factually inaccurate and generally misleading. For example, in an essay that I find otherwise impressive, and in a book with whose aims I am entirely in sympathy, the following statements appear:

> We know that during his captivity in Asia Minor in the 14th century, the Orthodox archbishop St Gregory Palamas, greatly impressed by the tolerance and kindness of the Muslims he met, became close friends with the son of the Turkish Emir, with whom he had many conversations, and in one of the letters which he wrote at that time, St Gregory expressed his hope that 'a day will soon come when we shall be able to understand each other'.[5]

The author of the passage is James Cutsinger, and he cites John Meyendorff, one of the leading authorities on Palamas during the past century, as his source.[6] Unfortunately, almost every clause in the sentence is contradicted or at least qualified by the descriptions that Palamas himself wrote of his captivity. Given the importance of Palamas and the significance of the surviving sources for the encounter between Christians and Muslims at a time when the teachings of Jalal al-Din Rumi, Ibn al-ʿArabi, Haji Bektash Veli, and other famous Sufis were of great influence in the Islamization of Anatolia and the Balkans, it seems advisable to return to the contemporary accounts of the captivity,[7] to see what they actually tell

article 'The Clash of Civilizations?', which was published by *Foreign Affairs* in 1993, and his subsequent book *The Clash of Civilizations and the Remaking of World Order* (New York: Simon & Schuster 1996). The term was first used, however, in a famous or indeed notorious article by Bernard Lewis entitled 'The Roots of Muslim Rage', in *The Atlantic Monthly*, vol. 266, No. 3 (September 1990), pp. 47–60. Even if much of the thesis has been dismissed as simplistic and tendentious, Robert Irwin has correctly observed that it is not a complete fantasy. See Robert Irwin, *For Lust of Knowing: The Orientalists and their Enemies* (London: Penguin 2006), p. 262.

5 James S. Cutsinger, 'Hesychia: An Orthodox Opening to Esoteric Ecumenism', in James S. Cutsinger, ed., *Paths to the Heart: Sufism and the Christian East* (Bloomington, Indiana: World Wisdom 2002), pp. 225–50, esp. p. 225.

6 John Meyendorff, *St. Gregory Palamas and Orthodox Spirituality* (Crestwood, New York: St Vladimir's Seminary Press 1974), p. 106.

7 Three primary sources survive for the experiences of Palamas in captivity. The letter that he addressed to the Church in Thessalonike of which he was archbishop was first published by K. Dyovouniotes, 'Gregoriou Palama epistole pros Thes-

us about the nature of religious dialogue at the time, and to assess whether what they purport to tell us is indeed an accurate reflection of relations between Muslims and Christians in the decades following Rumi's death.

A MASTER FOR EVERYONE?

The teachings of Jalal al-Din Rumi have long been seen as offering a bridge between Christianity and Islam, and between other faiths as well. His life has served as a demonstration that the day 'when we shall be able to understand each other' had already arrived at least a century before Palamas wrote his famous letters. Indeed the claim was being made shortly after Rumi's death in 1273, and perhaps even while he was alive. There are two obvious ways of considering whether this might actually be true. The first is to examine passages that appear in works of Rumi and assess how generous his intentions towards Christians appear to have been. The other is to examine passages in contemporary sources that describe attitudes to Rumi among those who were Christian, or attitudes to Christians among those who were close to Rumi, especially if either can be placed in the context of what we know from other sources was occurring in Anatolia.[8]

The *locus classicus* is undoubtedly the account of Rumi's funeral given by Ahmad Aflaki in his *Manaqib al-ʿarifin,* in which Jews and

salonikeis', *Neos Hellenomnemon* 16 (1922), pp. 7–21. A summary of the letter was sent to an unknown recipient and was published by M. Treu, 'Epistole Gregoriou tou Palama pros Dauid monakhon ton Disypaton', *Deltion tes historikes kai ethnologikes hetaireias* 3 (1890), pp. 229–34. An account of the theological debate in which Palamas participated in the presence of the Ottoman Emir Orhan was ostensibly written by the Armenian physician Taronites and published by A. I. Sakkelion, 'Gregoriou Thessalonikes tou Palama anekdotos dialexis', *Soter* 15 (1892), pp. 240–46. The standard edition of all three documents is now that of Anna Philippidis-Braat, 'La captivité de Palamas chez les Turcs: dossier et commentaire', *Travaux et mémoires* 6, (1979) pp. 109–22. The assumption that the summary was sent to a monk named David Disypatos, as Treu indicates in the title of his article, is dismissed by Philippidis-Brat on pages 133–34.

8 The former approach is perhaps best exemplified in an article written by Lloyd Ridgeon: 'Christianity as Portrayed by Jalāl al-Dīn Rūmī', in Lloyd Ridgeon, ed., *Islamic Interpretations of Christianity* (Richmond: Curzon 2001), pp. 99–126. An attempt at the latter was made by the present author during a conference in the Mevlevi Müzesi at Konya in December 2007: 'One Shrine Alone: Christians, Sufis, and the Vision of Mevlana', in Leonard Lewisohn, ed., *The Philosophy of Ecstasy: Rumi and the Sufi Tradition* (forthcoming).

Christians proclaim that in Rumi they found their true master, their Moses and their Jesus, a flute in tune with two hundred religions, the sun of truth, as essential for life as bread.[9] According to Aflaki, the members of the different communities and nations were present: Christians, Jews, Greeks, Arabs, Turks, and so on. As they marched forward, holding their sacred books in their hands, they read verses from the Psalms, the Pentateuch, and the Gospels, and uttered funeral lamentations in accordance with their own customs. Yet what is often overlooked in this passage is that Jews, Christians, and at least by implication the others as well, were required to offer an account of why they were there. Muslims in the funeral party demanded an explanation and indeed attacked them with clubs and with swords. Even if allowances are made for dramatic effect, this suggests that the question of confessional identity was not as irrelevant for those who followed Rumi while he was alive – or at least for Aflaki himself – as it might seem to many of us who are inspired by him now. The incredulous Muslims are not presented as a rabid mob and nothing more. When the various religious leaders are eventually summoned before the sultan and asked to explain themselves, the question is put to them: what possible connection can the funeral of Rumi have with them, as Rumi was obviously Muslim?

Indeed, the question seems perfectly reasonable. The attitudes that Rumi expresses toward Christ and toward Christians in his own writings do seem to be those of an orthodox Muslim rather than a figure of ecumenical significance for Christians or indeed anyone else. It would seem difficult to deny that Rumi regarded Jesus as a prophet, but nothing more, and that he saw Muhammad as a prophet of

---

9 The standard edition of the Persian text is Şams al-Dīn Aḥmed al-Aflākī, *Manāḳib al-ʿarifīn*, ed. Tahsin Yazıcı (Ankara: Türk Tarih Kurumu Basımevi 1959 and 1961). The editor also produced a Turkish translation: Ahmed Eflâkî, *Ariflerin Menkıbeleri (Mevlânâ ve Etrafındakiler)*, tr. Tahsin Yazıcı (Istanbul: Milli Eğitim Basımevi 1964). While earlier generations of Western scholars often resorted to the French translation of Clément Huart, *Les Saints des derviches tourneurs*, 2 vols. (Paris: E. Leroux 1918 and 1922), the English translation by John O'Kane has now replaced it: *The Feats of the Knowers of God (Manāqeb al-ʿārefīn)* (Leiden: Brill 2002). For convenience, the citations in the present article follow the numbering of the sections as they are given in O'Kane's English translation. As O'Kane himself remarks in note 2 on page ix, the numbering in Yazıcı's Turkish version is not always identical to his edition of the Persian, and the numbering in the Persian is occasionally out of sequence. The sections in O'Kane's translation that describe the death and funeral of Rumi are §565–88.

superior status. Although he compares prophets in general to fish who swim in the vast ocean of meaning, Muhammad is described as being different from any of the others. He is a pearl and is without equal.[10] He possesses completely and perfectly the Muhammadan Light, created before time, of which other prophets received only a portion.[11]

Even though Jesus ascended to the fourth heaven, Muhammad rose higher still, ascending through each of the heavens to stand in the presence of God.[12] While Jesus could walk upon water, the *Miraj* was proof that Muhammad could perform the even more astonishing miracle of walking in the air. Indeed, Rumi describes Muhammad as claiming that Jesus would have been able to make a Night Ascent of his own if only his faith had been stronger.[13]

Rumi criticizes Jesus for his practice of retiring to meditate in solitude, which he sees as the origin of the regrettable Christian institution of monasticism. In contrast, Muhammad was commanded by God to become a second Noah and guide the ark of the community. Muhammad was therefore not to isolate himself from the community as Jesus had done to pursue a spiritual vocation. Furthermore, he was to discourage others from doing so.[14] Rumi therefore describes a clear contrast between the religion of Jesus, which advocated withdrawal to caves and mountains, and Islam, a community of heroes and champions inspired by a Messenger who was a prophet of the sword.[15]

As well as claiming a superior status for Islam as a communal rather than a solitary religion,[16] Rumi also opposed monasticism because it meant that one simply removed oneself from temptation rather than struggling to overcome it. He was therefore opposed to celibacy, because he believed that chastity was a virtue that could only be practised by confronting lust, not by fleeing from it.[17]

Rumi denounced Christian churches because they were filled with idols, and noted that infidels were content to gaze upon painted

10 Jalal al-Din Rumi, *Kulliyat-i Shams ya Diwan-i kabir az guftar-i Mawlana Jalal al-Din Muhammad mashhur bih-Mawlavi, ba tashihat wa havashi*, 3rd ed., ed. B. Furuzanfar (Tehran: Sipihr 1363 A.Hsh./1984), no. 1700, vv. 17800–06.

11 Ibid., no. 1137, vv. 12051–52.

12 Ibid., no. 341, vv. 3685.

13 Jalal al-Din Rumi, *The Mathnawi of Jalálu'ddín Rúmí*, ed. and trans. Reynold A. Nicholson, 8 vols. (London: Luzac 1925–40), VI: 1186–88.

14 Ibid., IV: 1458–62.   15 Ibid., VI: 490–502.

16 Ibid., VI: 514–23.   17 Ibid., V: 574–78.

figures of the prophets.[18] He criticized the Christian priesthood as an attempt to impose an intermediary between man and God, and dismissed as preposterous the suggestion that a priest could dispense or withhold the mercy of God. He saw Christian practice as trivial, because it suggests that the reality of divine judgement can be avoided or ignored by relying on the presumption of other men.[19]

In the *Mathnawi*, Rumi repeats the conventional Muslim reply to the Christian assertion that the Hebrew Bible contains prophecies of Christ but the Greek New Testament contains no prophecies of Muhammad. He insisted that the original Gospels had contained prophecies about Muhammad. Christians had simply removed them, and thereby distorted the revelation of God.[20] Indeed, he follows the example of the Qur'an by describing Christians and Jews as engaging in intrigue against Islam.[21] An even more fundamental problem, however, was the undeniable fact that their religion, as the Qur'an made perfectly clear, violated the unity of God.[22]

If these views seem less ecumenical than Rumi is often assumed to have been, so too do later accounts that Frederick William Hasluck presented as evidence for what he described as a *'rapprochement'*[23] or 'religious compromise'[24] between Christianity and Islam at Konya. In addition to his famous account of the funeral of Rumi, Aflaki reports two miracles involving Rumi that occurred in the 'Monastery of Plato' not far from the city. In the first miracle, Rumi apparently visited the monastery and spent seven days and nights in a spring of icy water. At the end of the week, he emerged from the water unharmed and departed singing a hymn. The abbot of the monastery then swore that Rumi possessed the stature of the prophets in the Bible. Everything that he had read about Jesus was also true of Rumi, and everything that he had read about Abraham and Moses was true of Rumi as well.[25]

---

18 Ibid., v: 3599.

19 Ibid., v: 3257–84. However, in this passage he also suggests that it is possible, by virtue of the Christian believer's love, for divine grace to flow through mediation of the priest.

20 Ibid., I: 730–39.   21 Ibid., II: 2859.

22 *Kulliyat-i Shams, ghazal* 1876, v. 19763.

23 Frederick William Hasluck, *Christianity and Islam under the Sultans*, 2 vols. (Oxford: Clarendon Press 1929), esp. vol. 1, p. 373.

24 Ibid., p. 377.

25 Ibid., p. 372; Shams al-Dīn Aḥmed-e Aflākī, *The Feats of the Knowers of God*, §207.

In the second miracle, an elderly monk told dervishes who came to visit him that Rumi had spent forty days in meditation at the monastery. When the monk asked him if he believed that Islam was superior to Christianity, given that the Qur'an warns believers of the very real danger that the fires of Hell present even for those who are Muslim, Rumi took the cloak that the monk was wearing, wrapped it in his own cloak, and put them both into an oven. After the door had been opened and the cloaks removed, the monk could see that his cloak had been burned by the flames, but Rumi's had not. The monk proclaimed that he would now be Rumi's disciple.[26]

A third miracle was recounted to Hasluck when he visited the Greek monastery of St Chariton, also near Konya. It involved a mysterious old man who saved the son of Rumi when he fell from a cliff while hunting above the monastery. The old man was later identified from an icon inside the monastery as St Chariton himself. A mosque was cut into the rock beside the three churches in the monastery and every year, even in the early decades of the twentieth century, the Mevlevi shaykh would spend a night in prayer at the monastery mosque. He would also provide a gift of oil to the monastery every year.[27]

According to accounts that were current when Hasluck visited Konya itself, a Christian is buried next to Rumi in the Mevlevihane. Greeks claimed that he was the abbot of St Chariton, while Armenians claimed that he was a bishop named Yefsepi, or Eusebius. For their part, the Mevlevi claimed that he was a monk who had converted to Islam.[28]

Aflaki also describes Rumi meeting Syrian monks in a cave while he was making his way to Damascus. They apparently possessed marvellous powers, being able to read the thoughts of others, predict the future, and levitate. To impress Rumi, they told a child to rise into the air. He did so, but Rumi outdid them, keeping the boy suspended above the ground until he embraced Islam.[29]

Most of these encounters are reported in terms that are overtly, or at least implicitly, partisan. They describe relations between Christians and Muslims to support the claims of one side or another. Muslim

26 Hasluck, *Christianity and Islam under the Sultans*, p. 372; *The Feats of the Knowers of God*, §539.
27 Hasluck, *Christianity and Islam under the Sultans*, pp. 373–74.
28 Ibid., pp. 374–75.   29 *The Feats of the Knowers of God*, §7.

sources such as Aflaki will naturally assume the superiority of Muhammad or Rumi when compared to Jesus or any contemporary Christian. On the other hand, Christian traditions emphasize the power of Christian saints and the gratitude of prominent Muslims. The contrast is perhaps most obvious in the different accounts of the shrine in which Rumi is buried. Christians claim that a Christian lies beside Rumi, while Muslims claim that the Christian who was honoured with such intimacy had embraced Islam.

Nevertheless, it is important not to be overly pessimistic when examining these traditions. It would seem that it was possible to be a follower and indeed a prominent follower of Rumi without being Muslim. Shortly after Ghiyath al-Din Kay-Khusraw II succeeded ʿAla al-Din Kay-Kubad as sultan, he married Tamar, daughter of the Georgian queen, Rusudan, and a Seljuk prince who had become Christian to marry her. The princess arrived from Georgia dressed as a Christian and accompanied by clergy of senior rank, several priests, and a monk revered for his holiness. When the sultan died, Tamar accepted a second marriage to Parvana Muʿin al-Din, who administered the Sultanate of Rum for the Ilkhans after they extended their hegemony west into Anatolia. Aflaki describes Tamar as a disciple of Rumi, and as an intimate friend of Kyra Khatun, the wife of Rumi, as well as of Fatima Khatun, the wife of his son, Sultan Valad. Evidently, she contributed money and other supplies to Rumi and his followers, and after Rumi died, she provided a large donation to construct the shrine in which he is now buried. Her daughter, ʿAyn al-Hayat of Erzurum, is also said by Aflaki to have been affiliated with the Mevlevi.[30] Although claims have been made that the 'Georgian Lady' had converted to Islam,[31] Aflaki does not mention her conversion. In any case, the sharp demarcation that we often assume must have existed between Islam and Christianity was at some times and in some places understood in a very different way. It is not always clear from the historical record if certain individuals were Christian or Muslim, and it is certainly possible that they maintained one identity at one

---

30 Ibid., §62.

31 See Roderick Grierson, 'One Shrine Alone: Christians, Sufis, and the Vision of Mevlana', in *The Philosophy of Ecstasy: Rumi and the Sufi Tradition*, ed. Leonard Lewisohn (forthcoming) for an account of statements by the chronicler Bar Hebraeus, known in Arabic as Abu al-Faraj, who was Syrian Orthodox *maphrian* during the thirteenth century.

time and another at another, or that they might have converted and then reconverted without incurring obvious penalty.[32]

MYSTICAL VISION AND IMPERIAL DECLINE

With these questions in mind, the letters written by Palamas during his captivity offer a unique testimony. They reflect a central, yet often obscure, period in the transition from a largely Christian Anatolia to a largely Muslim Anatolia, and they contain the observations of one of the leading theologians of the time. Especially as they have been cited as a witness to intercommunal goodwill, it seems all the more important to examine them in some detail.[33]

Gregory Palamas had been born at Constantinople in 1296. His family was of senatorial rank, and he was educated in the imperial palace by Theodore Metochites, one of the most prominent Byzantine statesmen, patrons, and humanist scholars, famous for his work on Aristotelian philosophy and Ptolemaic astronomy.[34] While a simple contrast between the rationalism of Byzantine humanists and the

32 The question is discussed in more detail in Roderick Grierson, 'One Shrine Alone'.

33 All three sources began to receive critical attention sixty years ago from George Arnakis, first in a volume published in Greek about the early years of the Ottoman dynasty: *Hoi protoi Othomanoi*, Text und Forschungen zur byzantinisch-neugriechischen Philologie 41 (Athens 1947) esp. pp. 17–18, 89–90, 190; and then in two important articles published in English: 'Gregory Palamas among the Turks and Documents of His Captivity as Historical Sources', *Speculum* 26 (1951), pp. 104–18; 'Gregory Palamas, the Χιόνες, and the Fall of Gallipoli', *Byzantion* 22 (1952), pp. 302–12. The sources have subsequently been discussed by a number of prominent authorities on Ottoman history, notably by Paul Wittek 'Χιόνες', *Byzantion* 21 (1951), pp. 421–23 and more recently by Heath Lowry, *The Nature of the Early Ottoman State* (Albany: State University of New York Press 2003), esp. pp. 67, 79–80, 87. Eminent Byzantine historians have commented upon them, Speros Vryonis, in particular: *The Decline of Medieval Hellenism in Asia Minor and the Process of Islamization from the Eleventh through the Fifteenth Century* (Berkeley: University of California Press 1971,) esp. pp. 396–402, 426–27; as well specialists in Sufism such as Michel Balivet, ('Byzantins judaïsants et Juifs islamisés: des "Kühhân" (Kâhin) aux "Χιόναι" (Χιόνιος)', *Byzantion* 52 (1982), pp. 24–59, and experts in the history of Hesychast mysticism, the most famous among them being John Meyendorff, *Introduction à l'étude de Grégoire Palamas* (Paris: Éditions du Seuil 1959), esp. pp. 157–62; 'Grecs, Turcs et Juifs en Asie Mineure au XIVe siècle', *Byzantinische Forschungen* 1 (1966), pp. 211–17.

34 One of the most helpful introductions to the career of Theodore Metochites is still Ihor Ševčenko, 'Theodore Metochites, the Chora, and the Intellectual Trends of his Time', in *The Kariye Djami*, vol. 4, ed. Paul A. Underwood (Princeton: Princeton University Press 1975), pp. 17–91.

mysticism of a more conservative monastic party can be misleading, Palamas chose to abandon his studies before he embarked on philosophy. Inspired by Athonite monks whom he met in Constantinople, he departed for Mount Athos to pursue a life of ascesis and contemplation. After ten years on the Holy Mountain, the increasing threat of Turkish incursions convinced Palamas and a number of other monks that they should withdraw to the walled city of Thessalonike. Ordained as a priest in 1326, when he was thirty years old, he returned to Athos in 1331 and wrote a series of treatises in which he defended Hesychasm against attacks by a Greek monk from Calabria named Barlaam, who believed that his own version of Aristotelian scholasticism could serve as a vehicle to reunite the Catholic West and the Orthodox East.[35] The ensuing theological controversy was all the more bitter because it was conducted in the midst of a political struggle involving rivals for the imperial throne and their partisans within the Church, and because it could not be detached from the question of whether the emperor and patriarch should submit to papal authority and accept Latin doctrine in the hope of obtaining military aid from the West. As Rome rejected Hesychast mysticism, Hesychasts were obviously opposed to the idea of submitting to Rome. Others were willing to submit and therefore opposed the Hesychasts in turn. When Palamas was imprisoned by the patriarch of Constantinople in 1344, his crime was not only that he was a theologian who espoused Hesychast doctrine, but also that he was linked with one of the two rivals fighting for the imperial throne, John Kantakouzenos, who had allied himself to the Hesychast faction.[36]

35 The fundamental accounts of the life of Palamas, his contribution to Hesychast doctrine, and his controversy with Barlaam the Calabrian remain those of John Meyendorff, including *Grégoire Palamas* (Paris: Éditions de Seuil 1959), which was translated into English as *A Study of Gregory Palamas* (London: Faith Press 1964), *St. Grégoire Palamas et la mystique orthodoxe* (Paris: Éditions du Seuil 1959), which was translated into English as *St. Gregory Palamas and Orthodox Spirituality* (Crestwood, New York: St. Vladimir's Seminary Press 1974). A collection of his essays was published as *Byzantine Hesychasm: Historical, Cultural and Theological Problems* (London: Variorum Reprints 1974).

36 The political struggles in which Hesychasm and Palamas himself became embroiled are described by Donald M. Nicol in his *The Last Centuries of Byzantium, 1261–1453*, 2nd ed. (Cambridge: Cambridge University Press 1993) and *The Reluctant Emperor: A Biography of John Cantacuzene, Byzantine Emperor and Monk, c. 1295–1383* (Cambridge: Cambridge University Press 1996).

The struggle for the Byzantine Empire was by no means a simple conflict between two, or even three, parties. It was a process of complex manoeuvres between various factions within Byzantium itself that also involved military, ecclesiastical, and commercial interests in Catholic Europe, Orthodox rivals in Serbia and Bulgaria, and several Turkish emirates, including the Ottoman. Although at least one scholar has described the sources for the captivity of Palamas as evidence of a clash between mutually exclusive claims of competing theocratic empires,[37] what we know of the period from other accounts, and indeed what the sources themselves tell us, would seem to indicate a very different world in which almost nothing was mutually exclusive and almost everything the subject of negotiation or intrigue. Byzantium was no longer really an empire, the Ottoman emirate had not yet become an empire, and the role of religion or the compromises that various parties were prepared to make where religion was involved often seem to defy modern assumptions.

Such vicissitudes were in large part a legacy from the sack of Constantinople in 1204 by Frankish troops of the Fourth Crusade and the consequent establishment of a Latin Empire that endured until 1282. Parts of Byzantine territory near the Aegean that had not yet been occupied by Turks were nevertheless under Serbian, Bulgarian, Venetian, Genoese, Angevin, Catalan, Naxiote, or Templar control. The Venetians and the Genoese in particular were willing to form alliances with Byzantine factions or with Turks. In the midst of general disarray, the Ottoman emirate grew in what was in effect a power vacuum. This was not a straightforward 'Clash of Civilizations' in which a great Muslim empire challenged a great Christian empire and defeated it.

In 1345, Kantakouzenos formed close ties with the Ottoman emir Orhan, and the alliance that he cemented through the marriage of his daughter Theodora to Orhan during the following year enabled him to assume the offensive against those who were championing the cause of John V Palaiologos, notably his mother, the empress Anna of Savoy. Although both factions apparently sought military assistance from Orhan or indeed from other Turkish emirs, it was Kantakouzenos who prevailed. In 1347, relying on troops sent by Orhan, Kantakouzenos entered Constantinople. He released Palamas from prison,

37 Daniel Sahas, 'Gregory Palamas (1296–1360) on Islam', *The Muslim World* 73, (1983), pp. 1–21, esp. p. 13.

ensuring that he was consecrated archbishop of Thessalonike and his doctrines confirmed to be orthodox.

After marrying another daughter to John Palaiologos, Kantakouzenos declared himself to be senior emperor and relegated his new son-in-law to the status of junior emperor. However, as John Palaiologos grew older, he became increasingly keen to assume the status of senior emperor himself. His military offensive of 1352 ended in failure, again due to the alliance between Kantakouzenos and Orhan, and the Turkish troops on which Kantakouzenos could draw through this alliance. To punish his son-in-law, Kantakouzenos sent him into exile on the island of Tenedos. In the hope of escaping this fate, Palaiologos and his mother summoned Palamas to Tenedos and sent him to Constantinople as a mediator between the two factions. His education at the imperial palace and his elevation to senior ecclesiastical rank, not to mention his formidable intellect and his ties to Kantakouzenos, meant that he would have seemed an excellent candidate to undertake a diplomatic mission.

Into Captivity

Palamas and his retinue set out from Tenedos on an imperial trireme in 1354 and sailed as far north as Kallipolis, the modern Gallipoli. When they encountered a violent north wind, the captain anchored at Gallipoli to avoid shipwreck in the narrow straits. The city itself was now under Turkish control, however, having been occupied after its defensive walls were damaged in an earthquake, he kept his distance from the port and dropped anchor nearby.

By dawn, conditions were not much improved, and a new threat began to appear. From the deck of the ship, the passengers could see Turks gathering on the European shore. Before long, a number of boats set out, and although the passengers were convinced that they were hostile, the captain disagreed and refused to weigh anchor. As a result, the ship and everyone on aboard was captured.

The attitudes that Palamas held toward his captors are revealed at the beginning of his account, and they are very different from what has been suggested by at least some commentators. He sees his capture as the work of divine providence, because it has enabled him to report that Christians and Turks have been living alongside each other, a situation that will offer Turks no excuse when they face the judgement of God. They will not be able to plead ignorance in mitigation. Even 'the most barbaric among the barbarians' must accept the authority of Christ or be consigned to the fires of hell.[38]

Along with his retinue, Palamas was taken to Lampsakos, known in Turkish as Lapseki, on the Asian side of the strait. He was apparently suffering from exposure and was generally unwell. Concern shown by local Christians for the well-being of such an illustrious cleric encouraged the 'leader of the barbarians' to hope for an even larger ransom. Evidently, this 'leader' was Süleyman, the son of Orhan, who had been commanding Turkish forces in the region.[39] Rather than the equanimity with which Palamas was said to have looked upon Turks, he regarded their behaviour towards him as outrageous. He was not only mistreated physically, he was also taunted by Turks who told him that his capture was proof of the inefficacy of Christianity. The more that he saw, the more intransigent his views seem to have become. He was convinced that although they could not claim to be ignorant of Christ, the Turks nevertheless refused to accept him, and had therefore been consigned by God to all manner of vicious behaviour. In other words, precisely because they knew that Jesus was a prophet, but did not accept him as the Christ of the New Testament, they were punished by God.[40] The local Christians, however, were simply miserable. They begged Palamas for some kind of consolation, above all for an explanation of why God seemed to have abandoned them.[41]

When Palamas was taken to Pegae, known in Turkish as Biga, he found the journey very difficult. Despite the great cold, he was kept without shelter, and he was repeatedly threatened in the hope of increasing the size of his ransom. Once he arrived at Biga, however, he was delivered into the care of Mavrozoumis, whom Palamas describes as 'heteriarch'.[42] He was given food and shelter, and he was able to teach in the local church and to minister to the Christians of the city.

After three months, Palamas was taken to Bursa, a journey which took four days. Once again, he found himself in the care of local

38 Anna Philippidis-Braat, 'La captivité de Palamas', pp. 136–37.
39 Ibid., pp. 140–41, esp. n. 12; Rudi Paul Lindner, 'Anatolia, 1300–1451', in Kate Fleet, ed., *The Cambridge History of Turkey*, vol. I: *Byzantium to Turkey, 1071–1453*, (Cambridge: Cambridge University Press 2009), pp. 102–37, esp. p. 123.
40 Anna Philippidis-Braat, 'La captivité de Palamas', pp. 142–43.
41 Ibid., pp. 142–45.
42 Ibid., pp. 144–45. For a discussion of Mavrozoumis and his role in the Ottoman administration, see Heath W. Lowry, *The Nature of the Early Ottoman State*, pp. 87–89.

Christians, but he was moved after only two days to the camp of the Ottoman emir, itself a journey of two days. He describes it 'a hilly place, surrounded by mountains in the distance and made beautiful by thick-shaded trees; winds blow from one side and then from the other side of the mountain ridges, providing a cool draught that keeps the air around it refreshing even in summertime'.[43] This would be the setting for two of the three debates about the relationship between Christianity and Islam that many historians have found so encouraging.

A Conversation with Ismaꜥil

The first encounter occurred when Palamas was introduced to 'the grandson of the Great Emir', whose name was said to be Ismaꜥil. Food was brought to the two men while they sat on the grass, but as Palamas was an Athonite monk, and as their meeting took place on a Friday, he ate only fruit rather than meat. Ismaꜥil asked him about his diet, and when a servant who had been dispensing alms arrived, they began to discuss the importance of charity. The prince then inquired if Palamas accepted and loved Muhammad, the prophet of the Turks. When Palamas said that he did not, the prince asked why. Palamas replied that unless one believed the words of a teacher, it would be impossible to accept him as a teacher and therefore love him. Ismaꜥil then expressed incredulity at the crucifixion, remarking that Christians apparently loved Jesus but nevertheless believed that he was crucified. Palamas resolved the apparent contradiction, at least to his own satisfaction, by citing the voluntary nature of the martyrdom and the impassibility of a divine nature that was by definition beyond suffering. When Ismaꜥil criticized the Christian practice of venerating the Cross, Palamas explained that it was venerated as a symbol of the victory of Christ.

Ismaꜥil pressed on, however, and Palamas remarks that he evidently 'wanted to further ridicule and insult our beliefs'.[44] He accused Christians of believing that God had been married at some point. After all, they claimed that God had begotten a son. Palamas replied that Turks recognized Jesus as the Word of God and accepted that his

---

43 Ibid., pp. 146–47.   44 Ibid., pp. 148–49.

mother had been a virgin. If Mary gave birth to the Word of God without requiring a husband, it was surely all the easier to see that God himself did not require a wife to engender His own Word. Apparently Palamas was rather surprised at Isma'il's reaction to his reply, and notes that he did not respond with anger, even though those who knew him claimed that he had originally been unrelenting in his hostility to Christians. Unfortunately, as a heavy rain was beginning to fall, the conversation ended abruptly.

Late in the evening, the guards brought Palamas and his companions into the presence of Orhan Gazi himself, after which they were taken to be housed in a nearby residence for Byzantine ambassadors. Orhan was suffering from a liver complaint at the time, and the Armenian physician named Taronites[45] who was treating him remarked that Palamas too was unwell, but might recover if he were permitted to travel to Iznik, a city that he would find congenial. Orhan asked who Palamas was, and what sort of a man he was said to be. When Taronites told him, Orhan remarked, 'I too have wise and erudite men who will hold a discussion with him.'[46]

CHIONES

For the second of the debates, Orhan summoned a group of men named *Chiones*, whose identity has troubled several generations of scholars. Palamas describes them in contemptuous and aggressive terms as 'men who have studied and learned from Satan nothing except blasphemy and shamelessness towards Our Lord Jesus Christ, the Son of God'.[47]

In his own account of the proceedings, Taronites describes the *Chiones* trying to insist that a debate should simply not be held. When their complaint was rejected, they argued that a debate should at least not be held in the presence of Orhan himself. They apparently succeeded on their second attempt, and Orhan appointed several officials and a man whose name is given in Greek as Palapanis to preside over the discussion. This would appear to be Balaban, usually known in Ottoman sources by the diminutive Balabancık, a slave and a former Christian. He was a member of Orhan's inner circle, and had

45 Ibid., p. 114, esp. n. 20.   46 Ibid., pp. 168–69.   47 Ibid., pp. 150–51.

commanded one of the two fortresses that Orhan had built when he laid siege to Bursa.[48]

For his part, Palamas simply refused to debate with the *Chiones*. In fact, he claimed that he was only an insignificant figure compared to the full majesty and wisdom of the Church, and was therefore reluctant to engage in any debate. Furthermore, the officials who would judge the winner and loser of the debate belonged to the party of his adversaries. And in any case, Jesus himself refused to answer questions while he was a prisoner. Nevertheless, he recognized that the emir had ordered a debate, and he agreed that an emir should be kept informed of all the things that a ruler with authority over many races and religions needed to know. As for the *Chiones*, however, they seemed to be Jews, and Palamas was concerned to explain his faith to Muslims rather than to Jews.

Palamas then embarked on a metaphysical account of Christianity, carefully constructed to lead the discussion toward a point at which Muslims would be reassured that he was emphasizing the complete transcendence and absolute Unity of God. They might therefore be prepared to admit that Christ was the Word of God, and for this reason more than a mere prophet. At least according to the account that Taronites presents, Palamas succeeded in doing so. The Muslims who were present agreed that what he has said was true, and that they believed the same truth.

However, Palamas encountered greater resistance when he began to explain the Christian view of the process by which God saved the world. If the incarnation was a problem, the resurrection was even worse. Nevertheless, Palamas continued to build upon the agreed position that Christ was the Word of God.

When the *Chiones* interrupted, Palapanis told them to be silent. Instead, he informed Palamas that Orhan himself wanted Palamas to explain why Christians did not accept the Muslim prophet and love him, especially as Muslims accepted Jesus, loved him, respected him, confessed him to be the Word and the Breath of God, and placed his mother near to God. This was an extended version of the question that Isma'il had asked, and Palamas offered the same reply: those who do

---

48 Ibid., 168, n. 2. For a discussion of the identity of Balaban and the significance of his status as slave, see Heath W. Lowry, *The Nature of the Early Ottoman State*, p. 74.

not believe the words of a teacher cannot love the teacher himself, and Christians do not love Muhammad for this reason. He then cited verses from the New Testament that warned of false prophets who would come in the future.[49]

When the *Chiones* asked why Palamas had never been circumcised, given that God had commanded circumcision and that Jesus himself was circumcised, Palamas replied that neither Christians nor Turks kept the entire law that had been revealed to Moses. The *Chiones* then asked about Christian veneration of icons, given that the law revealed to Moses prohibited them. Palamas replied that Moses himself had depicted the cherubim in the temple. These images were not idols and they were not worshipped. Worship was directed to God the Creator.

Palamas evidently believed that his defence of the faith had been a success, but one of the *Chiones* stayed behind and struck Palamas in the eye. Others, however, rushed back to seize the culprit and deliver him to the Emir for punishment.

TASIMANES

At Iznik, while Palamas was waiting to be ransomed, he engaged in a third conversation about religious matters. He had been watching a Muslim funeral, and after finding an interpreter, he began a conversation with an Imam, whom he calls 'Tasimanes'.[50]

Palamas remarked that the Imam had obviously been addressing himself to God, but wondered what had he been saying. The Imam replied that he had been asking God to forgive the sins that the deceased had committed while he was alive. Palamas observed that this was all very well, but added that the judge who will decide the rewards and punishments of everyone, even according to Muslim doctrine, is Christ. The Imam must therefore have been addressing Christ as God, just as Christians do, believing that Christ is the Word of God is therefore indivisible from God. The Imam replied that Christ is a servant of God, rather than God himself. Palamas therefore reminded him that Abraham, who was the ancestor of Jews, Christians, and Muslims, said to God: 'You who judge the entire world,

---

49 Gospel of John 5.43; Epistle to the Galatians 1.8–9.
50 Paul Wittek, 'Χιόνες', p. 423, n. 3 discusses the derivation of Tasimanes from the Persian *danishmand*, meaning scholar.

will you not do right?'[51] This could only mean that the judge of the world is God himself. The Imam seemed unable to answer, and a crowd was beginning to gather. The Imam attempted another approach, telling Palamas that Muslims accepted all the prophets, including Jesus, and the four books that came down from Heaven, by which he meant the Torah, the Psalms, the Gospel, and the Qur'an. Why then did Christians not accept the Muslim prophet? Why did they not believe in his book, which had also come down from heaven?

This was the third occasion on which Palamas had been asked the question. He replied that none of the prophets had spoken of the coming of Muhammad, and Muhammad performed no miracles. The Imam offered the conventional Muslim reply that the Gospels had indeed spoken of Muhammad, but that Christians had removed any reference to him. Furthermore, the Muslim victory over the great empires of the world was itself a miracle as great as any performed by Moses or Jesus. Palamas rejected the claim that Christians had excised references to Muhammad in the Gospel. On the contrary, he maintained, the Gospel warned that false prophets would appear. As for the Muslim victories, they brought war, slaughter, and enslavement, and were therefore no better than the victories of Alexander. The teachings of Christ, on the other hand, had spread without force.

By now, however, the Turks who were listening had begun to take offence. The Christians tried to warn Palamas to stop. He therefore made a few banal and hopefully soothing remarks. The Turks replied that a time would come when they could all agree, and Palamas replied that he hoped the time would come quickly. Nevertheless, he added in his letter that he said this only because the New Testament states that in the future everyone will confess that Jesus Christ is Lord. In other words, Palamas's idea of agreement and the Turks' idea of agreement were very different.

A COMMON GROUND?

Anyone hoping for an inspiring account of goodwill across confessional lines may well be disappointed by the conversations described above. Nevertheless, it is worth recalling a remark by Daniel Sahas that we are hardly in a position to criticize Palamas. Discussions

---

51 Anna Philippidis-Braat, 'La captivité de Palamas chez les Turcs', pp. 154–5.

between Christians and Muslims today are often no more charitable and no more likely to escape the doctrinal constraints of the past. We seem to have made little progress.[52]

The first question to ask is whether the reports are actually genuine. Although the question was indeed raised by Martin Jugie eighty years ago, he did not pursue it at any length and no one else has been inclined to do so.[53] There seems no reason to suspect that the patriarch Philotheos or other contemporaries of Palamas knew of different versions.[54] The fact that Taronites appears to confirm everything that Palamas has written himself is not usually seen as an argument against the authenticity of the entire correspondence, as it is assumed that Palamas exerted at the very least some sort of editorial control over the text of the physician's account.[55]

Even if the accounts are genuine, however, are they accurate? In other words, do they record the conversations as they occurred, or are they rhetorical displays of arguments that Palamas wanted others to believe that he had made, or even of arguments that he thought that others should make if they were in a position to do so? Both are entirely possible. Palamas knew that enemies in Constantinople, such as the polymath Nikephoros Gregoras, were prepared to denounce him for his behaviour during captivity,[56] while the rate of conversion in territory occupied by the Ottomans was so rapid that the patriarch of Constantinople sent a letter to Iznik, the ancient Nicaea, urging the people to hold fast to their faith only a few years after the city had fallen.[57] For either reason, Palamas may have been keen to present himself as an example of unyielding resistance. This would also allow him to provide arguments that could be used by Christians whose beliefs were challenged, and to assure his readers that history was

52 Daniel Sahas, 'Gregory Palamas (1296–1360) on Islam', esp. p. 21.

53 Martin Jugie, 'Palamas Grégoire', in *Dictionnaire de Théologie Catholique*, (Paris: Letouzy et Ané 1932), vol. 11, pp. 1735–76.

54 Anna Philippidis-Braat, 'La captivité de Palamas chez les Turcs', p. 110.

55 Ibid., p. 116; Eva de Vries-van der Velden, *L'élite byzantine devant l'avance turque à l'époque de la guerre civile de 1341 à 1354* (Amsterdam: J. C. Gieben 1989), esp. pp. 198–99.

56 George G. Arnakis, 'Gregory Palamas among the Turks and Documents of His Captivity as Historical Sources', p. 116, n. 5 provides an account of scandalous accusations made against Palamas by the historian Nikephoros Gregoras, who opposed the Hesychast movement in general and detested Palamas.

57 Ibid., p. 114 and p. 118, n. 29.

really on their side. Furthermore, it is important to remember that Palamas was evidently writing while he was still in captivity. He might have hoped that an account of steadfast, and even heroic, behaviour would encourage readers who possessed sufficient wealth to pay his ransom.

We might be in a better position to decide if we knew more about the circumstances of the three debates, especially about the *Chiones* whom Orhan invited to his camp. The name is obscure and has occasioned three solutions of particular interest: Arnakis suggested that it derives from *akhiyan*, the Persian plural of *akhi*, and that they were representatives of the guilds of artisans.[58] Wittek replied almost immediately that the guilds were simply trade guilds, and that we would need to revise completely our understanding of their role in Anatolian society for this to be plausible. He therefore suggested that the *Chiones* were Muslim specialists in the law, and proposed a derivation from *khoja*.[59] Some thirty years later, Michel Balivet focused on the fact that Palamas denounced the *Chiones* as Jews, and suggested a derivation from *kahin*, proposing the existence of a circle or movement comprising Judaizing scholars devoted to astrology and other arcane disciplines.[60]

However, even a correct etymology of the word may or may not answer the question of who the *Chiones* were before their conversion, and the still more important question of who they were after it. They state clearly that they did convert, and they also state clearly that they converted to become Turks.[61] Difficulty has arisen because Palamas dismisses them by claiming that they seem to be Jews,[62] and because they themselves claim that their conversion to Islam was made easier because Muslims accept the law delivered to Moses on Mount Sinai.[63] But these are two different questions. It is certainly possible, although by no means certain, that they were Jews before their conversion, but the idea that they converted to Judaism as a way of gaining favour with Turks would seem preposterous, as well as unprecedented, despite the distinguished scholars who have suggested it.[64] The ques-

---

58 Ibid., pp. 113–14.   59 Paul Wittek, 'Χιόνες', pp. 421–23.

60 Michel Balivet, 'Byzantins judaïsants et Juifs islamisés: des "Kühhân" (Kâhin) aux "Χιόναι" (Χιόνες)', pp. 24–59.

61 Anna Philippidis-Braat, 'La captivité de Palamas', pp. 168–69.

62 Ibid., pp. 170–71.   63 Ibid., pp. 168–69, 172–73.

64 In particular, see John Meyendorff, 'Grecs, Turcs et Juifs en Asie Mineure au xiv[e]

tion is complicated by the fact that 'Jew' was used as an opprobrious epithet by Orthodox theologians, and the possibility that Palamas would have dismissed opponents as 'Jews' even though they were not.[65] It is worth remembering that Palamas regarded the *Chiones* and the Muslim dignitaries who presided over the debate as members of the same party or faction.[66] Furthermore, although Balivet simply claims that he is mistaken, the patriarch Philotheos states that the *Chiones* were converts from Christianity to Islam.[67]

If indeed the *Chiones* had become Muslim, this would seem to be far more important than what they had been before. Wittek's claim that the term is derived from *khoja* is philologically difficult, it seems to me, and is only occasioned by the fact that Wittek found the suggestion of Arnakis incredible because it would mean completely rewriting what he understood to be the history of the Akhis. But in fact, such a revision has now occurred. Instead of simply a trade guild, the Akhis are seen to be a mystical fraternity either similar to Sufis, or connected to Sufis, or in fact simply Sufis themselves.[68] However implausible Wittek found the suggestion, it would seem perfectly natural for Orhan to have summoned such people. There is certainly evidence that Orhan, who was believed to be the grandson of the famous shaykh Edebali, was regarded as a generous patron of Sufis and Akhis,[69] and the Maghrebian scholar and traveller Ibn Battuta describes the prominent role that Akhis played in the region only two decades before Palamas was taken captive.[70] Especially if the *Chiones*

siècle', pp. 211–17. The possibility has been dismissed by Steven Bowman, *Jews of Byzantium*, (Birmingham: University of Alabama Press 1985), pp. 69–70.

65 Ibid., p. 70.

66 Anna Philippidis-Braat, 'La captivité de Palamas', pp. 170–71.

67 Michel Balivet, 'Byzantins judaïsants et Juifs islamisés: des "Kühhân" (Kâhin) aux "Χιόναι" (Χιόνες)', pp. 24–59, esp. 25–33.

68 Ethel S. Wolper, *Cities and Saints: Sufism and the Transformation of Urban Space in Medieval Anatolia* (University Park, PA: Pennsylvania State University Press 2003), pp. 76–78.

69 It is worth noting that the oldest known Ottoman document, usually cited as the 'Mekece *Vakfiye*', is a foundation charter for a *tekke* issued by Orhan in 1324. See Heath W. Lowry, *The Nature of the Early Ottoman State*, pp. 75–77. For a more general discussion of sufism at the time, see Osman Türer, 'General Distribution of the Sufi Orders in Ottoman Anatolia', in *Sufism and Sufis in Ottoman Society*, ed. Ahmet Yaşar Ocak (Ankara: Turkish Historical Society 2005), pp. 219–26, esp. pp. 220–22.

70 George G. Arnakis, 'Futuwwa Traditions in the Ottoman Empire: Akhis, Bektashi Dervishes, and Craftsmen', *Journal of Near Eastern Studies* 12, (1953), pp. 232–47, esp. pp. 238–39.

were recent converts, one can imagine their reticence to engage with a theologian as skilled and as tenacious as Palamas, above all in the presence of an illustrious patron.

What is surprising, however – or perhaps more disappointing than surprising – is the fact that Palamas simply delivers an apologia: skilful but nevertheless conventional, an exercise in dogmatics rather than mysticism. As for the *Chiones*, they are represented as doing nothing to change the tenor of the debate. If they were indeed Akhis who were part of the mystical movement that spread Islam among the Christians or Jews of Anatolia by forming a hybrid or common ground between the religions, they give little evidence of it here, and Palamas was not in a mood to listen anyway.

The latter point is in itself important, and it should not be overlooked. Palamas, of course, may be forgiven for remaining opposed to any attempt at finding a common ground, at least as modern readers might imagine such a thing. He does grant a common heritage for Judaism, Christianity, and Islam, of course, but the shared legacy simply proves, as far as he is concerned, that Christianity is true and the others are defective. That being said, the question proposed by Isma'il, by Orhan, and by the Imam at Iznik is loaded: 'We accept your prophet, so why do you not accept ours?' While Muslims do accept the Qur'anic account of the prophet Jesus, they certainly do not accept the New Testament account of the crucified and resurrected Christ. For Palamas or for any Christian to accept the terms suggested by Isma'il, Orhan, or the Imam – or to accept the statements that Rumi had written a century earlier – would mean that they were no longer Christian but Muslim. This is not the middle ground that some who refer to the captivity of Palamas imagine, and it is certainly not a view in which Christianity and Islam are two equally valid paths to salvation. There may well have been Christians and Muslims who took this view, or something very close to it, but that is not what we find here and it is not what we find in the statements cited earlier from the writings of Rumi. In any discussion of this question, it is extremely important to determine if Christians and Muslims are actually talking about the same thing. Invariably, it seems to me, they are not.

With this in mind, one needs to be very careful in assuming too much about the tolerance that Ottomans adopted towards subject peoples. It was undoubtedly real, and it is certainly more attractive to a modern sensibility than prejudice and persecution, but it was hardly disinterested and there were limits to it. In a world in which the Ottoman dynasty and the followers at their disposal were very much outnumbered by indigenous or at least earlier inhabitants, a policy that reduced discrimination and encouraged a sense of common enterprise was obviously pragmatic. Furthermore, for anyone acquiring control over a large empire, it obviously made sense to retain as much of the previous administration as possible, confirming Mavrozoumis and others like him in the positions that they had occupied under the old regime. Eventually, however, the Ottoman state would become overtly Sunni and orthodox. While the latitude allowed to those who were neither, or whom the state judged to be neither, may still have been impressive by the standard of contemporary societies in Europe, it was nevertheless reduced.

The question is of great importance for the study of Ottoman history in general, because of the claim that the dynasty came to power as *ghazi*s dedicated to advancing Islam and eradicating infidelity by conquest.[71] The account of Palamas in captivity suggests that neither by their actions nor by their opinions were Ottomans, such as Orhan or his grandson Isma'il, simple 'warriors for the faith', as we might imagine such a term to mean today. The word *ghazi* has been much debated, but at the very least it would seem to be capable of interpretations that are different and perhaps not mutually exclusive, capable of meaning many things to many people.[72] On the other hand, the gloating that Palamas describes at the beginning of his account, in which he is told that his captivity proves the weakness of Christianity, suggests that a sense of triumphalism was not unknown.[73]

All this may seem to indicate attitudes on both sides that were far removed from Aflaki's famous account of the funeral of Rumi as it is usually understood, a celebration in which Jews and Christians, as well as Muslims, are depicted as finding in the person of Rumi their own prophets, their Moses or their Jesus.[74] It is worth making the

---

71 For a summary of different approaches to the subject, see Heath W. Lowry, *The Nature of the Early Ottoman State*, pp. 1–13.

72 Among other discussions, see Linda Darling, 'Contested Territory: Ottoman Holy War in Comparative Context', *Studia Islamica* 91 (2000), pp. 133–63, and Colin Imber, 'What Does *Ghazi* Actually Mean?', in Çigdem Balım-Harding and Colin Imber, eds., *The Balance of Truth: Essays in Honour of Professor Geoffrey Lewis* (Istanbul: Isis Press 2000), pp. 165–78.

73 Anna Philippidis-Braat, 'La captivité de Palamas', pp. 140–41.

74 *The Feats of the Knowers of God*, §565–88.

obvious point that Aflaki and other Mevlevi hagiographers were Muslim themselves. The situation might have seemed rather different if one were Christian and were witnessing the demise of a Christian empire and the transformation of a Christian society. The account of Palamas, and indeed a more careful reading of statements by Rumi or about Rumi, suggests that we should not simply be looking for evidence that confirms our own hopes and aspirations for the past as well as for the future.

Above all, we should at least make an attempt to understand the past as it appeared to those who lived in it. It is utterly misleading to claim, for example, that 'Palamas also described many interactions in the streets in which the relative merits of Islam and Christianity were compared, discussed, and accepted as alternative and compatible ways of approaching faith, so much so that Palamas assumed that the Turks and Byzantines were going to reach an inter-confessional concordat.'[75] He did not describe many interactions in the streets, and he described none in which Christianity and Islam were accepted as alternative and compatible ways of approaching faith. He only said that Turks and Byzantines were going to agree because his companions were afraid that his defence of Christian doctrine had offended the Turks and violence would ensue. In his letter, he is explicit about assuming that agreement would mean that Turks became Christian, not that Christians became Turks, or that some sort of hybrid would emerge.

So Palamas was not intent on learning from Muslims, or at least does not present himself as willing to learn from them. In any case, there is certainly nothing in these conversations that he could have taken away and used to construct a Hesychast theology. Furthermore, his teachings do not need to be explained by appealing to influences outside the Christian tradition. I hasten to add that there are Christian mystics who can only be explained in this way, but Palamas is not one of them. Above all, however, there is the problem of chronology. Palamas would die only four years after his release from captivity. All his great treatises, especially his robust defence of Hesychasm against the attacks by Barlaam the Calabrian, had been written before he was captured. Whether or not one believes that he was broken by his

75 Karen Barkey, *Empire of Difference: The Ottomans in Comparative Perspective* (Cambridge: Cambridge University Press 2008), esp. p. 61.

experiences in captivity, as indeed has been suggested,[76] his career as a great champion of Hesychasm was now at an end. There is no evidence of an essential treatise having been written after his captivity or of Palamas having rewritten Hesychast doctrines in any way as a result of anything that he learned during his captivity.

But even if there was no direct influence, does this mean that Palamas represents a Christian tradition completely distinct from others? On the contrary, I would argue. Jewish, Christian, and Muslim versions of mysticism are closely connected, and even in cases where there is no specific influence from one individual to another, they are all part of traditions that are mutually indebted to each other. Furthermore, the tantalizing question of the extent to which different mystical traditions may or may not point to the same experiences or the same fundamental truths is undoubtedly in need of further exploration. Even if the accounts of Palamas in captivity are valuable evidence for religious debate in the century following the death of Jalal al-Din Rumi, for the Ottoman policy of toleration, for its limits, and for Christian resistance to it or resentment of it, it seems to me that there is still work for those of us who find Aflaki's account of the funeral of Rumi inspiring, or at least intriguing. As Daniel Sahas reminded us twenty years ago, we need to try harder.[77]

SELECTED BIBLIOGRAPHY

Aflākī, Shams al-Dīn Aḥmad. *Ariflerin Menkıbeleri* (*Mevlânâ ve Etrafindakiler*), tr. Tahsin Yazıcı. Istanbul: Milli Eğitim Basımevi, 1964.

—. *Manāḳib al-ʿarifīn*, ed. Tahsin Yazıcı. Ankara: Türk Tarih Kurumu Basımevi, 1959 and 1961.

—. *The Feats of the Knowers of God* (*Manāqeb al-ʿārefīn*), trans. John O'Kane. Leiden: Brill, 2002.

Arnakis, George. 'Futuwwa Traditions in the Ottoman Empire: Akhis, Bektashi Dervishes, and Craftsmen', *Journal of Near Eastern Studies* 12, 1953, pp. 232–47.

—. 'Gregory Palamas among the Turks and Documents of His Captivity as Historical Sources', *Speculum* 26, 1951, pp. 104–18.

76 For example, Eva de Vries-van der Velden, *L'élite byzantine devant l'avance turque à l'époque de la guerre civile de 1341 à 1354*, esp. pp. 201–2.

77 Daniel Sahas, 'Gregory Palamas (1296–1360) on Islam', esp. p. 21.

—. 'Gregory Palamas, the Χιόνες, and the Fall of Gallipoli', *Byzantion* 22, 1952, pp. 302–12.

—. *Hoi protoi Othomanoi*, Texte und Forschungen zur byzantinisch-neugriechischen Philologie 41, Athens, 1947.

Balivet, Michel. 'Byzantins judaïsants et Juifs islamisés: des "Kühhân" (Kâhin) aux "Χιόναι" (Χιόνιος)', *Byzantion* 52, 1982, pp. 24–59.

—. 'Culture ouverte et échanges inter-religieux dans les villes ottomanes du XIVe siècle', in *The Ottoman Emirate (1300–1389)*, ed. Elizabeth Zachariadou, Rethymnon: Crete University Press, 1993, pp. 1–6.

Barkey, Karen. *Empire of Difference: The Ottomans in Comparative Perspective*. Cambridge: Cambridge University Press, 2008, esp. pp. 61–2.

Bowman, Steven. *Jews of Byzantium*. Birmingham: University of Alabama Press, 1985, esp. pp. 69–70.

Cutsinger, James S. ed., *Paths to the Heart: Sufism and the Christian East*. Bloomington, Indiana: World Wisdom 2002.

Darling, Linda. 'Contested Territory: Ottoman Holy War in Comparative Context', *Studia Islamica* 91, 2000, pp. 133–63.

Dölger, Franz. 'Zur Frage des jüdischen Anteils an der Bevölkerung Thessalonikes im 14. Jahrhundert', *Jewish Social Studies* 5, 1953, pp. 129–33.

Dyovouniotes, K. 'Gregoriou Palama epistole pros Thessalonikeis', *Neos Hellenomnemon* 16, 1922, pp. 7–21.

Ernst, Carl W. 'Traditionalism, the Perennial Philosophy, and Islamic Studies', *Middle East Studies Association Bulletin* 28, 1994, pp. 176–81.

Grierson, Roderick. 'One Shrine Alone: Christians, Sufis, and the Vision of Mevlana', in *The Philosophy of Ecstasy: Rumi and the Sufi Tradition*, ed. Leonard. Lewisohn. Forthcoming.

Hasluck, Frederick William. *Christianity and Islam under the Sultans*, 2 vols., Oxford: Clarendon Press, 1929.

Huart, Clément. *Les Saints des derviches tourneurs*, Paris: E. Leroux, 1918 and 1922.

Huntingdon, Samuel. *The Clash of Civilizations and the Remaking of World Order*, New York: Simon & Schuster, 1996.

Imber, Colin. 'What Does *Ghazi* Actually Mean?', in Çigdem Balım-Harding and Colin Imber, eds., *The Balance of Truth: Essays in Honour of Professor Geoffrey Lewis*, Istanbul: Isis Press, 2000, pp. 165–78.

Irwin, Robert. *For Lust of Knowing: The Orientalists and their Enemies*, London: Penguin, 2006.

Jugie, Martin. 'Palamas Grégoire', in *Dictionnaire de Théologie Catholique*, Paris: Letouzy et Ané, 1932, vol. 11, pp. 1735–76.

Kafadar, Cemal. *Between Two Worlds: The Construction of the Ottoman State*. Berkeley and Los Angeles: University of California Press, 1995, esp. p. 175.

Krausmüller, Dirk. 'The Rise of Hesychasm', in *Eastern Christianity*, ed. Michael Angold, Cambridge: Cambridge University Press, 2006, pp. 101–26.

Lewis, Bernard. 'The Roots of Muslim Rage' in *The Atlantic Monthly*, Vol. 266, No. 3, September 1990, pp. 47–60.

Lindner, Rudi Paul. 'Anatolia, 1300–1451', in *The Cambridge History of Turkey*, vol. I: *Byzantium to Turkey, 1071–1453*, ed. Kate Fleet. Cambridge: Cambridge University Press, 2009.

Lowry, Heath W. *The Nature of the Early Ottoman State*. Albany: State University of New York Press, 2003.

Meyendorff, John. 'Grecs, Turcs et Juifs en Asie Mineure au XIVᵉ siècle', *Byzantinische Forschungen* 1, 1966, pp. 211–17 (reprinted as Essay IX in John Meyendorff, *Byzantine Hesychasm: Historical, Cultural and Theological Problems*, London: Variorum Reprints, 1974).

—. *Introduction à l'étude de Grégoire Palamas*. Paris: Éditions du Seuil, 1959, esp. pp. 157–62 (translated into English as *A Study of Gregory Palamas*, London: Faith Press, 1964).

—. 'Palamas (Grégoire)', *Dictionnaire de Spiritualité*, vol. 12, Paris: Beauchesne, 1984, pp. 81–107.

—. *St. Grégoire Palamas et la mystique orthodoxe*, Paris: Éditions du Seuil, 1959 (translated into English as *St. Gregory Palamas and Orthodox Spirituality*. Crestwood, New York: St. Vladimir's Seminary Press, 1974).

Nasr, Seyyed Hossein. 'The Prayer of the Heart in Hesychasm and Sufism', *Greek Orthodox Theological Review* 31, 1986, pp. 195–203.

Nicol, Donald M. *The Last Centuries of Byzantium, 1261–1453*, 2nd ed., Cambridge: Cambridge University Press, 1993.

—. *The Reluctant Emperor: A Biography of John Cantacuzene, Byzantine Emperor and Monk, c. 1295–1383*, Cambridge: Cambridge University Press, 1996.

Ocak, Ahmet Yaşar. 'Les milieux soufis dan les territoires du beylicat ottoman et le problème des "Abdalan-i Rum" (1300–1389)', in Elizabeth Zachariadou, Rethymnon: Crete University Press, 1993, pp. 145–58.

Philippidis-Braat, Anna, 'La captivité de Palamas chez les Turcs: dossier et commentaire', *Travaux et mémoires* 6, 1979, pp. 109–222.

Prokhorov, G. M. 'Preniye Grigoriya Palamy "s khiony i turki" i problema zhidovskaya mudrstvuyushchikh', *Trudy otdela drevnerusskoy literatury* 27, 1972, pp. 329–69.

Ridgeon, Lloyd. 'Christianity as Portrayed by Jalāl al-Dīn Rūmī', in *Islamic Interpretations of Christianity*, ed. Lloyd. Ridgeon, Richmond: Curzon, 2001, pp. 99–126

Rumi, Jalal al-Din. *The Mathnawí of Jalálu'ddín Rúmí*, ed. Reynold A. Nicholson, 8 vols., London: Luzac, 1925–40.

—. *Kulliyat-i Shams ya Diwan-i kabir az guftar-i Mawlana Jalal al-Din Muhammad mashhur bih-Mawlavi, ba tashihat wa havashi*, ed. Badiᶜ al-Zaman Furuzanfar, 3rd ed., Tehran: Sipihr, 1363 A.Hsh./1984. 10 vols.

Sahas, Daniel. 'Captivity and Dialogue: Gregory Palamas (1296–1360) and the Muslims', *Greek Orthodox Theological Review* 25, 1981, pp. 409–36.

—. 'Gregory Palamas (1296–1360) on Islam', *The Muslim World* 73, 1983, pp. 1–21.

Sakkelion, A. I. 'Gregoriou Thessalonikes tou Palama anekdotos dialexis', *Soter* 15, 1892, pp. 240–46.

Ševčenko, Ihor. 'Theodore Metochites, the Chora, and the Intellectual Trends of his Time', in *The Kariye Djami*, vol. 4, ed. Paul A. Underwood. Princeton: Princeton University Press, 1975, pp. 17–91.

Treu, M. 'Epistole Gregoriou tou Palama pros Dauid monakhon ton Disypaton', *Deltion tes historikes kai ethnologikes hetaireias* 3, 1890, pp. 229–34.

Türer, Osman. 'General Distribution of the Sufi Orders in Ottoman Anatolia', in *Sufism and Sufis in Ottoman Society*, ed. Ahmet Yaşar Ocak. Ankara: Turkish Historical Society, 2005, pp. 219–226, esp. pp. 220–22.

de Vries-van der Velden, Eva. *L'élite byzantine devant l'avancé turque à l'époque de la guerre civile de 1341 à 1354*, Amsterdam, J. C. Gieben, 1989.

Vryonis, Speros. *The Decline of Medieval Hellenism in Asia Minor and the Process of Islamization from the Eleventh through the Fifteenth Century*, Berkeley and Los Angeles: University of California Press, 1971.

Wittek, Paul. 'Χιόνες', *Byzantion* 21, 1951, pp. 421–3.

Wolper, Ethel Sara. *Cities and Saints: Sufism and the Transformation of Urban Space in Medieval Anatolia*, University Park: Pennsylvania State University Press, 2003.

Zachariadou, Elizabeth. 'Religious Dialogue between Byzantines and Turks during the Ottoman Expansion', in *Religionsgespräche im Mittelalter. Wolfenbütteler Mittelalterstudien*, eds. Bernard Lewis and Friedrich Niewöhner, Wiesbaden: Otto Harrassowitz, 1992, pp. 289–304 (reprinted in Elizabeth Zachariadou, *Studies in Pre-Ottoman Turkey and the Ottomans*, Aldershot: Ashgate, 2007, Essay II).

—. 'Co-Existence and Religion', *Archivum Ottomanicum* 15, 1997, pp. 119–30.

—. 'Records of the Turkish Anatolian States, c. 1250–1330', in *Pragmatic Literacy, East and West, 1200–1330*, ed. Richard Britnell, Woodbridge: Boydell Press, 1997, pp. 199–205.

Homage to Professor Nicholson

BADIᶜ AL-ZAMAN FURUZANFAR

Translated from the Persian by Rasoul Sorkhabi

Translator's Note

Reynold Alleyne Nicholson (1868–1945), Professor of Persian Literature at Cambridge University, and Badiᶜ al-Zaman Furuzanfar (1903–1970), his counterpart at Tehran University, were regarded as the most eminent Rumi scholars of their day. To the former we owe the first scholarly edited version of Mawlana's *Mathnawi-yi maᶜnawi* ('Spiritual Couplets'), published in eight volumes from 1925 to 1940 in London (this included the first critical edition of the Persian text, the first full English translation, and a two-volume commentary). Prof. Furuzanfar accomplished the same daunting task and valuable service to Mawlana's *Divan-i Shams* ('Poetry Book Dedicated to Shams'), published in ten volumes from 1957 to 1967 by the University of Tehran.[1]

This article presents for the first time an English translation of Prof. Furuzanfar's speech delivered in October 1945 in Tehran to commemorate Nicholson's death (which occurred on 27 August of the same year). Furuzanfar also affectionately composed a poem in praise of Nicholson's contributions which comes at the end of his article, which however I have not translated. Wherever possible, I have closely followed Furuzanfar's original language, but have added a few footnotes to make the article more accessible to the general public; in places where it was required I have also added a few words in brackets to clarify otherwise obscure statements. Needless to say, for lovers of Rumi who do not have

---

1 The details of Badiᶜ al-Zaman Furuzanfar's own edition of the *Divan*, which includes Rumi's lyric poems (*ghazaliyat*) as well as strophe-poems (*tarjiᶜiyat*), and quatrains (*rubaᶜiyat*), are: *Kulliyat-i Shams ya Diwan-i kabir az guftar-i Mawlana Jalal al-Din Muhammad mashhur bih-Mawlavi, ba tashihat wa havashi*, 10 vols. in 9 (3rd ed., reprinted Tehran: Sipihr 1363 A.Hsh./1984).

access to modern Persian scholarship about the great Sufi poet, it will be fascinating to hear what one of the greatest Iranian scholars of the twentieth century thought of Nicholson and his achievement.[2]

*

Anyone who is familiar with Mawlana Jalal al-Din Muhammad Balkhi and has some knowledge of his works, including the *Mathnawi* and the *Divan,* is aware of the difficulties and hardships in [understanding] Mawlana's works, particularly his *Mathnawi*. Throughout the ages, from Mawlana's death until the present time, Sufi masters, eminent mystics, learned men and scholars have made efforts to explain and interpret the *Mathnawi*, and have written commentaries on this book, some detailed and some brief, some in prose and others in verse, in various languages including Persian, Arabic and Turkish. Nevertheless, the *Mathnawi*, this lovely witness of the divine beauty of the Unseen World (*ghayb*), has only lifted up a tiny corner of the veil concealing her face, so that many of the problems [in understanding the text] still remain unresolved.

It may be supposed that the main reason for these difficulties lies in our estrangement from the terminology of Sufism, the Sufi mystics and our insufficient knowledge of the fundamentals of Sufism. However, upon close examination and research it becomes obvious that the majority of our problems arise from the errors and unjustifiable distortions that either deliberately, or by accident, have found their way into the *Mathnawi* through accretions made by copyists and readers. For this very reason, even those who were familiar with Sufi terms and the fundamentals of Islamic mysticism have not been able to successfully tackle this issue.

Evidence [from secondary literature] clearly shows that ever since the brilliance of the *Mathnawi* began to be noticed, it was read in the [Sufi] gatherings of *Sama*[3] and spiritual joy (*hal*), and in Mawlana's

---

2 This article is taken from *Majmu'a-yi maqalat va ash'ar-i ustad Badi' al-Zaman Furuzanfar*, ed. 'Inayatu'llah Majidi (Tehran: Dihkhuda 1351 A.Hsh./1972), pp. 230–37. The speech was originally published in *Nama-yi Farhangistan*, vol. 4, no. 1 (Ordibihisht 1325 A.Hsh./April 1946), pp. 19–24. I am grateful to Leonard Lewisohn for critically reading and editing this translation. Dr Lewisohn has also written an informative article on this subject: 'Profile: Reynold Alleyne Nicholson', published in the *British Association for the Study of Religion Bulletin*, no. 77 (1996), pp. 4–10.

3 *Sama'* (literally 'listening') is a special type of Sufi gathering in order to listen to singing of mystical poetry and music, to invoke the Name of God (*dhikr*), and,

time, a group called the '*Mathnawi*-reciters' had a distinguished place among his fans and disciples, and this group in a way paralleled the professional Qur'an-reciters. After Mawlana's death, this tradition [of reading and recitation from the *Mathnawi*] at the site of his sacred mausoleum and in gatherings headed by his successors and designated representatives was quite prevalent. Given the importance of the *Mathnawi* and its impact on the hearts of spiritual wayfarers and seekers, other Sufi orders also used to recite the *Mathnawi* in their gatherings, and considering the tradition of ongoing commentary and exposition of the principles of Sufism that existed then, they continually used to read and recommend the reading of this poem to their disciples. Even Qutb ibn Muhyi Jahrumi, one of the important ascetics and Sufi masters of the fifteenth century, who observed the formal rituals in a somewhat rigid and dry manner, had made the reading of four books obligatory upon his followers who were known as the Brethren (*Akhwan*). One of these four books was the *Mathnawi*.

The Sufi Orders of our time too have included the *Mathnawi* as part and parcel of the basic principles of the spiritual work of their disciples. Thus on Thursday and Sunday nights [in Iran], wherever a gathering of Sufi seekers takes place, vocalists sing from this book with a heart-warming voice. Of course, those readers of the *Mathnawi* who live outside Iran and are not very familiar with the Persian language may not appreciate this tradition. It is also clear that those Sufi devotees who disregard the significance of words and outward expressions and consider themselves above and beyond all formal traditions and customs, will find the attempt [by the likes of Nicholson] to preserve [for posterity] the original text of the *Mathnawi* and establish an edition free from alterations and distortions, to be a useless endeavour.

Mawlana had gained vast knowledge through the works of poets preceding him, especially the Persian-speaking poets of northern Iran such as Nizami[4] and Khaqani,[5] and employed this knowledge in his

---

sometimes, to dance. This is especially an important tradition among the Mevlevi Sufis who are followers of Mawlana Rumi.

4 Nizami (1141–1209), an eminent Persian poet from Ganja (now in the Republic of Azerbaijan) well known for his romantic stories of lovers and for his clear Persian verse; his most celebrated work is the *Panj ganj* ('Five Jewels') or *Khamsa* ('Quintet') that included five books of verse: *Makhzan al-asrar* ('Storehouse of Secrets'), *Khusraw va Shirin* ('Khusrow and Shirin'), *Layli va Majnun* ('Leili and Majnun'), *Iskandar-nama* ('The Book of Alexander') and *Haft paykar* ('Seven Beautiful Bodies').

own poetry quite well. In this way, there were certain archaic and yet marvellously eloquent expressions in Mawlana's poetry which remained alien to the style of poets who came after the Mongol period.[6] Unravelling these expressions and terms is an extremely difficult task unless one undertakes an extensive investigation into the *Mathnawi* itself as well as examination of the works of Sana'i,[7] Khaqani and Nizami. Therefore, it is quite possible, as indeed quite often happened, that calligraphers and copyists made alterations in the *Mathnawi* so as to transform these – to their mind – strange expressions into familiar ones. Such erroneous scribal emendations have occurred in the works of most of the other poets, and their readers and copyists may have even judged these unwarranted alterations as a kind of service to the Persian language and to Rumi himself. In a similar manner, we can see in the manuscripts of Saᶜdi's *Gulistan* ('The Rose Garden')[8] how later copyists tried to make rhyme many sentences which originally did not fully rhyme, so that the more we refer to older manuscripts of the *Gulistan,* the fewer rhymed lines we encounter in the text.

Another reason [for our difficulties in reading the *Mathnawi*] is that during the Mongol period, with the disappearance of scholars, learned men and Persian texts, a gap between peoples living prior and after the Mongol period came into being, and this produced a huge contrast in

5 Khaqani (1121–1190) one of the eminent Persian poets from the classical times, who has left a *Divan* ('Book of Poetry') and used plain but powerful expressions especially in his quatrains. He is buried in Tabriz, Iran.

6 The Mongols under Genghis Khan invaded Persia in the early thirteenth century (a reason that is sometimes cited for the westward migration of Rumi's family). After decades of destruction and massacre, decades which overlap with Rumi's life in Anatolia, the Mongol (known as 'Il-Khanids') rulers finally converted to Islam, were Persianized, and established their courts on the model of Iranian dynasties before them. These new Mongol courts (and the later proto-Mongol dynasties of the Jalayirids, Inju'ids, Muzaffarids, etc.) in Iran continued to support Persian poetry and the arts and Iranian scholars during the fourteenth century. Here, Professor Furuzanfar seems to refer to the thirteenth-century period of Mongol rule in Iran.

7 Sana'i (d. ca. 1131) lived in Ghazna (now in Afghanistan) and is regarded as one of the earliest Persian Sufi poets who wrote in a style that was later carried on by ᶜAttar and Rumi. Aside from his *Divan*, his most important book is a *mathnawi* poem: *Hadiqa al-haqiqat* ('The Walled Garden of Truth').

8 Saᶜdi (1209–1292), a contemporary of Rumi from the city of Shiraz (where his mausoleum exists), was a world-traveller and poet. Aside from the *ghazal*s (lyrics) in his *Divan*, his two books: *Bustan* ('The Orchard', 1257) and *Gulistan* ('The Rose Garden', 1258) are regarded as masterpieces of Persian literature. Both works have been translated into English.

terms of ways of thinking and expression between these two generations of scholars, with the result that those who belonged to the later
generation became unable to understand Mawlana's intended words
and objectives. Consequently, because they considered Rumi's ideas
to be opposed to their own fundamental beliefs, they introduced
textual alterations and distortions into the *Mathnawi*. Putting that
problem to one side, when the Shi'ite sect came to predominate in
Iran, some Iranians even added verses of their own to the *Mathnawi*
and made alterations to its text so as to portray Mawlana's *Mathnawi*
as a Shi'ite work.

We come to another point here. Mawlana did not, in any way,
consider himself as being bound down and shackled to following the
rules of rhyming, scansion, or other poetic devices and crafts which
the poets considered to be the fundamental principles of poetry and
verse, and at times Mawlana even ignored these rules. Therefore,
some copyists and fans of Mawlana's works, either having good
intentions or else assuming that some errors had been committed by
ignorant copyists of the past, themselves made certain alterations in
the poems, especially with regard to rhythm and rhyme. The scale of
this problem becomes even more severe and shocking when we read
in the work of Aflaki[9] that some copyists in Mawlana's own day had
already tried to change the wording of his poems. One instance is
given of a scribe by the name of Shaykh Fakhr al-Din Sivasi, who was
among Mawlana's followers and a copyist of the *Mathnawi*.[10] He is
reported to have deliberately made changes to some verses of the
Mathnawi to suit his own tastes while copying it down, and in Aflaki's
opinion, his attempt at these inappropriate alterations eventually
drove him insane. Mawlana apparently composed the following
ghazal in reference to him:

9 Shams al-Din Ahmad Aflaki (d. 1360) was an admirer of Mawlana, a disciple of his
   Order and close to his family, who compiled the *Manaqib al-ʿarifin* which contains
   biographies of Mawlana, his family members, friends and disciples. The full text of
   this fourteenth-century Persian work has recently been translated by John O'Kane
   as *The Feats of the Knowers of God* (Leiden: Brill 2002).
10 This incident is recorded in the *Manaqib al-ʿarifin* edited by Tahsin Yazıcı (Ankara:
   Turk Tarih Kurumu Basimeri, 2nd ed., 1976–1980), 2 vols. (reprinted: Tehran: Dunya-
   yi Kitab 1375 A.Hsh./1983), vol. 1, pp. 238–39.

O Lovers! O Lovers! A young fellow has gone insane!
His wash-tub fell off our roof [he's disgraced]; he's gone to the
     lunatic asylum.[11]

In the first book of the *Mathnawi*, there is a story about a scribe commissioned to note down the revelation of the Qur'an [as it was being
revealed to the Prophet] by the name of Abdu'llah ibn Saʿd ibn Abi
Sarh[12] who became a heretic [because he deliberately changed expressions in the divine Scripture], and it is possible that here there can be
found an allusion to the case of Shaykh Fakhr al-Din Sivasi as well.

When we examine and compare the earliest manuscripts of the
Mathnawi with each other, most of which can be assumed to have
been written down by Rumi's earliest copyists or disciples, and
consider some of the textual variations that are apparent between
them, it seems that (or at least the question arises as to whether) it is
conceivable that over a period of no shorter than twelve years [that
Mawlana spent on the *Mathnawi*], Mawlana himself made some
modifications to the structure and verses of the book. Although it is
difficult to answer this question, an examination of the earliest manuscripts indicates that this hypothesis – that is, that some of the revi-
sions of the *Mathnawi*'s verses were made by the hand of Mawlana
himself – is a definite possibility, if not probability.

Taking this into consideration, we find that devotees and lovers of
Mawlana's works have from time to time made enormous efforts to
compare and collate the *Mathnawi*'s various manuscripts in order to
produce an edition of the *Mathnawi* that is free from error, so that the
complexities, mysteries and difficulties of the poem may be resolved.
Among these men was ʿAbdu'l-Latif ʿAbbasi, a scholar from the first
half of the seventeenth century, who wrote two books on the explanation of verses and interpretation of terms in the *Mathnawi*.[13] For

---

11 The opening lines of the *ghazal* are recorded as above by Aflaki. In Furuzanfar's
   edition of the *Divan*, the first words of the *ghazal* (no. 526, vol. 2, p. 3) read: 'O
   young fellows! O young fellows!' (*Ay luliyan, ay luliyan*), not 'O lovers! O lovers!'
   (*Ay ʿashiqan, ay ʿashiqan*) as Aflaki has recorded it. The Persian word *Luli* means a
   gypsy, and by extension, a young, smart-looking, carefree man.
12 ʿAbdu'llah ibn Saʿd ibn Abi Sarh was a scribe of the Qur'an in Medina during Prophet
   Muhammad's lifetime, who attempted to make alterations in the Qur'an while copying it down. After being caught, he fled to Mecca.
13 ʿAbdu'l-Latif ibn ʿAbdu'llah ʿAbbasi Gujarati (d. ca. 1638) was an eminent Rumi scholar
   from the Mughul period of India. He edited a comprehensive version of the *Math-*

several years, beginning in 1617, he compared and contrasted over eighty manuscripts of the *Mathnawi* and produced a comprehensive copy with explanatory notes on the margins of the manuscript. Several copies of this edition are still extant in libraries in Tehran and the one kept at the National Library is possibly the original autograph manuscript. Despite his painstaking efforts, many problems still remain with Abdu'l-Latif's version of the *Mathnawi*, since many unwarranted modifications and changes that had been made to Rumi's verses by the previous copyists were incorporated therein.

From these introductory remarks it seems absolutely necessary both for [the sake of preserving the literary heritage of] the Persian language and for lovers infatuated with Mawlana's poetry that an edition of the *Mathnawi* should be produced which is more reliable than the previous editions and which is the product of analysis and comparison of the variable readings of all the available manuscripts, especially those manuscripts closer to Mawlana's time and hence probably less subject to modification and change. I regret to say that Iranians did not take the pioneering steps necessary to perform this service, and even the printed edition of ʿAla al-Dawla, which is by far better than any other edition in print, did not accomplish this task.[14]

The late and great Professor Nicholson, in whose commemoration this gathering has been held, accomplished this great service over a long period of time and prepared a version of the *Mathnawi* that is undoubtedly the best, the most complete, accurate and reliable version that anyone can obtain of its text.

The first time Nicholson demonstrated his interest in Mawlana was when he published several lyrics (*ghazal*) from the *Divan*, which was

---

nawi called *Nuskha-yi nasikh* ('A Copy to Replace All Copies'), and also published two commentaries in Persian on it: *Lata'if al-maʿnawi* (printed in Lucknow, 1875) and *Mir'at al-Mathnawi* (printed in Lucknow, 1877 and Cawnpore, 1905). In his book *Rumi: Past and Present, East and West* (Oxford: Oneworld 2000), Franklin Lewis writes: '[ʿAbdu'l-Latif] used eighty manuscripts, but seems to have added verses from all of them without removing any lines; rather than a proto-critical edition, then, this is a compendium of lines attributed to Rumi in a wide variety of faulty exemplars of the text' (p. 306).

14 This is in reference to the first printed copy of the *Mathnawi* in Iran: *Mathnawi-yi maʿnawi*, commissioned by Muhammad Rahim Khan ʿAla al-Dawla, calligraphed by Tahir ibn Ahmad Kashani, with a verse index by Muhammad Tahir Mustawfi Kashani, printed in Tabriz 1264 A.H./1847 A.D., but its third printing in 1299/1881 in Tehran was more influential among Iranian scholars of the late nineteenth century.

printed in 1898.[15] From that year until his death approximately forty-seven years later, he devoted his precious life to the cause of publishing Sufi texts, reviving the works of Mawlana Jalal al-Din, research on Sufism and commentary on the *Mathnawi*. In his last letter to me he stated that owing to long years of studies his eyesight has become weak and feeble and that he was unable to read fine print. Nevertheless, he went on to inform me that he was devoting his time to investigating and studying the *Discourses* (*Maqalat*) of Shams-i Tabrizi.

With the enthusiasm and devotion that is the hallmark of true researchers, and through his own diligence, hard work, precision and carefulness, this eminent professor published an edition of the *Mathnawi* that is based on a comparative evaluation of several manuscripts which were written within a span of one hundred years following the death of its author [Mawlana], recording therein the variant readings of all the different manuscripts that he had consulted. The manuscripts to which Prof. Nicholson had access were as follows:

1   The Bulaq manuscript printed in 1268 A.H./1852 AD that was based on a very ancient manuscript
2   The British Museum manuscript dated 718/1319
3   The Munich Museum manuscript dated 15 Dhu'l-Hijjah 744/29 April 1344
4   A private manuscript owned by the editor [Nicholson] dated 7 Rabiʿ al-Akhar 743/17 September 1439
5   Another British Museum manuscript that includes the first and the second *daftar*s [of the *Mathnawi*], which, according to Nicholson, was apparently written in the 14th century AD.
6   Another Munich Museum manuscript whose copyist: Musa ibn Hamza ibn Yahya al-Mawlawi, concluded the writing thereof on 4 Sha'ban 706/8 February 1307 in Damascus
7   The Cairo manuscript dated 674/1275, only two years after Mawlana's death
8   The Nafidh Pasha Mosque manuscript written on 15 Rabiʿ al-Awwal 680/2 August 1281
9   Another manuscript dated 687/1288 whose copyist, Hasan ibn

15 Reynold A. Nicholson (trans. and ed.), *Selected Poems from the Divani Shamsi Tabrizi* (Cambridge: Cambridge University Press 1898).

Husayn al-Mawlawi, copied it out from a manuscript presented to him

10 A manuscript from the Mevlana Museum dated 677/1278, that is, five years after Mawlana's death, copied down from a manuscript that belonged to Husam al-Din Chelebi, which is the most important manuscript of the *Mathnawi* extant in the world

11 Another British Museum manuscript dated 695/1296, the date of which appears to have been altered

Gentlemen! You will acknowledge that such an edition [of the *Mathnawi*] that was prepared and edited by way of comparison with all the above-mentioned manuscripts is indeed unique. All these manuscripts are, in their own way, very good extant copies of the *Mathnawi*, but Nicholson's edition is superior to them because it incorporates all of them while recording all their variant readings and differences.

In studying this venerable edition [by Nicholson], I acknowledge that I have learned that many of the difficulties in the *Mathnawi* (as noted above) are due to errors and alterations which various copyists have introduced into the poem's text. The more I read this edited version, the more I am convinced of its accuracy and significance. I should also point out that the fine and elegant printing of this book, accompanied by indices found at the rear of the sixth volume, adds even greater value to this work.

Regarding Professor Nicholson's English translation of and commentary on the *Mathnawi*, my respected colleague Dr Suratgar will share with you the necessary remarks.[16] For my part, ever since I came to know Mawlana's works, due to the affiliation to the rites and practices of Sufism that we share in common,[17] I maintained a strong

16 Dr Lutf ʿAli Suratgar, born in Shiraz in 1901, was a poet and professor of English literature at the University of Tehran. He studied at the University of London, where his Ph.D. thesis was on 'Traces of Persian Influence upon English Literature during the Fifteenth and Sixteenth Centuries' (University of London, 1939). He married an English woman: Lady Olive Hepburn, who later wrote *I Sing in the Wilderness: Account of the Persian Scene* (1951). His speech on Prof. Nicholson's English translation of the *Mathnawi*, to which Professor Furuzanfar refers above, was published in *Nama-yi Farhangistan*, vol. 4, no. 1 (Ordibihisht 1325 A.Hsh./April 1946), pp. 27–35. Dr Suratgar died in 1969.

17 The author uses the term *ham-khirqagi* here, an untranslatable compound phrase literally meaning: 'sharing the same Sufi mantle', implying their shared commitment to the principles and ideals of the Sufi way.

connection with the late Professor Nicholson, and all through these years kept up an ongoing correspondence with him about Rumi and his works. And today I am extremely saddened by his death because the Iranian nation has lost one of the contributors to its literature, the Iranian Academy[18] has lost one of its members, and I also have lost a friend and a collegial scholar whose love for Mawlana's work took precedence over mine.

18 The Iranian Academy (*Farhangistan*) was founded in 1935 to advance research on the Persian literature and language. It published the journal *Nama-yi Farhangistan*.

Depictions of the Islamization of the Mongols in the *Manāqib al-ʿārifīn* and the Foundation of the Mawlawī Community[1]

JOHN DECHANT

Although research into the Islamization of the Mongols, by which I mean the process of how they converted to Islam and integrated into Muslim communities, or even formed their own distinct Muslim communities, has made great strides in recent years, many works have yet to receive much, if any, attention for this endeavour. One such work is Shams al-Dīn Aḥmad-i Aflākī's *Manāqib al-ʿārifīn*, 'The Feats of the Knowers of God', a hagiography of the Sufi poet Mawlānā Jalāl al-Dīn-i Rūmī (1207-1273) and his immediate familial and spiritual ancestors and successors.[2] As a hagiography, the primary purpose of the *Manāqib al-ʿārifīn* is the glorification of Islam and the early Mawlawī saints. Describing the spread of Islamization is but one of the ways Aflākī works to achieve this goal: he writes that Rūmī and the other Mawlawī saints Islamized and made disciples of thousands, including Greeks, Armenians, Jews, and even sea creatures and a river monster.[3]

---

1   I would especially like to thank Professors Devin DeWeese, Franklin Lewis, Paul Losensky, John Woods, and of course Leonard Lewisohn, for all their help and guidance in producing this research. An earlier version of this essay was presented at the Sixteenth Annual Central Eurasian Studies Conference at Indiana University, February 2009.
2   Although I have consulted and do cite from the original Persian text, Shams al-Dīn Aḥmad-i Aflākī, *Manāqib al-ʿārifīn*, ed. Tahsin Yazıcı (Ankara: Türk Tarih Kurumu Basımevi 1959), for this article, all translations will be taken directly from John O'Kane's recent English translation, Shams al-Dīn Aḥmad-i Aflākī, *The Feats of the Knowers of God* (*Manāqeb al-ʿārifīn*), (Leiden: Brill 2002).
3   Aflākī at one point asserts that 'from the time of Mowlānā's appearance until the day of his death, eighteen thousand infidels found the faith and became disciples. And they are still becoming disciples', Aflākī, *Manāqib al-ʿārifīn*, ed. Yazıcı, 2, p. 611; and idem, *The Feats of the Knowers of God*, trans. O'Kane, p. 419. For examples of the

But of all the peoples Islamized in the text, Aflākī's treatment of the Mongols probably does the most to advance the primacy of Islam and the claim of sainthood for the book's subjects. The *Manāqib al-ʿārifīn* Islamizes the Mongols in a number of ways, such as how it portrays many non-Muslim Mongols as nonetheless good monotheists, Mongol converts as sincere and devoted in their new faith, and Islamized Mongol Khāns as the rightful rulers of the Islamic world. In portraying the Mongols in seemingly contradictory ways, the text succeeds in framing everything the Mongols do, from their successes and failures on the battlefield to their conversion, as well as their rise and fall from power, as being a result of the spiritual authority of God and His (Mawlawī) saints; thus in effect, further Islamizing the Mongols beyond conversion, in that Mawlawī involvement integrates them into both an overall Islamic narrative and the new Islamic community forming around the Mawlawī founders.

Many scholars have painted the Islamization of the Mongols and other Inner Asian nomads to fit certain stereotypes, in turn questioning the sincerity of their conversion as either superficial or violently fanatical.[4] For instance, scholars such as V. L. Ménage have concluded that nomadic Mongols and Turks converted to Islam because of what they believed to be the similarities between shamanism and the 'deviant' forms of Sufism that flourished at the time, and therefore their conversion had nothing but 'a veneer of Islam'.[5] Recent scholars such as Devin DeWeese on the other hand have argued that it is not necessary to ascertain the convert's 'actual' sincerity and 'true' motivation behind their conversion;[6] he instead proposes that we look at conversion narratives for how they portray these issues and values:

conversion of the Greeks, Armenians, Jews, sea creatures and a river monster, see respectively: Aflākī, *Manāqib al-ʿārifīn*, ed. Tahsin Yazıcı 1, pp. 552–53, 80–81, 2: pp. 610–11, 1, pp. 368–70, 2, pp. 608–09; and idem, *The Feats of the Knowers of God*, trans. John O'Kane, pp. 382–83, p. 60, 418–19, 254–56, 417–18.

4 Devin DeWeese, *Islamization and Native Religion in the Golden Horde: Baba Tükles and Conversion to Islam in Historical and Epic Tradition* (Pennsylvania: Pennsylvania State University Press 1994), p. 4. See also: Reuven Amitai-Preiss, 'Sufis and Shamans: Some Remarks on the Islamization of the Mongols in the Ilkhanate', in *Journal of the Economic and Social History of the Orient* 42, no. 1 (1999), p. 41.

5 V. L. Ménage, 'The Islamization of Anatolia' in *Conversion to Islam*, ed. Nehemia Levtzion (New York: Holmes & Meier Publishers, Inc. 1979), pp. 59–60.

6 Devin DeWeese, 'Islamization in the Mongol Empire', in *The Cambridge History of Inner Asia: The Chinggisid Age*, ed. Nicola Di Cosmo, Allen J. Frank, and Peter B. Golden (Cambridge: Cambridge University Press 2009), p. 121.

'Conversion narratives are themselves central elements in the process of Islamization, as the community articulates its Islamicness and either stresses its break with the past or finds common ground with pre-Islamic traditions or values.'[7] Conversion involves communal change, whereby either the convert leaves their original community behind for the Islamic *umma*, or a non-Muslim community converts, perhaps very gradually, transforming, and in many cases strengthening, their community identity. As per that communal change, DeWeese contends that it is often the case that 'Sufism, in the form of the charismatic person (and family) of a *šayḫ*, provides a focus for collective identity whereby whole communities are brought into the fold of Islam, with details of observance and ritual to be worked out later.'[8] The community's historical memory of how they understand that Islamization to have occurred and who precipitated that process, as opposed to what 'really' happened, becomes a central element in that community's identity; how people believe a historical event happened, even if those beliefs are completely false, still in itself effects how history progresses.[9] Therefore, legendary narratives like the *Manāqib al-ʿārifīn*, according to István Vásáry, 'should be taken as facts regarded through the prism of the age, and not untruth as opposed to truth'.[10] Along with the need to boast of one's spiritual protagonist in order to promote their cult over rivals, understanding an author's 'prism of the age', that is, their temporal context and world view, explains how and why a hagiographer like Aflākī deals with

---

7 DeWeese, *Islamization and Native Religion in the Golden Horde*, p. 10.

8 Devin DeWeese, 'Yasavī Šayḫs in the Timurid Era: Notes on the Social and Political Role of Communal Sufi Affiliations in the 14th and 15th Centuries' in 'La civiltà timuride come fenomeno internazionale' ed. Michele Bernardini, special issue, *Oriente Moderno*, n.s., 15, no. 2 (1996), p. 188. See also: Devin DeWeese, '"Stuck in the Throat of Chingīz Khān": Envisioning the Mongol Conquests in Some Sufi Accounts from the 14th to 17th Centuries' in *History and Historiography of Post-Mongol Central Asia and the Middle East: Studies in Honor of John E. Woods*, ed. Judith Pfeiffer and Sholeh A. Quinn (Wiesbaden: Harrossowitz Verlag 2006), p. 55.

9 DeWeese, *Islamization and Native Religion in the Golden Horde*, p. 22.

10 István Vásáry, '"History and Legend" in Berke Khan's Conversion to Islam', in *Aspects of Altaic Civilization III* (= PIACC XXX), ed. Denis Sinor (Bloomington: Indiana University, Research Institute for Inner Asian Studies 1990), pp. 230–31. Victoria Holbrook likewise touches on these issues in her discussion of what she calls 'textual play' in Mawlawī sources. See: Victoria Holbrook, 'Diverse Tastes in the Spiritual Life: Textual Play in the Diffusion of Rumi's Order', in *The Heritage of Sufism*, vol. 2, *The Legacy of Medieval Persian Sufism (1150–1500)*, ed. Leonard Lewisohn (Oxford: Oneworld Publications 1999), p. 100.

historical issues in a non-positivistic fashion. What a modern reader might see as fiction is instead Aflākī's attempt to make sense of historical events based upon his religious assumptions, primarily in this case the spiritual station of the Mawlawī family, as well as the political and social realities of his lifetime.

Aflākī began to write the *Manāqib al-ʿārifīn* in 1318 and finished it sometime before his death on 15 June, 1360,[11] decades after the Mongol conquest and the Islamization of the Īlkhāns. As we will see, the 'prism of this age' of Islamized Mongol rule greatly impacts Aflākī and his values, seen in his portrayal of the Mongol conquests, non-Muslim Mongols and the Mongol rulers. One needs only to compare the *Manāqib al-ʿārifīn* to an earlier hagiography of Rūmī, the *Risāla-yi Sipahsālār* of Farīdūn b. Aḥmad Sipahsālār,[12] to appreciate the difference the conversion of the Mongols, and a few decades of time between their initial bloody conquests, had made on the Muslims of a later period. The most obvious difference between the two authors' portrayals of the Mongols is that while Sipahsālār has only one major story about a Mongol interacting with Rūmī's family, Aflākī has several, including two expanded versions of the same story told by Sipahsālār, all three of which are compared in the table on pages 140–41. All three versions relate that Gaykhātū (spelled 'Kayghātū' in the texts), the Mongol viceroy of Anatolia from 1284 to 1291, and afterwards the Īl-Khān from 1291 to 1295,[13] arrives with an army intending to kill and plunder the inhabitants of Konya, who pray at the tomb of

---

11 Franklin D. Lewis, *Rumi: Past and Present, East and West: The Life, Teachings and Poetry of Jalāl al-Din Rumi*, revised ed. (Oxford: Oneworld Publications 2008), pp. 243–50; Aflākī, *Manāqib al-ʿārifīn*, ed. Yazıcı, 1, p. 4; and idem, *The Feats of the Knowers of God*, trans. O'Kane, p. 3.

12 'The Treatise of Sipahsālār', retitled by the modern editor, Saʿīd Nafīsī, as *Zindigīnāma-yi Mawlānā Jalāl al-Dīn-i Mawlawī* or 'The Book of the Life of Mawlānā Jalāl al-Dīn-i Mawlawī'. Farīdūn b. Aḥmad Sipahsālār, *Zindigīnāma-yi Mawlānā Jalāl al-Din Mawlawī*, ed. Saʿīd Nafīsī (Tehran: Intishārāt-i Iqbāl 1363). Franklin Lewis explains that the exact duration of Sipahsālār's life remains a mystery. He claims to have known Rūmī for forty years before his death in 1273, meaning that he too would have lived during some of the darkest days of the Mongol conquests. Yet his *Risāla* also chronicles the lives of Rūmī's grandsons, Amīr ʿĀrif (d. 1320) and Amīr ʿĀbid (d. 1338). Altogether, that means Sipahsālār would have to have lived well over one hundred years of age, which seems unlikely. See: Lewis, *Rumi*, pp. 243–51.

13 Peter Jackson, 'Gaykātū Khān', in *Encyclopaedia Iranica*, vol. 10 (2001), pp. 344–45. It is unclear whether the story, if based on actual events, takes place during Gaykhātū's reign as viceroy or Khān.

Rūmī for help. The night before the siege, Rūmī appears to Gaykhātū in a dream and threatens him. Gaykhātū awakes in fear, and comes to see the error of his ways. He enters Konya as a pilgrim and visits Rūmī's shrine, then departs the city, leaving it unharmed.

We can deduce that Aflākī copied his first version of the Gaykhātū story directly from Sipahsālār's *Risāla,* since except for the differences noted in the table below, his re-telling follows Sipahsālār's almost word-for-word, and because he also attributes that version to the same Amīr Muḥammad-i Sukūrjī, someone who he was unlikely to have ever met.[14] Yet as shown in the table, Aflākī makes some important additions and changes, and includes another version of the story, all of which betray 'the prism of his age'. Sipahsālār experienced the Mawlawī community in its earliest stages when the infidel Mongols were ravaging Anatolia and the Muslim world. He would have known a Rūmī who in all likelihood saw himself more as a simple preacher, and not the world-renowned leader of an established Sufi order, as his son and grandson, Sulṭān Walad and Amīr ʿĀrif, were the ones who established the *ṭarīqa*.[15] Aflākī, on the other hand, lived and wrote long after the Mongol invasion, and was a disciple of Rūmī's grandsons, the ones

14 'Sukūrjī' likely comes from the Mongol title *sükürchi*, or 'parasol holder', i.e. a symbolic court position of high status that brings with it special proximity to the ruler, akin to an official cup-bearer in Iranian kingly tradition. Rashīd al-Dīn makes a brief mention of someone by that same name also attached to Gaykhātū, as his *shaḥna* ('viceroy' or 'lieutenant') in Baghdad. According to Rashīd al-Dīn, Gaykhātū's cousin Bāydū sends some men to kill Sukūrjī in Baghdad as his first open act of rebellion, which would ultimately lead to the overthrowing of his cousin. Although he gives no specific date for the murder, Rashīd al-Dīn notes that it occurs after Bāydū's release from Gaykhātū's custody on 11 July, 1294, but before Gaykhātū sends two of his amīrs to confront his rebellious cousin on 17 March, 1295. See: Rashīd al-Dīn Faḍl Allah, *Compendium of Chronicles*, trans. W. M. Thackston, Sources of Oriental Languages and Literatures, no. 45, part 3 (Cambridge, Massachusetts: Harvard University Department of Near Eastern Languages and Civilizations 1999), 3, pp. 583–86. The Christian historian Bar Hebraeus also mentions that in 1295, Bāydū killed 'the captain of the soldiers' in Mosul, 'And he also sent and killed the man who held a similar post in Baghdad', probably referring to Muḥammad-i Sukūrjī. See: Bar Hebraeus, *The Chronography of Gregory Abūʾl Faraj the son of Aaron, the Hebrew Physician, commonly known as Bar Hebraeus, being the First Part of his Political History of the World*, trans. Ernest A. Wallis Budge (London: Oxford University Press 1932), I, pp. 497–98. Since Aflākī began to write his *Manāqib al-ʿārifīn* in 1318, twenty-three years after Sukūrjī's assassination, and died in 1360, sixty-five years after Sukūrjī, Aflākī probably never received the story firsthand from Sukūrjī and therefore took it from Sipahsālār's *Risāla*.

15 Lewis, *Rumi*, pp. 423–26.

A COMPARISON OF THE IMPORTANT DIFFERENCES IN THREE
VERSIONS OF THE GAYKHĀTŪ TALE

VERSION:	SIPAHSĀLĀR'S ACCOUNT*
Narrator:	Amīr Muḥammad-i Sukūrjī
Rūmī referred to as:	'Khudāwandgar'
Gaykhātū referred to as:	'Prince Kayghātū'
Rūmī appears to Gaykhātū in a dream and:	leaves his tomb, unwraps his turban, encircles the city with its cloth, and puts his finger on Gaykhātū's throat.
Rūmī says to Gaykhātū in the dream:	'Oh Turk [*turk*]! Give up [*tark*] this idea and undertaking, otherwise, you will not escape with your life'
After Gaykhātū awakens from his dream trembling in fear, he:	summons his courtiers, who tell him: 'We were worried about this matter, but from fear of bondage we could not make a proposal.'
While performing pilgrimage at Rūmī's tomb, Gaykhātū:	bestows great wealth on those present.

* Sipahsālār, *Zindigīnāma*, pp. 103–04.
§ Aflākī, *Manāḳib al-ʿārifīn*, ed. Yazıcı, 1, 331–33; and idem, *The Feats of the Knowers of God*, trans. O'Kane, pp. 229–31.
‡ Aflākī, *Manāḳib al-ʿārifīn*, ed. Yazıcı, 2, 611–13; and idem, *The Feats of the Knowers of God*, trans. O'Kane, pp. 419–21.

AFLĀKĪ'S FIRST ACCOUNT[§]	AFLĀKĪ'S SECOND ACCOUNT[‡]
Amīr Muḥammad-i Sukūrjī, 'the intimate disciple of Solṭān Valad'	Akhī Aḥmad-Shāh
'Mawlānā'	'Mawlānā', also 'great sultan' and 'true sovereign'
'the esteemed Prince of the World, Keyghātū Khān'	'Keyghātū Khān'
leaves his tomb, unwraps his 'blessed' turban, encircles the city with its cloth, and strangles Gaykhātū.	strangles Gaykhātū.
'Oh ignorant Turk [turk]! Give up [tark] this idea and undertaking. Take back your Turks [turkān] to your lady [tarkān] as quickly as possible. Otherwise, you will not escape with your life.'	'Konya belongs to us! What business have you with the people of Konya?'
summons his noyans and courtiers, who tell him: 'We were worried about this matter. This city and this clime belong to Mawlānā, and whoever sets out to attack this region [dīyār], no member [diyyār] of his lineage remains and he is destroyed. But out of fear of the king it was impossible to speak.'	seeks forgiveness and permission to enter the city, which is granted by Sulṭān Walad. He visits Akhī Aḥmad-Shāh, and again sees the man from his dream. The Akhī tells him the man is Rūmī. Gaykhātū renounces his 'bad intentions', adopts the Akhī as his 'father' and asks to see Sulṭān Walad.
becomes of disciple of Sulṭān Walad, 'performed sacrifices and gave out alms' on those present, and departs 'with a happy heart'.	'felt devotion and became a disciple [of Sulṭān Walad, who] placed a Mawlawī hat on the khān's head and bestowed much favor on him.' Walad performs samāᶜ and recites a quatrain exhorting the khān to 'Let the world be. The world doesn't belong to you.' Gaykhātū then 'shed tears and was filled with great joy. Thus he kissed Solṭān Valad's hand and departed in a state of absolute serenity.'

actually responsible for the creation of the Mawlawī Order.[16] Therefore, Aflākī goes to much greater lengths to Islamize the Mongols and make Rūmī and Sultān Walad into greater saints and heroes. Aflākī introduces Gaykhātū with grander titles, which shows a much better recognition of Mongol political legitimacy, and mentions the Mongol title of *noyan*, reflecting a better knowledge and appreciation of Mongolian customs. While Sipahsālār calls Rūmī by his more personal nickname 'Khudāwandgar', Aflākī refers to him by the title 'Mawlānā', and moreover uses the adjective 'blessed' to describe his turban, altogether painting Rūmī differently as a saintly head of a Sufi Order.[17] By having Rūmī strangle Gaykhātū in the dream and use even more word-plays, the *Manāqib al-ʿārifīn* makes Rūmī into much more of a 'manly' hero and a poet than the *Risāla* does (themes which we will explore in greater detail below). Both of Aflākī's versions make a number of explicit statements to assert that Rūmī and his family, not the Mongols, have authority over Konya. Finally, Aflākī has Gaykhātū become a disciple of Sultān Walad, implicitly making him a Muslim, and uses imagery to portray the Mongol as sincere in his conversion, especially in the version attributed to Akhī Ahmad-Shāh.

Clearly, the additions Aflākī makes to Sipahsālār's version of the Gaykhātū story explain that Aflākī lived and wrote in a time in which he could conceive of the Mawlawī founders and the Mongols very differently than Sipahsālār. Other than explaining how Aflākī saw Rūmī as more of a grand saint, this 'prism of the age' of Islamized Mongol rule also explains the *Manāqib al-ʿārifīn's* treatment of the Mongol invasion. As Aflākī lived long after the danger of the Mongol conquests subsided, he could discuss the dispensation not out of terror for his life, but out of the hindsight of the rise of the Mawlawī community, the Islamization of the Mongols, and the ultimate fall of the Īl-Khānid dynasty. For instance, Rūmī's father Bahā' al-Dīn Walad

---

16 For instance, it was Amīr ʿĀrif who requested that Aflākī write the *Manāqib al-ʿārifīn*. Aflākī, *Manāqib al-ʿārifīn*, ed. Yazıcı, 1, p. 4; idem, *The Feats of the Knowers of God*, trans. O'Kane, p. 3; and Lewis, *Rumi*, p. 249.

17 The *Manāqib al-ʿārifīn* explains that Rūmī's father, Bahā' al-Dīn, 'addressed him with the title "Khodāvandgar"'. Aflākī, *Manāqib al-ʿārifīn*, ed. Yazıcı, 1, p. 73; and idem, *The Feats of the Knowers of God*, trans. O'Kane, p. 55. Likewise, Franklin Lewis explains Rūmī was known as 'Khudāvandgar' by 'many of Rumi's Persian-speaking disciples' (such as Sipahsālār), while starting with his hagiographies, he is known as 'Mawlānā'. Lewis, *Rumi*, p. 10. Aflākī therefore by changing Rūmī's title shows that he lives in a later time in the development of the Mawlawī Order.

(c. 1152–1231) warns both the Khwārazmshāh[18] and the ʿAbbāsid Caliph that, as he tells the court in Baghdad:

Now I announce to you the glad tidings that those with slanted eyes whose wrath is fiery – I mean the army of the Mongols – are about to arrive. Divine judgement decrees that they make a martyr of you and kill you in an utterly miserable and wretched manner. They will exact revenge from you on behalf of Moḥammad's religion.[19]

These stories both inflate the saint's spiritual power and act as a warning to the audience. Aflākī puts Bahā' al-Dīn in the company of several Qur'ānic prophets, notably Noah, Hūd, Ṣāliḥ, and Moses, all of whom warned a sinful ruler and/or population of a coming chastisement from God to punish their wickedness or immorality. Such a theme is not unique to the *Manāqib al-ʿārifīn*. Devin DeWeese, in his article 'Stuck in the Throat of Chingīz Khān', explains that in one sense, such stories describe the Mongols as serving as God's tool for punishing a sinful Muslim population.[20] But in another sense:

To the extent that the stories were intended for a Sufi audience, they work by demanding that those who hear them reorder their understanding of the real so that what appeared to be forces of desolation and destruction could be envisioned with Khiżr leading them, or Najm al-Dīn Kubrā calmly letting them pass. The stories naturally stem from, and support, an interiorized, mystical understanding of the world, and if what the Mongols could destroy was not what was real and essential, then it was hardly a difficult leap to see arbiters of the real, whether Khiżr, a saint, or the *rijāl al-ghayb* ['the unseen men'], lending a hand in undermining what obscured the real from Muslims.[21]

18 Aflākī, *Manāqib al-ʿārifīn*, ed. Yazıcı, 1, p. 15; and idem, *The Feats of the Knowers of God*, trans. O'Kane, p. 13.
19 Aflākī, *Manāqib al-ʿārifīn*, ed. Yazıcı, 1, pp. 19–20; and idem, *The Feats of the Knowers of God*, trans. O'Kane, p. 17.
20 DeWeese, '"Stuck in the Throat of Chingīz Khān"' p. 27.
21 Ibid., p. 52.

For example, at one point in the *Manāqib al-ʿārifīn*, Rūmī miracu-lously saves the city of Konya from the Mongol army of Bāyjū ('Bājū' in the text), the Mongol commander behind the victory at Köse Dagh in 1243 and responsible for the subjugation of Anatolia.[22] Despite the peace, Bāyjū is still ordered to destroy Konya's walls, an order which he proceeds to carry out. When some of the residents start to com-plain, Rūmī replies:

> Let them destroy the battlements because it is assured for Konya's people that the city of Konya will be guarded and protected by another tower and curtain, not by this tower and battlement of stone which can be destroyed by a small cause and devastated by the least earthquake. For if it were not for the spiritual power of the men of God, in the end like the fortified city of the people of ʿĀd and Thamūd: *uppermost nethermost*,[23] it would have been turned upside down, and human beings would have wept over its ruins and its former days.[24]

Rūmī then bestows on Konya the title of the '"City of the Friends of God", for every born person who comes into existence in this city will be a Friend of God'.[25] He explains that the body of the deceased saint Bahā' al-Dīn, buried in Konya, and his family, will forever protect the city,

> For even if some of the city falls into ruin, is obliterated and decreases, it will not be completely destroyed. Indeed, if it does fall into ruin, our treasure will still be buried there . . . Even if the Tatars destroyed the world through war, / The ruins would contain your treasure. Why be sad?[26]

---

22 Christopher P. Atwood, *Encyclopedia of Mongolia and the Mongol Empire* (New York: Facts On File, Inc. 2004), p. 29; Rashīd al-Dīn, *Compendium of Chronicles*, 2, p. 487.

23 A reference to the Qur'ān, 11:82, which refers to God's destruction of the 'people of Luṭ [Lot]' for their sins'. 'ʿĀd and Thamūd' likewise refer to other peoples mentioned in the Qur'ān who God destroys, despite the warnings given by the prophets Hūd and Ṣāliḥ, respectively.

24 Aflākī, *Manāqib al-ʿārifīn*, ed. Yazıcı, 1, pp. 258–60; and idem, *The Feats of the Knowers of God*, trans. O'Kane, p. 180.

25 Aflākī, *Manāqib al-ʿārifīn*, ed. Yazıcı, 1, pp. 261; and idem, *The Feats of the Knowers of God*, trans. O'Kane, p. 181.

26 Aflākī, *Manāqib al-ʿārifīn*, ed. Yazıcı, 1, pp. 262; and idem, *The Feats of the Knowers of God*, trans. O'Kane, pp. 182. Jalāl al-Dīn-i Rūmī, *Kulliyāt-i Shams yā Dīvān-i kabīr*, ed.

The Mongols only destroy things that are not 'real', something which humans turn to rely on instead of faith in God, such as the city walls. Rūmī therefore allows the demolition to continue, knowing that real protection comes from the Real, faith in God. Aflākī further supports this idea by presenting the following couplets penned by Rūmī shortly afterwards in the text:

> I have received an order from the Qān of all Qāns.
>> This Bājū and Bātū I know not, I know not!
> What Rūmī-faced [beauties], what hidden Turks I have!
>> What's the fault? This Hulagu I know not, I know not![27]

Here, Rūmī and Aflākī again use the Mongols in order to invoke God. No matter how powerful the Mongols may appear to be, they are nothing in comparison to God, 'the Qān of all Qāns'. A Knower of God like Rūmī does not need to 'know' the Mongols. Neither the women nor the Turkish armies the Mongols have in the 'real' world can match up to the metaphorical 'Rūmī-faced [beauties]' and army of Turks that a Knower of 'the Real', a Knower of God, possesses. To Aflākī, this makes his hero, Rūmī, much more powerful than any Khān.

Stories of the Mongol invasion also serve the purpose of making Rūmī and his family into great heroes and defenders of the faith. 'Manliness' (*mardī*) is a constant theme throughout the text; in a few anecdotes Rūmī confronts the Mongols in a heroic way, as he does when Gaykhātū attempts to conquer Konya. When, in the above mentioned story, Bāyjū's army laid siege to the city, Rūmī merely went to perform his sunrise prayers on top of a hill overlooking Bāyjū's camp. Aflākī then adds: 'At that time the Mongol army was ignorant of the light of Islam and safety based on good faith and oaths. Indeed, in several cities of Islam they had destroyed madrasas, mosques and minarets.'[28] Seeing Rūmī's blatant defiance, the Mongols, including

---

B. Furūzānfar (Tehran: Intishārāt-i Dānishgāh-i Tihrān 1344 A.Hsh./1965), 3:142, v. 14040. Later in Ṣalāḥ al-Dīn-i Zarkūb's chapter, Aflākī again mentions the same event, and adds that Rūmī also includes Ṣalāḥ al-Dīn as another reason why Konya will be protected. See: Aflākī, *Manāqib al-ʿārifīn*, ed. Yazıcı, 2, p. 722; and idem, *The Feats of the Knowers of God*, trans. O'Kane, p. 503.

27 Aflākī, *Manāqib al-ʿārifīn*, ed. Yazıcı, 1, pp. 261–62; and idem, *The Feats of the Knowers of God*, trans. O'Kane, pp. 181–82. Poetry: Rūmī, *Kulliyāt-i Shams*, 3:206, v. 15235.

28 Aflākī, *Manāqib al-ʿārifīn*, ed. Yazıcı, 1, pp. 258; and idem, *The Feats of the Knowers of God*, trans. O'Kane, p. 179.

Bāyjū himself, tried to fire arrows and charge up the hill against him, but they find themselves unable to pluck their bows or move their horses, or even themselves, leading Bāyjū to conclude: 'That man in truth belongs to the Yaratghān [Creator]. His anger must be avoided. In whatever city or province there is a man like this, those people will not be conquered by us.'[29] Therefore the Mongols, '*ignorant* of the light of Islam and *safety* based on good faith and oaths [emphasis mine]', were defeated by Rūmī, a heroic saint who by contrast *knew* the light of Islam and provided *safety* to the city because his good faith ensured that God would protect the land and people under his spiritual dominion. Further underscoring Rūmī's heroism and 'manliness', Aflākī follows the anecdote with a comment by a dervish: 'It's amazing how our Khodāvandgār was not afraid of the army of Bāyjū and on that day of upheaval stood praying on top of that hill. What bravery and courage! It has been established that our Khodāvandgār is a great champion.'[30]

Another anecdote goes to even greater lengths to portray Rūmī as a *mujāhid*, or holy warrior. The text describes how a visibly disturbed Rūmī approached a disciple of his who raised horses. 'Covered in sweat and in an awesome state' Rūmī requested a good horse be saddled for him, which he used to ride off 'in the direction of the *qibla*'. He returned that night 'covered in dust', while the 'horse with a body like an elephant was emaciated and bent double'. The same thing happened the next two days. When he returned after the third day, Rūmī, now relaxed, said: 'Good news, good news, oh group of revellers!/That dog from Hell has gone back to Hell.'[31] Out of awe for his spiritual master, the disciple who raised the horses refrained from asking what exactly happened, but a few days later, he received word that the Mongols under

> General Ketbūghā advanced to Damascus with a huge army. At the time when the army had laid siege to Damascus, the people of Damascus saw Mowlānā there with their own eyes. He arrived to

29 Aflākī, *Manāqib al-ʿārifīn*, ed. Yazıcı, 1, pp. 258–59; and idem, *The Feats of the Knowers of God*, trans. O'Kane, pp. 179–80.
30 Aflākī, *Manāqib al-ʿārifīn*, ed. Yazıcı, 1, pp. 261–62; and idem, *The Feats of the Knowers of God*, trans. O'Kane, p. 181.
31 Jalāl al-Dīn Rūmī, *The Mathnawi of Jalálu'ddín Rúmí*, ed. R. A. Nicholson (London: Gibb Memorial Series, New Series 4, 1925–40), I: 1354.

give help to the army of Islam and they smashed the Mongols who were then completely routed and departed in utter defeat.[32]

Just as with the story of Bāyjū, Aflākī uses the Mongols in order to portray Rūmī as a true Islamic hero, supporting the rectitude of his hero and the task with a variety of details. Aflākī describes Rūmī, about to undertake the mission, as 'covered in sweat'. Sweat in hagiographies often represents exerting oneself for a righteous cause and even a form of penance, especially in contrast to the sweating that sinners will suffer in the heat of the fires of Hell.[33] By sweating, Rūmī showed his spiritual credentials, as well as the effort he put into a holy cause, by fighting the Mongols, both of which help portray him as a manly warrior-hero. He then departed towards the scene of the action in Syria, which is also conveniently the direction of the *qibla*, meaning that fighting the Mongols must have been a righteous cause, because in doing so Rūmī set out in the righteous direction. Rūmī later returns unscathed but for the dust that covered him, while the horse is ravaged. This detail, emphasized by the fact that Rūmī repeats it in the next two days, illustrates Rūmī's heroic and manly strength and endurance, which stems from his spirituality. Finally, after the last ordeal, he declared the news that, 'That dog from Hell has gone back to Hell', implicitly calling the Mongol general Kitbūghā a dog from Hell, and therefore an enemy worthy of fighting against.

The prism of the age of Islamic Mongol rule also allows Aflākī to Islamize several Mongols associated with the slaughter of Muslims, by portraying them as monotheists and Knowers of God. After describing how Rūmī single-handedly held off the Mongol army of Bāyjū, Bāyjū accepts defeat and describes Rūmī as a man who 'belongs to the Yaratghān [Creator]', a not-so-subtle recognition of Rūmī's status as a *walī*, a 'friend [of God]' or a saint, but also an acknowledgment of Bāyjū's own monotheism. In an even greater recognition of Bāyjū's status, Aflākī writes that '[Mawlānā] even said several times about Bāju: "Bāju is a Friend [*walī*] of God but [*walī*] he doesn't know it."'[34]

---

32 Aflākī, *Manāqib al-ʿārifīn*, ed. Yazıcı, 1, pp. 93–95; and idem, *The Feats of the Knowers of God*, trans. O'Kane, pp. 68-70.

33 See: DeWeese, *Islamization and Native Religion in the Golden Horde*, p. 245.

34 Aflākī, *Manāqib al-ʿārifīn*, ed. Yazıcı, 1, p. 259; and idem, *The Feats of the Knowers of God*, trans. O'Kane, p. 180.

In one conversion narrative, 'a fierce Mongol with drawn sword' confronts Rūmī's spiritual guide, Sayyid Burhān al-Dīn, while the latter is entranced in a mystical state. The Mongol barks: 'Hey! Who are you?' to which Burhān al-Dīn replies, 'Don't say hey! You may have donned [pūshīda] the appearance of a Mongol, but you're not concealed [pūshīda] from me. I know who you are.' The Mongol then descends from his horse, bows his head and shortly thereafter departs. Prompted by questions about the Mongol by some Sufis in attendance, Burhān al-Dīn explains that 'He is one of those concealed by the domes [qibāb] of God, who has become hidden in a tunic [qabā].' Finally, the Mongol returns and offers him some dinars. 'He bared his head, became Sayyed's disciple, and then departed.'[35] So while many modern positivistic scholars describe Mongols concealing themselves in only a thin tunic of Islam, this story shows how Aflākī paints the Mongols as doing quite the opposite. John O'Kane notes that the word 'domes' (qibāb) references a well-known hadith: 'My Friends (concealed) under My domes and only I know them.'[36] Aflākī argues that this Mongol, having hidden in a 'tunic' of a Mongol, was really a Muslim underneath, a fact apparent to pious Muslims and agents of conversion like Burhān al-Dīn. Therefore, when the Mongol converts, he finds that thin veneer removed.

The Manāqib al-ʿārifīn also portrays Hülegü (r. 1256–65) as a worshipper of God. While many sources remember Hülegü as an enemy of Islam for his conquest of Baghdad, Rūmī in the text paints the Khān and his approach to the siege as a role-model for proper Sufi behaviour. Rūmī explains that despite the greatest efforts of the Mongol army, Hülegü could not manage to attain victory. So he prohibited everyone in his army, including the horses, from eating for three days, calling on everyone to 'beseech his Yaratghān [Creator] for the conquest of Baghdad and the Khān's victory. Perhaps the Opener [mufattih] of Gates will confer victory [fatūhī] on us and a benefaction [futūhī] will be obtained, for the caliph is exceedingly rich and very shameful.' Three days later when the fast ended, the Khān ordered his court scholar and advisor, Naṣīr al-Dīn Ṭūsī, to draft an ultimatum to send to the

---

35 Aflākī, Manāqib al-ʿārifīn, ed. Yazıcı, 1, pp. 66–67; and idem, The Feats of the Knowers of God, trans. O'Kane, p. 49. Sipahsālar includes the same story in his text, matching Aflākī almost word for word: Sipahsālar, Zindigīnāma, p. 169.
36 Aflākī, The Feats of the Knowers of God, trans. O'Kane, p. 707, n. 48.

caliph: 'submit and . . . [do not] act insolently, for this is the judgement of the Yaratghān.' The Khān also instructed that if the caliph complied, 'he will obtain good fortune and an honorific robe, but if he does not come, I know he will not endure.' Ṭūsī furthermore filled the letter with Qur'ānic verses exhorting the caliph to give in. But the caliph refused to surrender and proceeded to act insolently to Hülegü's messenger, the Mongol general Kitbūghā. Later that day the Mongols successfully captured Baghdad and the caliph. As Rūmī comments,

> Now if not eating and fasting has this great effect on the affairs of unbelievers in religion and those rude persons with no religious certainty so that they attain their goal and become victorious, imagine the things it can bestow on behalf of helpers endowed with discrimination and pious supporters.

Hülegü then had the caliph, who 'was a glutton and accustomed to all kinds of delicacies and fine luxuries', imprisoned without food for three days. After the caliph bawled and beseeched him out of hunger; Ṭūsī notified the Khān, who replied by having three food-bowls, filled with pearls, precious stones, and gold and silver coins, all from the caliph's own coffers, delivered to the prisoner. The caliph, who thought that the Khān had sent some of his own food, realized the joke was on him when the attendants removed the lids and mocked his fate. Aflākī reports that Hülegü then chastised the caliph, telling him: 'When you had sufficient bread, why did you act proudly and not give thanks to the Yaratghān for such blessings and behave with ingratitude? It was inevitable that you be caught in this hardship and misfortune.' The anecdote ends with Aflākī explaining that all of this happened exactly as Rūmī's father predicted it would.[37]

In the above story Hülegü acts as a guide for piety, an important hagiographical role, as Rūmī uses the Khān 'on behalf of the excellence of hunger and not eating.'[38] Although recognizing the Khān as an unbeliever, a rude person, 'with no religious certainty', Aflākī and Rūmī show that Hülegü approached his problems in a pious, Sufi-like

---

37 Aflākī, *Manāqib al-ʿārifīn*, ed. Yazıcı, 1, pp. 202–05; and idem, *The Feats of the Knowers of God*, trans. O'Kane, pp. 140–42.

38 Aflākī, *Manāqib al-ʿārifīn*, ed. Yazıcı, 1, p. 204; and idem, *The Feats of the Knowers of God*, trans. O'Kane, p. 141.

way, in contrast to the caliph. The forced abstention from food for three days tormented the caliph, who beseeched Ṭūsī and the Khān for help, whereas Hülegü voluntarily fasted for three days and beseeched God for help. The story presents Hülegü as an example of someone submitting to the will of God and receiving the benefits, as opposed to the caliph, who did not submit to God's will and as a result suffered God's wrath, just as Rūmī's father warned would happen and as Hülegü also noted at the end of the story. Finally, on another metaphorical level, Hülegü, through his pious invocations and deeds, gained power and authority over the domain of Baghdad, similar to how Rūmī, by his pious invocations and deeds gained spiritual power and authority over the spiritual domain of Konya.

Thus far, Aflākī has portrayed the Mongols in a variety of ways that often seem to conflict with one another. In the above story, the *Manāqib al-ʿārifīn* describes Kitbūghā as the messenger who delivered a letter filled with Qurʾānic verses that commanded the caliph to submit to the will of God: a very pro-Islamic theme that hearkens to the model of the Prophet. But as described earlier, the text also paints Kitbūghā as an enemy of Islam and a 'dog from Hell' whom Rūmī sent 'back to Hell' during his miraculous defence of Damascus. The text has also portrayed the Mongols as Bahāʾ al-Dīn Walad's divinely sent chastisement of the wicked, natural monotheists, and sincere converts to Islam. These discrepancies can be explained in two ways. First, Aflākī probably did not mean to portray the Mongols as some monolithic group.[39] Second, more vexing discrepancies such as the two contrasting portrayals of Kitbūghā should be understood through the purpose and values of the text and the 'prism of Aflākī's age'. As the primary focus of this hagiography is not the Mongols, but Islam and

39 This approach I owe mainly to Judith Pfeiffer, who in her study of the conversion of Aḥmad Tegüder cautions those studying Islamization against generalizing conversion motives. She writes: 'I would suggest to investigate the individual lives of such persons to allow to draw the first lines of a more complex – if seemingly less complete – picture.' Judith Pfeiffer, 'Conversion to Islam Among the Ilkhans in Muslim Narrative Traditions: The Case of Aḥmad Tegüder' (Ph.D. diss., the University of Chicago, 2003), p. 155. Likewise, Angus Stewart comes to a similar conclusion in his study of how modern writers have unrealistically portrayed the assassination of an Armenian king at the hands of a Mongol convert to Islam as evidence that all or most Mongol converts were violent fanatics, urging us instead to look at individual motives. See: Angus Stewart, 'The Assassination of King Hetʿum II: The Conversion of The Ilkhans and the Armenians', in *Journal of the Royal Asiatic Society* 15, no. 1 (2005), p. 60.

the Mawlawī saints, the only things Aflākī needs to portray consistently are the Mawlawī family's claim to sainthood and the truth of their faith. Beyond that, Aflākī has free rein to portray the Mongols in any way that supports those main values. It is beyond the scope of this article, if not nearly impossible, to determine the Mongols' actual sincerity in their conversion. However, the depiction of the sincerity of the Mongols in the text reveals the nature of Aflākī's devotion to the Mawlawī saints, which constrains him from portraying the convert as anything but a good and sincere convert, because to do otherwise would taint his protagonists' claim to sainthood and their ability to act as guides for the true faith. At the same time, Aflākī's portrayal of the Mongols before and after their conversion to Islam does have some consistency in that in all instances the fate and actions of the Mongols are linked to those of Rūmī's family. To put it another way, Aflākī Islamizes the Mongols by incorporating them into the Islamic narrative, whose main characters are the Mawlawī saints.

Sulṭān Walad makes disciples of two other Mongols by way of making obedience to the Chinggisid ruler similar to obedience to God. Amīr-i Kabīr Īranjīn Noyan asks Sulṭān Walad for his opinion on the beliefs of the Buddhist priests or *bakhsī*s. Sulṭān Walad explains the unity and omnipotence of God, and that 'the people of the Sunna and the Community . . .have been victorious over all creeds and religions', similar to how the Mongols have been victorious over all peoples. Walad also describes that just as how a Mongol's obedience lies with his lord up to 'the supreme Khāqān', so too a believer is subservient to God, 'the greatest Khāqān'. Walad's answer so impresses Īranjīn Noyan that he converts on the spot and becomes a disciple. The Mongol explains that although he had asked many the same question, 'I never received from any great man an answer with such clarity as I received today. Through the favor of God and your spiritual power I have turned my face to the religion of Islam. I have taken a dislike to those other gods and have become a Muslim.'[40] Shortly thereafter in the text, Aflākī presents a similar story where Sulṭān Walad makes a disciple of the Mongol who Ghāzān put in charge of Anatolia, Upushghā Noyan. Aflākī says: 'They called him [Upushghā] the Beardless Prophet. And he was a man of great authority, a Muslim, generous

40 Aflākī, *Manāqib al-ʿārifīn*, ed. Yazıcı, 2, pp. 797–99; and idem, *The Feats of the Knowers of God*, trans. O'Kane, pp. 556–58.

by nature, and of pure belief.' Upushghā asks Sulṭān Walad why his disciples cry out and weep when he preaches. Walad replies:

> In a situation in which a messenger from the king of the age came and gave you good news, saying: 'The Supreme Khān shows kindness toward you and he has bestowed great favor on you', would you not become delighted due to extreme joy and express gratitude and bestow thanks offerings? In this way the prophets and the Friends of God – peace be upon them – having brought the Word of God like an envoy, reveal God's secrets full of light and bring good news.

Upushghā summarily becomes a disciple of Walad and gives him a thousand dinars.[41] As he did with Īranjīn Noyan, Sulṭān Walad describes Islam in familiar language, comparing God to something like the Supreme Khān, further Islamizing the Mongols by fitting Mongolian terms into the narrative. Finally, the story provides yet another example of how Aflākī does not portray Mongol converts as shamanists with a 'veneer of Islam': Īranjīn Noyan renounces his former beliefs, while Upushghā Noyan is 'a Muslim . . . of pure belief' even before he meets Walad.

The *Manāqib al-ʿārifīn* makes a case for the sainthood of Rūmī's family by stressing their relationship with many members of the Mongol royal house and inducting them as disciples.[42] We have already seen how the text explains that Sulṭān Walad made a disciple of Gaykhātū, and treated him favourably; likewise, Aflākī describes a close relationship between Gaykhātū's wife, Pāshā Khātūn, and Rūmī's grandson, Chalabī Amīr ʿĀrif.[43] The *Manāqib al-ʿārifīn* also portrays probably the most famous Mongol convert to Islam, Ghāzān Khān (r. 1295–1304), as a Mawlawī disciple. Ghāzān received news of how Amīr

---

41 Aflākī, *Manāqib al-ʿārifīn*, ed. Yazıcı, 2, pp. 818–19; and idem, *The Feats of the Knowers of God*, trans. O'Kane, pp. 571–72.

42 The one notable exception to Īl-Khāns mentioned in the text is Aḥmad Tegüder, who as Judith Pfeiffer has noted, has received little respect in many sources. She specifically points out how Rashīd al-Dīn does not depict his practice of Islam properly, and how no Īl-Khānid source refers to his murder as 'martyrdom'. See: Pfeiffer, 'Conversion to Islam Among the Ilkhans in Muslim Narrative Traditions: The Case of Aḥmad Tegüder', pp. 313 and 332, respectively.

43 Aflākī, *Manāqib al-ʿārifīn*, ed. Yazıcı, 2, pp. 888–91; and idem, *The Feats of the Knowers of God*, trans. O'Kane, pp. 621–23.

ʿĀrif made a disciple of his chief falconer, and a member of the Saljūqid noble family and 'a firm believer, sincere, a knower of God', by way of returning a prized lost falcon. As Aflākī explains: 'so great a chief huntsman [*mīr-i shikārī*] became the prey of our prince [*shikār-i mīr-i mā*].' Ghāzān honoured the falconer according to Mongol customs and appointed him among his circle of attendants and advisors. Eager to meet Amīr ʿĀrif, Ghāzān also had the falconer try to talk Rūmī's grandson into meeting with him. Although Amīr ʿĀrif refused, 'the king's desire increased a thousandfold'. In order to lure the dervish into his presence, Ghāzān's wife, Īltirmish Khātūn, arranged a *samāʿ*-session and invited Chalabī by way of the son of the Shaykh al-Islam. Amīr ʿĀrif arrived, performed, recited a number of quatrains, and:

> In this way the Khān, with a hundred hearts and souls, became a supporter of this sultan [Amīr ʿĀrif]. He looked on from a distance and was overcome with wonder. In the end, Īltermesh Khātūn gave away so many gifts and robes of honor and became one of the disciples. The son of the Sheykh al-Eslām also became a disciple . . . And the sovereign of Islam, out of his love for them, conceived an immense attachment for the family of Mowlānā and awoke from sleep.

Aflākī explains that Ghāzān became captivated by Rūmī's poetry, especially one ghazal, which he ordered stitched into a mantle with gold thread:

> When from the friends' vat I draw a cup of manliness
>   I put wholly out of action both worlds and 'the hidden'.
> You fear the Tatars because you don't know God
>   But I raise against the Tatars two hundred banners of faith.[44]

According to Ghāzān, 'Mowlānā of Rūm composed this ghazal for me because in this day and age it was I who raised the banner of faith among the Mongols, and this group has just now become Muslim.'[45]

44 Rūmī, *Kulliyāt-i Shams*, 3:296, v. 16752.
45 Aflākī, *Manāqib al-ʿārifīn*, ed. Yazıcı, 2, pp. 844–49; and idem, *The Feats of the Knowers of God*, trans. O'Kane, pp. 589–93.

The above anecdote presents Islamization in a number of ways. First, Amīr ʿĀrif made a disciple of the falconer, 'a firm believer, sincere, a knower of God' who became an 'intimate courtier' of the Khān, thus by his presence adding more Islamic legitimacy to the court. The story shows that Aflākī credited the Mongols of Ghāzān's reign as becoming true Muslims who sincerely joined the Mawlawī community, not as shamans pretending to be converts: both 'the sovereign of Islam', Ghāzān Khān, and his wife, felt drawn to the charismatic Shaykh, Amīr ʿĀrif, because of his Islamic spiritual powers. The Khān's attachment to Rūmī and his family caused him to awake 'from sleep', to open his eyes to God, and more fully accept Islam. Aflākī's story attributes much of this success to Rūmī and ʿĀrif's poetic skills. Ghāzān became captivated with a ghazal which he believed honoured him for Islamizing the Mongols, an interpretation Aflākī does not refute. While I might instead suggest a reading of the poetry as another reference to the Sufi reliance on God discussed above, Ghāzān's claim should remind us that when reading hagiographies, we are not necessarily reading 'actual' history. Charles Melville has convincingly argued that despite claims like this one, Ghāzān's conversion did not precipitate the Islamization of his army. Instead, the opposite is true: Ghāzān, manoeuvring for the throne against Bāydū, converted in order to win over the support of the large number of soldiers who had already converted in both camps.[46] By having Ghāzān claim responsibility for this Islamization as demonstrated through poetry Rūmī had long since composed, Aflākī has the deceased saint foresee and honour the future king, sanctifying the former and legitimizing the latter.

Aflākī again represents the Mawlawī saints as committed to guiding the Mongols Khāns towards God in a story about Öljeytü (r. 1304–16), the successor to the throne after his brother Ghāzān, and a convert to Shīʿī Islam. Aflākī describes how Öljeytü levelled curses on the Prophet's Companions and sought to dig a tunnel in Medina to remove the bodies of ʿUmar and that of Rūmī's ancestor, Abū Bakr[47] from their resting places besides Muḥammad. Öljeytü even prohibited the imams

46 Charles Melville, 'Padshah-i Islam: the Conversion of Sultan Mahmud Ghazan Khan', in Pembroke Papers 1 (1990), pp. 161, 163, and 166. See also: DeWeese, 'Islamization in the Mongol Empire', p. 123.

47 This claim is repeated many times in the Manāqib al-ʿārifīn, the first instance being at the very beginning of the text itself, in the chapter on Rūmī's father, describing his lineage: Aflākī, Manāqib al-ʿārifīn, ed. Yazıcı, 1, p. 8; and idem, The Feats of the Knowers of God, trans. O'Kane, p. 7.

of Anatolia from uttering the names of Abū Bakr and ʿUmar. Dismayed by the recent turn of events, Sulṭān Walad instructed his son Chalabī Amīr ʿĀrif to proceed to Sulṭāniyya, telling him, 'Help will come from friends to an afflicted friend.' Although Walad's passing delayed the journey, he reminded his son on his deathbed, 'ʿĀref, do not neglect Kharbanda Khān [Öljeytü],' ʿĀref and a party soon set out eastward, but while in a mystical state during a *samāʿ*-session along the journey, ʿĀrif learned of Öljeytü's death.[48] Nevertheless, the party continued on to Sulṭāniyya, where ʿĀrif consoled the mourners through *samāʿ* and poetry, declaring: 'Although the king is dead, our King remains.'[49]

The *Manāqib al-ʿārifīn* does not describe Öljeytü's conversion to Shīʿism as superficial or a thin veneer over shamanist practices, but rather as a sincere conversion, albeit to 'heretical' Shīʿa doctrine. Aflākī illustrates a variety of ways in which Öljeytü took his faith and its ideology seriously and points out the fact that both Walad and Amīr ʿĀrif were concerned with the Khān's Shīʿism, not shamanism. Although the story features a Mongol adopting a 'false' doctrine of Islam, the story also shows the degree to which Walad and Amīr ʿĀrif accepted the Mongols as their responsibility. Walad perceived his relationship with the Mongols not as an antagonistic one, but as a friendly one between members of the same community. He says, 'Help will come from friends to an afflicted friend' and has enough concern for the Khān that he thinks of him on his deathbed and urges his son not to forget the Khān. Finally, Amīr ʿĀrif explains: 'Although the king is dead, our King remains', a reference to a well-known tradition where after the death of Muḥammad, Abū Bakr declared: 'O people, those who worshipped Muḥammad, [must know that] Muḥammad is dead; those who worshipped God, [must know that] God is alive [and] immortal',[50] linking the deeds and sayings of Amīr ʿĀrif to the first caliph, from whom Rūmī and his family claimed descent.

---

48 Likewise, Chalabī Amīr ʿĀrif also learns about Ghāzān's death while in a mystical state of being during a *samāʿ*-session; see Aflākī, *Manāqib al-ʿārifīn*, ed. Yazıcı, 2, pp. 857–58; and idem, *The Feats of the Knowers of God*, trans. O'Kane, p. 599. While other sources explicitly state that Öljeytü died a Shīʿī or reconverted to Sunnism before his death, Aflākī makes no such claim. See: Judith Pfeiffer, 'Conversion Versions: Sultan Öljeytü's Conversion to Shiʿism (709/1309) in Muslim Narrative Sources', in *Mongolian Studies* 22 (1999), p. 43.

49 Aflākī, *Manāqib al-ʿārifīn*, ed. Yazıcı, 2, pp. 858–62; and idem, *The Feats of the Knowers of God*, trans. O'Kane, pp. 600–602.

50 al-Ṭabarī, Abū Jaʿfar Muḥammad b. Jarīr, *The History of al-Ṭabarī*, vol. 9, *The Last*

In stories like these, Aflākī represents the Mongols as the rightful rulers of the Islamic world. He explains that after the Turkish Qaramānid dynasty gained control of the city of Konya, they complained to Rūmī's grandson Chalabī Amīr ʿĀrif, 'You do not want us who are your neighbors and supporters but you definitely favor the foreign Mongols.' Chalabī answered that 'Whomever God wishes and whomever He entrusts with His sovereignty, we are on that person's side and we want him.' Then, after reciting, 'When the bondsman is content with God's predestination,/He becomes a willing bondsman under His command,'[51] he added, 'This being the case, God Most High does not want you but He favors the army of the Mongols. He has taken sovereignty away from the Saljūqs and given it to the family of Chengīz Khān, in accordance with: *God gives His kingship to whom He will.'*[52] The Qaramānids took over Konya in the year 1313,[53] so after the Īl-Khānid rulers had converted to Islam, meaning that Aflākī at this point recognizes the Mongols as the righteous scions of Islamic rule, and therefore fully Islamized.

Despite these positive depictions of Muslim Mongol leadership, towards the end of the text Aflākī portrays some of the Mongols as straying from the path. In one such story, Temür-Tāsh, the son of the Mongol Amīr Chūpān and as of the year 1322, the viceroy of Rūm,[54] mistreated Rūmī's grandson and Amīr ʿĀrif's half-brother and successor, Chalabī Amīr ʿĀbid (d. 1338). Although Aflākī portrays Temür-Tāsh in many ways as a good ruler and Muslim, he also points out Temür-Tāsh's hubristic flaws. Aflākī notes that Temür-Tāsh claimed to be the 'Lord of the Happy Conjunction [*ṣāḥib-i qirān*]' as well as the Mahdi. Aflākī further recounts that 'For the sake of acquiring wealth and obtaining their interests, [all the prominent men of Rūm] went to great lengths in praising this leader', and that 'In absolute love Temür-Tāsh very much wished that Chalabī ʿĀbid and all the family's offspring would enter the train of that company as well

Years of the Prophet, trans. Ismail K. Poonawala (Albany: State University of New York Press 1990), pp. 185, 87.

51 Rūmī, *The Mathnawi of Jalālu'ddin Rúmi*, III: 1906.

52 Aflākī, *Manāqib al-ʿārifīn*, ed. Yazıcı, 2, pp. 925–27; and idem, *The Feats of the Knowers of God*, trans. O'Kane, pp. 647–48. Italics: Qur'ān 2:247.

53 Claude Cahen 'Konya' in *EI²*, vol. 5 (1986), p. 253.

54 J. A. Boyle, 'Dynastic and Political History of the Īl-Khāns', in *The Cambridge History of Iran*, vol. 5, *The Saljuq and Mongol Periods*, ed. J. A. Boyle (Cambridge: Cambridge University Press 1968), p. 409.

and would attend on him in circumstances of hardship and ease, at home and abroad.' But because of Temür-Tāsh's excessive pride and his increasingly self-centred and greedy court circle, 'Chalabī ʿĀbed displayed affection from a distance and frequented their gatherings less often. Naturally, Temür-Tāsh was annoyed and felt displeasure at this.' So Temür-Tāsh, seeking to get rid of Chalabī ʿĀbid, ordered the dervish to go to the Ūj (the western frontier) and urge the Turkish beys in the area to submit to Temür-Tāsh's rule. If he would not be killed in the process of the dangerous mission, the troublesome Chalabī ʿĀbid would either end up helping Temür-Tāsh expand his realm, or else find himself exiled from his centre of power and influence in Konya; Temür-Tāsh makes it clear that if Chalabī ʿĀbid fails, he 'should settle in that region'. After trying and failing to excuse himself from the mission, Chalabī ʿĀbid decided that to prevent the crisis from worsening and for the sake of his followers, and implicitly the ultimate survival of his family and community, he had no choice but to go. Although Aflākī notes that Chalabī ʿĀbid continued to put his faith in God and God's friends, he left Konya 'moaning and letting out shouts . . . And due to the pain in his heart he fetched up a sigh and said: "When we come back, not one of these persons will remain." Thus, through the decree of the Omnipotent King, when we returned from visiting the region of Ūj, no one was left in Konya except Amīr Ẓahīr al-Dīn, the son of Tāj-Qezel [a local notable].' Aflākī adds that apparently everyone had gone to Syria, the realm of the Mamlūks and beyond the control of Temür-Tāsh, as 'that company of nobles had all been expelled'.[55] Temür-Tāsh, as the self-proclaimed 'Lord of the Happy Conjunction' and Mahdi, thus disrespected the Mawlawī Order by trying to subordinate the community and its rightful leader to his own false claim to spiritual authority. Consequently, although not reported in the text, Temür-Tāsh eventually found himself chased out of power in Anatolia and executed at the hands of the Mamlūks in 1328.[56]

In the following anecdote, Chalabī Amīr ʿĀbid and Amīr ʿĀrif's son Amīr ʿĀlim Chalabī 'Shāhzāda' meet in Tabriz with Shams al-Dīn Amīr Muḥammad, the Īl-Khān vizier and son of Rashīd al-Dīn to discuss

---

55 Aflākī, *Manāqib al-ʿārifīn*, ed. Yazıcı, 2, pp. 976–80; and idem, *The Feats of the Knowers of God*, trans. O'Kane, pp. 684–86.
56 Boyle, 'Dynastic and Political History of the Īl-Khāns', p. 411.

'particular matters regarding which the dervishes were in need'. However, the vizier showed little regard for his esteemed visitors or their
affairs, and did nothing. As Aflākī explains: 'Indeed, this was the cause
of the decline of their kingdom and dominion. Their good fortune was
reversed, and the scoundrels of that region [diyār] fell upon one
another and not a single one [diyyār] remained.'[57] The word-play
used here fulfils, and refers back to, the above mentioned story of
Gaykhātū, when the Khān's courtiers told him that since the region
belonged to Mawlānā, 'whoever sets out to attack this region [diyār],
no member [diyyār] of his lineage remains and he is destroyed'.[58]

At this point, Aflākī immediately moves to explain how this caused
the decline of the kingdom and dominion of the Mongols. After these
stories, Aflākī revisits the broader history of the Mongols in the
Islamic world, and concludes that they were once willed by God to
succeed, yet were destined to fall because the Mongols and their supporters inevitably strayed from God by turning against the Mawlawī
family. For Aflākī, the lynchpin behind the Mongols' rise, conversion
and fall was their relation to the saints and heroes of the text, the
pious family of Rūmī, the descendants of Abū Bakr. In one anecdote
placed late in the text, the Saljūqid administrator Muʿīn al-Dīn
Sulaymān Parwāna asked Rūmī: 'When will the period of the House of
Chengīz Khān, which you referred to as: "Our Army", draw to a close,
and how will their end come about?' Rūmī replies:

> When the Great Master [Bahā' al-Dīn] – God be pleased with him –
> became sore at heart because of the Khvārazamshāh's disagree-
> able behavior which had taken a bad form, and being very
> annoyed, departed from Balkh, he invoked God in accordance
> with His name the Avenger to take revenge on those innovators
> on the road of the *sharīʿat*, for *God is All-powerful, the Avenger.*[59]
> When God Most High had brought forth the enormous Mongol
> army from the east, they destroyed the capital city Balkh, as well
> as Khorasan.[60]

57 Aflākī, *Manāqib al-ʿārifīn*, ed. Yazıcı, 2, pp. 980–81; and idem, *The Feats of the Knowers
   of God*, trans. O'Kane, pp. 686-87.
58 Aflākī, *Manāqib al-ʿārifīn*, ed. Yazıcı, 1, pp. 331–33; idem, *The Feats of the Knowers of
   God*, trans. O'Kane, pp. 229–31; and Sipahsālār, *Zindigīnāma*, pp. 103–104.
59 Qur'ān, 3:3, 5:96.
60 Aflākī, *Manāqib al-ʿārifīn*, ed. Yazıcı, 2, pp. 981–82; and idem, *The Feats of the Knowers
   of God*, trans. O'Kane, pp. 687–88.

He then recited a *hadīth* where God tells Muḥammad that,

I possess an army which I have given an abode towards the east, and I have called them the Turks. I created them with (both) My wrath and My anger, and I will inflict them upon whichever of My bondsmen and bondswomen neglects my command, and I will take revenge on the latter by means of them.

But Rūmī continued that the Mongols in turn will fall when they neglect God's command. He specifically noted:

The occasion of the decline of that group's dominion will be when they show contempt for our sons and successors and grand-children, and treat them unjustly and cause them hardship and are negligent in paying them proper respect, and disdain to revere our descendants out of despotism and high-handedness. Inevitably God – *He is sublime and exalted* – will become jealous and make an exemplary punishment out of them for those endowed with sight.[61]

Next, Aflākī reiterates that 'Likewise, from the outset, the cause of the Mongols coming forth was the prayer of Bahā'-e Valad and the afflic-tion of his blessed heart by the Khwārazmshāh and his supporters' and comments:

the cause of the overturning of the House of Chengīz Khān and the decline of that group's dominion was also the affliction of the blessed heart of their offspring. Moreover, the indication which Mowlānā gave to the Parvāna's question turned out to be true. And this is a wondrous miracle in the world. Understand it in seriousness and seek good fortune from God! This was so in order to make known to mankind how close the House of Ṣeddīq [Abū Bakr's descendants, i.e. Rūmī's family] is to the Glorious Presence and that their prayers are answered in all circumstances.[62]

61 Aflākī, *Manāqib al-ʿārifīn*, ed. Yazıcı, 2, p. 982; and idem, *The Feats of the Knowers of God*, trans. O'Kane, p. 688.
62 Aflākī, *Manāqib al-ʿārifīn*, ed. Yazıcı, 2, pp. 985-86; and idem, *The Feats of the Knowers of God*, trans. O'Kane, pp. 690–91.

In other words, Aflākī uses the Mongols' entire existence in the Islamic world, from their rise to their fall, as proof and support for the claim of sainthood of Rūmī's family. At the same time, the Mongols are Islamized as they are integrated into an Islamic narrative, from their coming to the Islamic world to their fall from grace, as well as the Islamic narrative of the rise of the Mawlawī community.[63]

As a hagiography, the *Manāqib al-ʿārifīn* depicts Rūmī and his family as the charismatic focus around which a community forms. Scholars traditionally credit the crafting of the organization of the Mawlawī Order to the leadership of Sulṭān Walad and Amīr ʿĀrif.[64] The *Manāqib al-ʿārifīn* was a major part of that project, as the newly emerging Mawlawī community was built around the cult and practices established by their saints, but also the historical memory of the saints' deeds. Amongst the many spiritual deeds that the Mawlawī family were remembered for, their interactions with the Mongols did much to help establish their credibility as saints. Mawlawī disciples or others reading or hearing a recitation of the *Manāqib al-ʿārifīn* would have seen how integral Rūmī and his family were to the whole history of the Mongols in the Islamic world. They would have seen that the Mongols were Islamized, in that they were an important part of the Islamic stories of the disciples' most cherished saints and heroes. Concurrently, as the text was written during and after the height and decline of Īl-Khānid rule after their conversion to Islam, Aflākī is able to portray the Mongols in a more Islamic fashion. He has different Mongols fulfil several Islamic purposes, such as enacting God's rage through the prayers of Bahā' al-Dīn, reducing the peoples' reliance on things other than God, and playing the roles of the enemy for Rūmī to

---

63 Aflākī is not the only writer to attribute his understanding of the Islamization of the Mongols to Rūmī's foresight: the anonymous author of the Chaghatay Turkic work *Tavārīkh-i guzīda-yi Nuṣrat-nāma*, a work sponsored by Muḥammad Shïbānī Khān and finished in 1504, writes that Rūmī predicted how the Mongols would become Muslims 'just as when gold is produced through alchemy'. See: *Tavārīkh-i guzīda-yi Nuṣrat-nāma*, London, British Library MS Or. 3222, ff. 4a–5a; DeWeese, 'Islamization in the Mongol Empire', p. 134.

64 Claude Cahen, *Pre-Ottoman Turkey: A general survey of the material and spiritual culture and history c. 1071–1330*, trans. J. Jones-Williams (New York: Taplinger Publishing Company 1968), p. 351; F. Lewis, *Rumi*, pp. 425–26; Speros Vryonis, Jr., *The Decline of Medieval Hellenism in Asia Minor and the Process of Islamization from the Eleventh through the Fifteenth Century* (Berkeley: University of California Press 1971), pp. 385–86.

become a heroic *mujāhid*, but elsewhere role-model for proper Sufi behaviour. Aflākī portrays the Mongols who convert to Islam and become Mawlawī disciples as sincere in their belief, and not shamans hiding behind 'a veneer of Islam'. Likewise, he attributes the fall of their rule to their descendants' insincerity towards the Mawlawī family. All of this serves to buttress Aflākī's hagiographic goals and values, which in turn serve to further Islamize the Mongols. Aflākī is able to make the Mawlawī family central to the historical memory of this community through the saints' interaction with the Mongols, who were the main power of their age, and thus that historical memory adds Islamic legitimacy, or illegitimacy when it comes to their fall, to the Mongols. Regardless of the fact that few, if any, of these stories might be 'true' in a positivistic sense, they help to establish the Mawlawī Order's identity, as well as lend it the legitimacy that helped it to become so successful in its diffusion as a Sufi Order and community.[65]

BIBLIOGRAPHY

Primary Sources

Aflākī, Shams al-Dīn Aḥmad-i. *The Feats of the Knowers of God (Manāqeb al-ᶜarefīn)*, trans. John O'Kane. Leiden: Brill, 2002.

—. *Manāqib al-ᶜarefīn*, ed. Tahsin Yazıcı. 2 volumes. Ankara: Türk Tarih Kurumu Basımevi, 1959.

Bar Hebraeus. *The Chronography of Gregory Abū'l Faraj the son of Aaron, the Hebrew Physician, commonly known as Bar Hebraeus, being the First Part of his Political History of the World,* trans. Ernest A. Wallis Budge. 2 volumes. London: Oxford University Press, 1932.

Rashīd al-Dīn Faḍl Allah. *'Compendium of Chronicles'*, trans. W. M. Thackston. *Sources of Oriental Languages and Literatures,* no. 45. 3 volumes. Cambridge, Massachusetts: Harvard University Department of Near Eastern Languages and Civilizations, 1999.

---

65 Holbrook, 'Diverse Tastes in Spiritual Life', p. 106. For example, Speros Vryonis has argued that Rūmī's success in dealing with the Mongols gave him the authority to intervene and bring about the conversion of non-Mongolian Christians in Anatolia. See Vryonis, *The Decline of Medieval Hellenism*, pp. 271–72.

Rūmī, Jalāl al-Dīn. *Kulliyāt-i Shams yā Dīvān-i kabīr*, ed. B. Furūzānfar. Tehran: Intishārāt-i Dānishgāh-i Tihrān, 1344 A.Hsh./1965.

—. *The Mathnawí of Jalálu'ddín Rúmí,* ed. Reynold Nicholson. London: Gibb Memorial Series, 1925–40.

Sipahsālār, Farīdūn b. Aḥmad. *Zindigīnāma-yi Mawlānā Jalāl al-Din-i Mawlawi,* ed. Saʿīd Nafīsī. Tehran: Intishārāt-i Iqbāl, 1363.

al-Ṭabarī, Abū Jaʿfar Muḥammad b. Jarīr. *The History of al-Ṭabarī.* Vol. 9, *The Last Years of the Prophet,* trans. Ismail K. Poonawala. Albany: State University of New York Press, 1990.

Tavārīkh-i guzīda-yi Nuṣrat-nāma. London, British Library MS Or. 3222.

Secondary Literature

Amitai-Preiss, Reuven. 'Ḡāzān Khan'. In *Encyclopaedia Iranica* III (1989), pp. 381–83.

—. 'Sufis and Shamans: Some Remarks on the Islamization of the Mongols in the Ilkhanate'. *Journal of the Economic and Social History of the Orient* 42, no. 1 (1999), pp. 27–46.

Arnold, T. W. *The Preaching of Islam: A History of the Propagation of the Muslim Faith.* New York: Charles Scribner's Sons, 1913.

Atwood, Christopher P. *Encyclopedia of Mongolia and the Mongol Empire.* New York: Facts on File, Inc., 2004.

Bausani, A. 'Religion under the Mongols'. In *The Cambridge History of Iran.* Vol. 5, *The Saljuq and Mongol Periods,* ed. J. A. Boyle. Cambridge: Cambridge University Press 1968, pp. 538–49.

Biran, Michal. 'The Chaghadaids and Islam: the Conversion of Tarmashirin Khan (1331–34)'. *Journal of the American Oriental Society* 122 (2002), pp. 742–52.

Boyle, J. A. 'Dynastic and Political History of the Īl-Khāns'. In *The Cambridge History of Iran.* Vol. 5, *The Saljuq and Mongol Periods,* ed. J. A. Boyle. Cambridge: Cambridge University Press 1968, pp. 303–421.

Cahen, Claude. 'Konya'. In *Encyclopaedia of Islam* [= *EI*²] vol. 5 (1986), pp. 253–56.

—. *Pre-Ottoman Turkey: A general survey of the material and spiritual culture and history c. 1071–1330,* trans. J. Jones-Williams. New York: Taplinger Publishing Company, 1968.

DeWeese, Devin. *Islamization and Native Religion in the Golden Horde: Baba Tükles and Conversion to Islam in Historical and Epic Tradition.* University Park, Pennsylvania: Pennsylvania State University Press, 1994.

—. 'Islamization in the Mongol Empire'. In *The Cambridge History of Inner Asia: The Chinggisid Age,* ed. Nicola Di Cosmo, Allen J. Frank, and Peter B. Golden. Cambridge: Cambridge University Press, 2009, pp. 120–34.

—. 'The *Mashā'ikh-i Turk* and the *Khojagān*: Rethinking the Links Between the Yasavī and Naqshbandī Sufi Traditions'. *In Journal of Islamic Studies* 7, no. 2 (1996), pp. 180–207.

—. '"Stuck in the Throat of Chingīz Khān": Envisioning the Mongol Conquests in Some Sufi Accounts from the 14th to 17th Centuries'. In *History and Historiography of Post-Mongol Central Asia and the Middle East: Studies in Honor of John E. Woods,* ed. Judith Pfeiffer and Sholeh A. Quinn. Wiesbaden, Germany: Harrossowitz Verlag, 2006, pp. 23–60.

—. 'Yasavī Šayḫs in the Timurid Era: Notes on the Social and Political Role of Communal Sufi Affiliations in the 14th and 15th Centuries'. In 'La civiltà timuride come fenomeno internazionale', ed. Michele Bernardini, special issue, *Oriente Moderno,* n.s., 15, no. 2 (1996), pp. 173–88.

Fragner, Bert G. 'Ilkhanid Rule and its Contributions to Iranian Political Culture'. In *Beyond the Legacy of Genghis Khan,* ed. Linda Komaroff. Leiden: Koninklijke Brill NV, 2006, pp. 68–80.

Gibb, H. A. R. *Mohammedanism: An Historical Survey.* London: Oxford University Press, 1949.

Grousset, René. *The Empire of the Steppes: A History of Central Asia,* trans. Naomi Walford. New Brunswick, New Jersey: Rutgers University Press, 1970.

Hodgson, Marshall G. S. *The Venture of Islam: Conscience and History in a World Civilization.* Vol. 2, *The Expansion of Islam in the Middle Periods.* Chicago: University of Chicago Press, 1978.

Holbrook, Victoria. 'Diverse Tastes in the Spiritual Life: Textual Play in the Diffusion of Rumi's Order'. In *The Heritage of Sufism.* Vol. 2, *The Legacy of Medieval Persian Sufism (1150–1500),* ed. Leonard Lewisohn, Oxford: Oneworld Publications, 1999, pp. 99–120

Humphreys, R. Stephen. *Islamic History: A Framework for Inquiry* (Revised Edition). Princeton: Princeton University Press, 1991.

Jackson, Peter. 'Gayḵūt Khan'. In *Encyclopaedia Iranica* III (1989), pp. 344–45.

Karamustafa, Ahmet T. *God's Unruly Friends: Dervish Groups in the Islamic Later Middle Period, 1200–1550.* Oxford: Oneworld Publications, 2006.

Köprülü, Mehmed Fuad. *Islam in Anatolia and the Turkish Invasion (Prolegomena),* trans. Gary Leiser. Salt Lake City: University of Utah Press, 1993.

Lane, George. *Early Mongol Rule in Thirteenth-Century Iran: A Persian Renaissance.* New York: RoutledgeCurzon, 2003.

Levtzion, Nehemia. 'Toward a Comparative Study of Islamization'. In *Conversion to Islam,* ed. Nehemia Levtzion, New York: Holmes & Meier Publishers, Inc. 1979, pp. 1–23.

Lewis, Bernard. 'The Mongols, the Turks, and the Muslim Polity'. In *Islam in History: Ideas, People, and Events in the Middle East,* 2d ed. Chicago: Open Court Publishing Company, 1993, pp. 179–98.

Lewis, Franklin D. *Rumi: Past and Present, East and West: The Life, Teachings and Poetry of Jalāl al-Din Rumi,* revised ed. Oxford: Oneworld Publications, 2008.

Melville, Charles. '*Padshah-i Islam*: the Conversion of Sultan Mahmud Ghazan Khan'. In *Pembroke Papers* 1 (1990), pp. 159–77.

Ménage, V. L. 'The Islamization of Anatolia'. In *Conversion to Islam,* ed. Nehemia Levtzion, New York: Holmes & Meier Publishers, Inc., 1979, pp. 52–67.

Morgan, David. *Medieval Persia 1040–1797.* London: Longman Group UK Limited, 1988.

Pfeiffer, Judith. 'Conversion to Islam Among the Ilkhans in Muslim Narrative Traditions: The Case of Aḥmad Tegüder'. Ph.D. diss., the University of Chicago 2003.

—. 'Conversion Versions: Sultan Öljeytü's Conversion to Shi'ism (709/1309) in Muslim Narrative Sources'. In *Mongolian Studies* 22 (1999), pp. 35–67.

—. 'Reflections on a "Double Reproachment": Conversion to Islam Among the Mongol Elite During the Early Ilkhanate'. *In Beyond the Legacy of Genghis Khan,* ed. Linda Komaroff, Leiden: Brill, 2006, pp. 369–89.

Renard, John. *Islam and the Heroic Image: Themes in Literature and the Visual Arts.* Macon, Georgia: Mercer University Press, 1999.

Schimmel, Annemarie. *And Muhammad is His Messenger: The Veneration of the Prophet in Islamic Piety.* Chapel Hill, North Carolina: University of North Carolina Press, 1985.

Stewart, Angus. 'The Assassination of King Hetʿum II: The Conversion of The Ilkhans and the Armenians'. In *Journal of the Royal Asiatic Society* 15, no. 1 (2005), pp. 45–61.

Vásáry, István, '"History and Legend" in Berke Khan's Conversion to Islam'. In *Aspects of Altaic Civilization* III (= PIACC XXX), ed. Denis Sinor. Bloomington: Indiana University, Research Institute for Inner Asian Studies, 1990.

Vryonis, Speros Jr. *The Decline of Medieval Hellenism in Asia Minor and the Process of Islamization from the Eleventh through the Fifteenth Century.* Berkeley: University of California Press, 1971.

A *Ghazal* from Rumi's *Divan-i Shams-i Tabrizi*

I am am I

Translated by Paul Losensky

How faded and indistinct I am!
How will I see me as I am?

You told me, 'Bring out the secrets.'
But just where is the out
in this in and out I'm in?
I am motion in quiesence.
How can my moving spirit be still?
Within itself my sea is drowned –
wondrous strange the shoreless sea I am.

Do not seek my here or my hereafter:
Neither is neither here nor there
in that world I am.

Like non-being, free from gain or loss,
a rarely balanced balance sheet I am.

'Soul,' I said, 'you are my essence.'
'When I'm so obvious,'
it replied, 'What essence am I?'
'But you are it!' I insisted,
and it replied, 'Ha! Be silent!
The it that I am won't be spoken.'
I said, 'If it won't be spoken,
see the speech-less speaker I am.'

In self-effacement, I was turning
into the footloose moon.
See the trackless sprinter I am.
The shout was heard, 'Why do you run?'
Look how hidden in plain sight I am.

When I saw Shams-i Tabrizi –
peerless sea and mine and treasure I am.[1]

---

1 *Kulliyāt-i Shams ya Dīvān-i kabīr*, ed. B. Furūzānfar (Tehran: Amīr Kabīr 1355 A.Hsh./ 1976), vol. 4, ghazal 1759, pp. 79–80. In the *Manāqib al-ʿārifīn*, the following strange tale of the circumstances that occasioned Rumi's composition of this poem is related: 'The sultan's wife Gorjī Khātūn – *God have mercy on her* – was among the sincere supporters and a close disciple of Mowlānā's family. She continually burned in the fire of her passion for Mowlānā. As it happened, she had the intention of going to Kayseri, and the sultan could not do without her because she was a distinguished person with firm opinions. But she could not bear the burden of the fire of separation. In that era there was a painter who was a second Manes when it came to portrait painting (*ṣūratgarī*) and the depiction of beings endowed with form (*taṣvīr-e moṣavvarāt*). He used to say: "In his art Manes (Mānī) would be at a loss (*forū mānī*) before our drawing." And he was called ʿEyn al-Dowla-ye Rūmī. Gorjī Khātūn gave him presents and ordered him to make a drawing of Mowlānā's appearance on a sheet of paper and to depict him and draw him as required in the extreme of beauty. That way the drawing would be her consoler on her travels.

'Thus ʿEyn al-Dowla came to Mowlānā with several officials (*amīn*) to inform him of the matter. He lowered his head and stood at a distance. Before he said anything, Mowlānā exclaimed: "It's alright if you're able." ʿEyn al-Dowla brought some sheets of *makhzanī* paper, took his pen in his hand and turned to face Mowlānā who was standing up. The drawer took a look and began to depict his appearance. He drew a very lovely picture on a sheet of paper. The second time he looked, he saw that what he had seen at first was not the same. On another sheet of paper he drew another drawing. When he was finished with the picture, Mowlānā displayed a different form again.

'In the end, he sketched different pictures on twenty sheets of paper, and as often as he looked he beheld a different portrait of the figure. He was taken aback in bewilderment, let out a shout, and fell into a swoon. He broke his pens. Like someone who is helpless, he prostrated himself. That moment Mowlānā began to recite this ghazal.' – Shams al-Dīn Aḥmad-i Aflākī, *The Feats of the Knowers of God* (*Manāqeb al-ʿarefīn*), trans. John O'Kane (Leiden: Koninklijke Brill NV 2002), pp. 292–93.

A Syntactic Analysis of Metaphorical Phrases in R. A. Nicholson's Translation of the *Mathnawi*

BEHROOZ MAHMOODI-BAKHTIARI
and
REZA ABBASI

INTRODUCTION

Mawlana Jalal al-Din Rumi is one of the most creative figures in Persian literature, and in particular, his great work, the *Mathnawi* is a wonderful treasury of imaginative phrases, adages, proverbs and aphorisms in Persian. Only a few poets in Persian literature match Rumi's inspired innovations in language, with respect to the invention of strange compounds, new words and unique grammatical structures.

Although translations of the *Mathnawi* have been rendered into a number of languages including Arabic, Turkish and French, the most famous translation by far is that of the celebrated English orientalist, Reynold A. Nicholson who spent the last twenty-five years of his life editing the Persian text of the *Mathnawi* before writing a full translation and commentary on it in English.[1] In particular, the meticulous accuracy of Nicholson's translation has been praised by scholars and students of the poem in both the East and the West.

The abstruseness of the *Mathnawi*'s phraseology, and the presence in it of so many difficult words and phrases, which even the most educated classes find hard to understand, is well known in Persian literature, hence the composition of so many commentaries on it written by eminent mystics and scholars who have spent lifetimes

1 See Marta Simidchieva, 'Mawlana Jalal al-Din Rumi of R. A. Nicholson', *Mawlana Rumi Review*, vol. 1 (2010), pp. 33–68.

exploring its great ocean of knowledge and seeking to understand its prolific meanings. The abundance of calligraphed manuscripts of the *Mathnawi* in the world's great libraries provides further testimony to its popularity and importance.

In this study, I have tried to examine and analyze some aspects of the *Mathnawi*'s creativity within the domain of metaphorical phrases in the poem, exploring from the linguistic point of view the use of metaphor in Nicholson's translation. The use of metaphor is of course a frequent feature of classical Persian literary texts. Some features of Persian poetry are exclusive to Persian literature (such as the complexities of the end-rhyme), but other properties (such as the use of imagery) are global and can be found in most world literature.

Metaphor, which is usually defined as a word or a phrase in a sentence that makes the reader/listener think in order to discover the real meaning (sense) of that word or phrase,[2] is frequently found in Persian literary texts. In the following example for instance, the statement: 'John is like a lion', which implies by extension that 'John is as brave and powerful as a lion', makes use of the device of simile so that the reader or listener need not himself compare John with a lion. If on the other hand one says that 'John is a lion', the listener or reader is forced to think and use her or his reasoning to discover why and to what extent 'John' and 'lion' are comparable.

In a metaphorical phrase, the semantic relationship between the components of the phrase is a figurative one, that is to say, one of the components of the phrase is not used in its usual semantic form, but is given a quality which basically does not exist in it. For instance, in the phrase 'sea of knowledge', the depth and expansion of one's knowledge is metaphorically analogized with a sea.

THEORIES OF METAPHORS IN TRANSLATION STUDIES

Although the connection between metaphor and translation is hard to demonstrate, some scholars of translation have attempted to compose theoretical models to analyze how the translation of metaphors from one language to another is effected.[3] In the field of translation studies,

2 As P. Newmark, *A Textbook of Translation* (London: Prentice Hall 1988), p. 104, says: 'metaphor is the application of a word or collocation to what it does not literally denote'.

3 See E. Nida, *Towards a Science of Translating* (Leiden: E. J. Brill 1964) and M. Dagut,

one of the most common models presented is that by Newmark and Larsen (1984)[4] who have enumerated the following steps:

a) Retaining the same Source Language (SL) metaphorical image in the Target Language (TL)

b) Replacing the SL metaphorical image with a TL simile, but keeping the image

c) Replacing the SL metaphorical image with a different TL one

d) Retaining the same SL metaphorical image but explaining its sense

e) Converting the SL metaphor into the literal sense of the metaphor in the TL

f) Omitting the metaphor altogether in the TL

Other scholars have argued that the translation of metaphor is not possible using such a series of abstract rules, but rather one needs to pay attention to the structure and function of metaphor according to its content.[5]

METAPHORICAL PHRASES IN THE *MATHNAWI*

Throughout the roughly twelve thousand verses of the first three books of Rumi's *Mathnawi*, one encounters many beautiful metaphors, each of which individually reflects the poet's intention. Below I have tried to analyze the various methods adopted by Nicholson in his translation of metaphorical phrases in this huge collection. After a careful study of all the existing verses in the first three books of the *Mathnawi*, 595 different metaphorical phrases were identified. Basing my research on the corpus and data within these three books, by

---

Can Metaphor Be Translated? (Babel: International Journal of Translation, XXII (1), 1976), pp. 21–33.
4 See P. Newmark, *A Textbook of Translation* (London: Prentice Hall 1988), pp. 108–11.
5 Mary Snell-Hornby, *Translation Studies* (Amsterdam: John Benjamins Publishing Co. 1998), p. 58.

making a comparison of the phrases with their equivalents in the translation done by Nicholson, I discovered three basic patterns:

- The 'phrase to phrase' pattern where the translator has connected the base of a phrase to its genitive word either by using a preposition such as: 'of', 'in', 'to', 'for' and so forth.

- The 'phrase to word' pattern in which the components of a metaphorical phrase (base and genitive word) have been translated either into a single noun or else into a noun with an adjective.

- The 'phrase to sentence' pattern, in which a phrasal verb (a phrase with a linking or main verb) is designated for a metaphorical phrase.

Since these patterns at first sight may seem hard to grasp, at least for those readers unfamiliar with the jargon of translation studies, examples of each of these patterns, along with a precise description of them, is given below:

'PHRASE TO PHRASE' PATTERNS

Although the literal translation of a metaphorical phrase may fail to express the beauty of the original or convey it to the reader, the use of this pattern is at the very least an indication of the accuracy and fidelity of the translator to the source text. According to the data of this study, this model had the highest rate (90.08 per cent) of the three patterns of translating metaphors used in Nicholson's translation of the *Mathnawi*. By using this method, Nicholson, as translator, obviously intended to keep the spirit of the metaphor in the translation alive and to convey it to the reader of the target text, thus demonstrating his fidelity to the source text and preserving both the external 'form' and the internal 'sense' of the metaphor in the voyage from source to target text.

The animation or lack thereof of this type of pattern of translation is quite interesting and noteworthy here. Studying this pattern of translation revealed its division into two different 'styles' that may be regarded as one of the major findings of my study.

The first style, which occurs in 501 cases of the translation, is configured in the format of 'X-word + preposition + Y-word', indicating that the translator chose genitive words linked by 'of' that are grammatically considered 'inanimate' and 'spirit-less', as the use of this construction often indicates that the words involved are non-living entities.

The second style, which occurs in 35 other cases, is the format of 'X-word's Y-word', indicating that the translator chose genitive words linked by ''s' that are grammatically considered 'animate' and 'living entities'. The category, 'animacy', is one among several, which determine the use of either the 'of' genitive or ''s genitive'.

The following verses[6] provide samples of the first style ('X-word + preposition + Y-word') of translation:

(I:3) *sina khwaham sharha sharha az faraq   ta biguyam sharh-i dard-i ishtiyaq*

I want a bosom torn by severance, that I may unfold (to such a one) the pain of love-desire.

(II:51) *hiss-i abdan qut-i zulmat mikhwarad   hiss-i jan az afitabi micharad*

The bodily sense is eating the food of darkness; the spiritual sense is feeding from a Sun.

(III: 135) *dar ʿazab-i munkar-ast an jan-i u   kazhdum-i gham dar dil-i ghamdan-i u*

His soul is in hateful torment, the scorpion of grief is in his grief-laden heart.

The following verses give some examples from the remaining 35 cases of the 'X-word's Y-word' pattern of translation, and shows how the translator chose genitive words that are more 'animate' and 'living':

---

6 Since the database in this section was very large, only a few samples have been selected here to illustrate my point.

(I:388) *har shabi az dam-i tan arwah ra   mirahani mikani alwah ra*

Every night Thou freest the spirits from the body's snare, and dost
erase (the impressions on) the tablets (of the mind).

(II:96) *ayina-yi jan nist illa ru-yi yar   ru-yi an yari kih bashad
z-an diyar*

The soul's mirror is naught but the face of the friend, the face of that
friend who is of yonder country (the spiritual land).

(III:71) *mihr-i dana'iyash jushid u biguft   khwush salamashan
u chun gulbun shiguft*

His wisdom's love was stirred (within him), and he gave them a fair
greeting and blossomed like a rose-bush.

'PHRASE TO WORD' PATTERNS

In a few cases, the metaphorical phrases (7.23 per cent) have been
translated into a lexical item. In these examples we find a metaphorical phrase translated into either a single unit or into a phrase with a
complementary equivalent in parenthesis:

(I:1745) *gharq-i haq khwahad kih bashad gharqtar   hamchu mawj-i
bahr-i jan zir u zibar*

He that is drowned in God wishes to be more drowned, (while) his
spirit (is tossed) up and down like the waves of the sea.

(II: 3218) *dil nigah darid ay bi-hasilan   dar hudhur-i hadhrat-i
sahibdilan*

Keep watch over your hearts, O fruitless ones, in the presence of
the majesty of the men of heart (saints).

There are also some instances of 'converted' adjectives, that is to say,
a word which is not an adjective used as an adjective without undergoing any morphological change:

(I:25) *jism-i khak az 'ishq bar aflak shud   kuh dar raqs amad u chalak shud*

Through Love the earthly body soared to the skies: the mountain began to dance and became nimble.

(II:940) *ruz-i marg in hiss-i tu batil shavad   nur-i jan dari ki yar-i dil shavad?*

On the day of death this sense-perception of yours will vanish: have you the spiritual light that should be the companion of your heart?

(III:774) *pas biguftandash kih tavusan-i jan   jilvaha darand andar gulsitan*

Then they said to him, The spiritual peacocks have displays (with the Beloved) in the Rose-garden.

'PHRASE TO SENTENCE' PATTERNS

The 'phrase to sentence pattern' is one in which a metaphorical phrase is rendered within a clause in a sentence by use of (1) a linking verb or (2) a main verb, since this is the only way the translator could convey the 'sense' of the literary text. Since an acceptable literary translation is usually considered to be one through which both 'meaning' and 'style' are conveyed from source to target text, an eminent translator such as Nicholson inevitably did not make use of this style of translation very much (in fact, it occurs only 2.69 per cent) since this pattern is incapable of conveying the style used in the source text. The following verses and their translation show his use of this pattern:

(1) Sentences containing a linking verb:

(I:1575) *qissa-yi tuti-yi jan z'in-san buvad   ku kasi ku mahram-i murghan buvad*

Such-like is the tale of the parrot which is the soul: where is that one who is the confidant of (the spiritual) birds.

(II:186) *muftariq shud afitab-i janha   dar darun-i rawzan-i abdanha*

The Sun, which is the spirits, became separated (broken into rays) in the windows, which are bodies.

(III:2712) *chun shuma dar dam-i in ab u gilid   kay shuma sayyad-i simurgh-i dilid*

Since ye are entrapped by this water and earth, how are ye hunters of the Símurgh (which is) the heart.

(III:4167) *rahmatash bar qahr az an sabiq shudast   ta kih sarmaya-yi wujud ayad bih dast*

His (God's) mercy (eternally) preceded His wrath in order that the stock-in-trade, (which is) existence, should come to hand (be acquired).

(2) Sentences containing a main verb:

(I:1439) *az manazilha-yi janash yad dad   vaz safarha-yi ravanash yad dad*

He (Umar) reminded him of the stages traversed by the soul, and he reminded him of the journeys of the spirit.

(II:95) *ayina-yi ahan barayi pustha'st   ayina-yi simayi jan sangin baha'st*

The mirror of iron is (only) for husks (external forms); the mirror that shows the aspect of the heart is of great price.

A Statistical Analysis of the Results

Exploring the data gleaned from our analysis of these three patterns of translation in the corpus examined reveals the following figures and percentages:

	PHRASE TO SENTENCE	PHRASE TO WORD	PHRASE TO PHRASE
NUMBER OF OCCURRENCES	16	43	536
PERCENTAGES	2.69	7.23	90.08

My study of the first three books of the *Mathnawi* revealed altogether 595 metaphorical phrases. After reviewing the data and comparing them with their equivalents in the translation done by Nicholson, three major translation styles can be observed: In 536 cases, there is evidence of the 'phrase to phrase' pattern; in 43 cases, one finds the 'phrase to word' pattern; and finally, in 16 cases the 'phrase to sentence' pattern occurs. This result is illustrated by the table below:

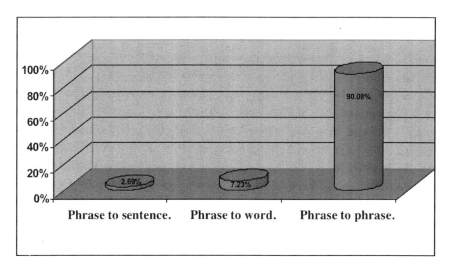

Some Preliminary Findings

The data provided by this study revealed that the major method used by Nicholson to translate the metaphorical phrases of *Mathnawi* was that of 'literal translation', that is to say the format of 'X-word + preposition + Y-word' for inanimate genitive words, and 'X-word's Y-word', for animate ones. In spite of the above, some different cases were observed as follows:

X-Word + Preposition + Y-Word Pattern Instead of X-Word's Y-Word Pattern

In order to connect a living or animate genitive word to its base, the translator has used the 'X-word + preposition + Y-word' pattern. The criterion used in judging this point is the record of decisions made by the translator in regard to words such as: God, soul, spirit and so on, which are obviously animate. The examples below give evidence of this pattern:

(I:323) *an sharab-i haq khitamash mushk-i nab   bada ra khatmash buvad gand u ʿazab*

The wine of God, its seal (last result) is pure musk, (but) as for (the other) wine, its seal is stench and torment.

(II:287) *ta bar-amad afitab-i anbiya   guft ay ghish dur shaw safi biya*

Until the sun of the prophets rose and said, Begone, O alloy! Come, O thou that art pure!

(III:689) *bada-yi haq rast bashad nay durugh   dugh khurdi dugh khurdi dugh dugh*

The wine of God is true, not false: thou hast drunk buttermilk, thou hast drunk buttermilk, buttermilk, buttermilk!

X-WORD'S Y-WORD PATTERN INSTEAD OF
X-WORD + PREPOSITION + Y-WORD PATTERN

Moreover, in a few cases, the translator has reversed the above-mentioned pattern, and used the 'X-word's Y-word' style for inanimate, spiritless genitive words. The following cases are some examples of this usage:

(I:3660) *chun shuma tarik budam dar nahad   vahy-yi khurshidam chinin nuri bidad*

Like you, I was dark in my nature: the Sun's revelation gave me such a light as this.

(II:422) *bang-i sag hargiz risad dar gush-i mah   khasa mahi ku buvad khass-i ilah*

Does the dog's bark ever reach the moon's ear, especially that Moon who is the chosen of God?

(III:71) *mihr-i dana'iyash jushid u biguft   khush salamashan u chun gulbun shiguft*

His wisdom's love was stirred (within him), and he gave them a fair greeting and blossomed like a rose-bush.

SUBSTITUTING A COMMA FOR A PREPOSITION

There are also a few cases in which the translator has replaced the preposition between the two components of a metaphorical phrase with a comma:

(I:1540) *var pazira'i chu bar-khwani qasas   murgh-i janat tang ayad dar qafas*

But if you are accepting (the Qurán), when you read the stories (of the prophets), the bird, your soul, will be distressed in its cage.

(II:1446) *gav-i nafs-i khwish ra zutar bikush   ta shavad ruh-i khafi zinda u bih hush*

Kill most quickly the <u>cow, your fleshly soul</u>, so that the hidden spirit may become alive and conscious.

(III:391) *bardarid an gusfandan ra bih khashm   kay zih <u>chupan-i khirad</u> bastand chashm*

In wrath he tore to pieces those sheep which shut their eyes to the <u>shepherd, Wisdom</u>.

SUBSTITUTING A HYPHEN FOR A POSSESSIVE

In addition, there were other cases where the translator replaced the possessive between the two components of a metaphorical phrase with syntactically related nouns connected with a hyphen:

(I:1352) *<u>nafs-i khargushat</u> bih sahra dar chara   tu bih ghaʿr-i in chah-i chun u chira*

Thy <u>hare-soul</u> is feeding in the desert, (whilst) thou art (lying) at the bottom of this well of How? and Why?

(II:3706) *<u>murgh-i janha</u> ra darin akhar zaman   nistashan az hamdigar yik dam aman*

In these latter days the <u>soul-birds</u> have no security from each other for a moment.

(III:3978) *zan sabab janash vatan did u qarar   andarin <u>surakh-i dunya</u> mushvar*

On that account his spirit, mouse-like, deemed its home and abode to be in this <u>world-hole</u>.

Prepositions Other than 'Of'

In some cases it was observed that the preposition 'of' has been replaced with other prepositions such as 'to', 'with', 'for', 'in', 'over' in connecting the two components of a metaphorical phrase.

– To

(1:303) *hiss-i dunya nardiban-i in jahan   hiss-i dini nardiban-i asiman*

The worldly sense is the ladder to this world; the religious sense is the ladder to Heaven.

– With

(1:1109) *ta chih ʿalamha'st dar sawda-yi ʿaql   ta chih ba pahna'st in darya-yi ʿaql*

Think, what worlds are in commerce with Reason! How wide is this ocean of Reason!

– For

(1:1816) *gah tanaquz gah naz u gah niyaz   gah sawda-yi haqiqat gah majaz*

Now self-contradiction, now disdain, now supplication, now passion for reality, now metaphor (unreality).

– In

(1:1366) *quwwatam bakhshid u dil ra nur dad   nur-i dil mar dast u pa ra zur dad*

He (God) bestowed power on me and gave light to my heart: the light in my heart gave strength to hand and foot.

– Over

(1:1678) *sahib-i dih padishah-i jismha'st   sahib-i dil shah-i dilha-yi shuma'st*

He that owns a village is king over bodies; he that owns a heart is king over your hearts.

USE OF IDIOSYNCRATIC EQUIVALENTS

While reviewing the 'phrase to word' pattern, perhaps due to lack of a proper equivalent or perhaps because a good idiosyncratic equivalent term already existed in English for the phrasal form, we can see how the translator uses a single word to bear the whole meaning of the metaphorical phrase, as in the example below where 'people of the pen' is rendered as 'secretaries':

(I:3152) *mushrif u ahl-i qalam bar dast-i rast   zank ʿilm-i khatt u thabt in dast ra'st*

On the right hand are the chancellor and the secretaries, because the science of writing and book-keeping belongs (in practice) to this hand.

AN UNUSUAL PATTERN

In relation to 'the phrase to sentence pattern', one exceptional instance should be mentioned. In this case, the concept and notion of the metaphor has been kept intact, but the exact format has undergone significant syntactic alteration:

(III:1943) *an-kih dar fatwa imam-i khalq bud   gu-yi taqwa az firishta mirubud*

That one who in giving legal judgments was the Imam of the people and in piety bore away the ball from the angels.

CONCLUSIONS

The main conclusion of our syntactical analysis has been to demonstrate that the dominant, and – percentage-wise – greatest tendency of Nicholson in his translation of the *Mathnawi*'s metaphorical phrases was towards employment of the 'phrase to phrase' pattern. This pattern somehow seemed better suited to the literal, 'word for word' style of translation that Nicholson favoured. One might thus posit that this pattern probably comprises the most accurate method of translation of a concept from source to target language.

However, due to the lack of good equivalent terms or the translator's failure to find the proper equivalents for metaphorical phrases in the target language, in a few cases, the translator did occasionally incline to use the two other models, that is, the 'phrase to word pattern' and the 'phrase to sentence pattern' in conformity with the subtleties of English idiom and usage which sound right to the English ear.

Nicholson resorted to the phrase to phrase style of translation because it would seem that the accurate rendition of the source text in English was best fulfilled thereby; in other words loyalty to the source text is preserved above all through this pattern, although in the process the original beauty of the text may be diminished. This kind of translation has been in general much recommended for translation of sacred scriptures from one language to another – and who would deny that the *Mathnawi* belongs to that genre?

BIBLIOGRAPHY

Abrams, M. H. *A Glossary of Literary Terms*. Boston: Earl McPeek, 1999.

Adams, Hazard. *The Interests of Criticism*. New York: Harcourt Brace and World Inc., 1998.

Baker, Mona. *In Other Words: A Course Book on Translation*. London: Routledge, 1992.

Berry, M. *Introduction to Systemic Linguistics*. London: Batsford, 1977.

Brannigan, John. *New Historicism and Cultural Materialism*. London: Macmillan Press, 1991.

Brower, R. *On Translation*. Oxford: OUP, 1966.

Catford, J. C. *A Linguistic Theory of Translation*. Oxford: OUP, 1965.

Chao, Yuen Ren. *A Grammar of Spoken Chinese*. San Francisco: University of California Press, 1968.

Cook, G. *Discourse*. Oxford: OUP, 1989.

Dagut, M. 'Can Metaphor Be Translated?' In *Babel: International Journal of Translation*, XXII (1), 1973, pp. 21–33.

Garravittta, Petter. *Italian Theory and Criticism-Twentieth Century*. Baltimore, Maryland: Johns Hopkins' University Press, 1973.

Ghorashi, M. *Translating Children's Literature, Problems and Solutions*. Tehran: Intisharat-i Sanam, 1385 A.Hsh./2006.

Giles, D. *Basic Concepts and Models for Interpreter and Translator Training*. Amsterdam: John Benjamins Publishing, 1995.

Halliday, M. A. K., & R. Hasan. *Cohesion in English*. London: Longman 1997.

Hoey, M. *Patterns of Lexis in Text*. Oxford: OUP, 1991.

Ilyas, A. *Theories of Translation: Theoretical Issues and Practical Implications*. Mosul: University of Mosul, 1989.

Lakoff, G. and M. Johnson. *Metaphors We Live By*. Chicago: University of Chicago Press, 2003.

Larson, Mildred L. *Meaning-Based Translation*. New York/London: University Press of America, 1984.

Mandelblit, N. *The Cognitive View of Metaphor and Its Implications for Translation Theory*. Maastricht: Universitaire Press, 1995.

McCarthy, M. *Discourse Analysis for Language Teachers*. Cambridge: Cambridge University Press, 1993.

Mulla-nazar, H. *Principles and Methodology of Translation*. Tehran: SAMT, 2001.

Newmark, P. *Approaches to Translation*. Oxford: Pergamon Press, 1982.

—. *A Textbook of Translation*. London: Prentice Hall, 1988.

Nida, E. *On Translation*. Beijing, China: Translation Publishing Corp., 1984.

—. *Towards a Science of Translating*. Leiden: Brill, 1964.

Nunan, D. *Discourse Analysis*. London: Penguin Group, 1993.

Rumi, Jalal al-Din. *Mathnawi-yi ma'nawi*. Ed. R.A. Nicholson. Tehran: Karavan, 1995.

—. *The Mathnawi of Jalálu'ddín Rúmi*, edited from the oldest manuscripts available with critical notes, translation, and commentary by Reynold A. Nicholson. London: Luzac, 1925–1940. 8 vols.

Snell-Hornby, Mary. *Translation Studies*. Amsterdam: John Benjamins Publishing Co., 1998.

Book Reviews

Alberto Fabio Ambrosio, *Vie d'un derviche Tourneur: Doctrine et rituels du soufisme au XVIIe siècle*. Paris: CNRS Editions 2010. 418 pages, 29 €.

Reviewed by Nayla Tabbara

Published in Paris by the Centre of National Scientific Research (CNRS) this book renders a vivid and detailed portrayal of the ideal of the Sufi dervish in the sixteenth- and seventeenth-century Ottoman world, vis-à-vis other ideals, namely those of the men of political power, the Islamic religious scholars (ʿulama), the preachers (vaʿiz) and the pseudo-Sufis.

The book also focuses on the Mevlevi practice of *Samaʿ*, especially as seen through the writings of Ismaʿil Ankaravi (d. 1041/1631), a Mevlevi Sufi master. Yet the author's methodology is quite unconventional, combining two methods of interpreting the reality of the Sufi experience, namely study of the historical and socio-political context on the one hand, and the phenomenological approach on the other. The mixture of methodologies makes this book an important contribution both to the study of Sufism and of the underlying societal power dynamics of the early, pre-modern Ottoman world.

So as to guide the reader to understand the ethos of the Mevlevi Sufi way the author offers an analysis on the various political dynamics operating in the history of the period. For instance, he describes the sociological and political issues at stake in the sixteenth and seventeenth centuries in Ottoman lands. This was a time of instability for the Ottoman Empire on the economic level (a monetary and land ownership crisis), political level (a succession of depositions of sultans, internal revolts and tensions on both the eastern and north-western borders of the empire) and social level where the traditional Muslim scholars (ʿulama) point their finger at religious innovations as being the hidden cause behind the instability. If the coffee houses, which are seen as a cause of social agitation, are closed, most of the blame will be placed on the shoulders of Sufis, for they are seen as the innovators *par excellence*. This blame then influences various political decisions made by the state, whereas until then the Sufis and the sultans had maintained a harmonious relationship.

The anti-Sufi polemics thus begin in the Ottoman world in the sixteenth century, a polemical debate that is played out on both the socio-political and the theological levels. The author's approach allows the reader to understand that things are never black and white, but that alongside decapitations of some Sufi shaykhs, one finds examples of official celebrations where Sufis' attendance is a central part of the ceremony and required protocol. On the more theoretical level, the author grants the reader a full overview of the debates between the Sufis and their formalist opponents and a summary of anti-Sufi writings that stirred this debate. By the middle of the seventeenth century, those debates become transformed into a matter of opposing ideological positions. Here, *fatwa*s issued by rigorist ʿ*ulama* will prohibit the entering of Sufi *tekke*s, followed by other *fatwa*s declaring the illegality of *Sama*ʿ. Although the State did not interfere earlier in these debates, at this point official edicts are issued for the demolition of *tekke*s, and in 1666 a decree (*firman*) prohibiting *Sama*ʿ and calling for the demolition of *tekke*s is officially promulgated.

However, this does not stop Sufism from spreading, and indeed remaining a strong voice in the empire. In fact, it is in this context that the writings of Ankaravi will appear. The anti-Sufi polemics of the period provide, as the author explains, a good chance for Sufis to write defences of their practices and to reflect more deeply on their ultimate meaning and purpose. This in turn will help Sufi *tekke*s find a more meaningful social framework for their adherents, as the *firman* for the demolition of *tekke*s will be revoked a few decades later. In Ankaravi's writings, especially *Minhacuʾl-fukara* and *Huccetuʾl-sema*, which are both analysed in depth, he explains the meaning of the values, practices, terminology and symbols of the Sufis. In the midst of these political crises and in the face of the general religious instability, Ankaravi seems to have chosen a middle way which was rooted in his spiritual commitment to Mevlevi Sufism and the strength of its symbolic language, for that symbolic language was tolerated by the popular preachers, the ʿ*ulama* and the state.

Yet the central importance of Ambrosio's work lies in the fact that it explains, between the lines, why Sufism was really attacked. Here the author, after presenting the history of *Samaᶜ*, a review of all the various texts written for and against it, its high historical moments, and its 'hermeneutics' linking geometry, cosmology and anthropology, puts forward his own original conclusion: that the struggle between the Sufis and anti-Sufi formalist *ᶜulama* must not be comprehended within the framework of societal power dynamics, but more on the level of symbols. It is a struggle between two different definitions of man. On the one hand, the definition advanced by the *ᶜulama*, of a man exoterically in obedience to the literal letter of both the divine law and the law of sultans and the *ᶜulama*, a man who is living in a world of multiplicity, and on the other hand, the definition presented by the Mevlevi Sufis of a man who understands the spirit of divine law esoterically, while putting it into practice by means of brotherhood and compassion in the Sufi way, thus reaching a unity with all creation. It is this ideal of the Sufi, this definition of man, portrayed in the image of the whirling dervish who, in his ecstasy, sees the unity of all through the light of God, sees the face of God in all there is, and becomes himself the locus of that unity, that the anti-Sufis tried to eliminate, yet without success.

İstanbul Mevlevihaneleri/Mawlawi Lodges of Istanbul, ed. Alper Çeker, Araştırma Yayınları Serisi VII (Istanbul: İstanbul Büyükşehir Belediyesi, Kultur A. Ş. Yayınları 2010). 359 pp.[1]

Reviewed by Roderick Grierson

The dust-cover of this glamorous and occasionally gorgeous new album of photographs announces an optimistic programme:

Elinizdeki eser günümüzde yeniden restore edilen bu mevlevihanelerin kültür tarihini konu alan eşsiz bir çalışmadır. (The work that you are holding is an unrivalled study focusing upon the cultural history of these Mevlevihanes, which are being restored again in our own day.)

However, a truncated and therefore slightly different version is given in the English translation that appears on the dust cover beneath the Turkish: 'This book is an excelent [sic] study about the history of these Mawlawi Lodges.' The original Turkish might have clarified the intentions of the editor and publisher in a way that foreign readers would have found helpful, especially if they had assumed that a book about Mevlevihanes would largely concern the past. The present book, or at least the photographs that provide its most attractive feature, are largely concerned with the present or even with the future, suggesting an enthusiasm for restored premises, new cultural centres, and foreign visitors.

Although the dust cover bears the title *Mawlawi Lodges of Istanbul,* the cover itself and the title page display the words *İstanbul's Mawlawi Lodges.* This may seem a punctilious and even trivial observation, but it is not the only sense in which the dust cover seems to belong to a rather different book. The name Handan Dizdarzade, which appears on the dust cover and is often cited by booksellers as the author, is not mentioned anywhere else, even when 'the author' is cited in the text. Futhermore, the style of the dust cover is completely unlike the design of the book itself. On a rich and sombre background of blue

1 Although the book is selling in Istanbul for prices between 100 TL and 120 TL, it can also be found at a substantial discount in İstanbul Kitapçısı on İstiklal Caddesi and in several other bookshops in the vicinity. For readers who do not live in Turkey, copies can be found online at a current price of €70.

and black, the designer has placed one of the most famous archival photographs depicting a group of Mevlevi, all of whom adopt the formal and indeed rigid poses required by the technology of the day: three *semazen*s, two *neyzen*s, a *kanuncu*, and a *hafiz* or *Mesnevihan*. The package suggests a study filled with antiquarian detail, and indeed the book is announced as the seventh in a series of research publications issued under the auspices of the Municipality of Istanbul and with the guidance of acknowledged authorities such as İskender Pala. While the text does contain historical material that is not readily available in English, its main attraction is almost purely visual: a large number of recent photographs by Halit Ömer Camcı that are colourful and dramatic, often impressive, and sometimes beautiful, even if they are occasionally overwhelmed by the opulence of the book itself.

Camcı works in a style very different from Shems Friedlander, the photographer most admired in the West for the portraits of Mevlevi that he produced over thirty years ago. Camcı's plates are not only in colour, rather than black and white, he has also made less attempt to create a series of contemplative and apparently timeless images by eliminating quotidian distractions. Instead, many of his photographs offer an accurate and revealing depiction of modern Turkey, with its new concrete constructions, automobiles, national flags, and perform-ances of *sema* for tourists who gather in outdoor venues as well as Mevlevihanes.

While Camcı's photographs are indeed very interesting, some of them appear with disconcerting frequency. The most familiar is printed on pages 14, 41, 51, 59, and across pages 318 and 319, and is included again among a selection on the endpapers, both front and back. There are almost no captions, however, which is likely to be frustrating for readers who are not already familiar with the locations. The impact of the photographs is also diminished, at least to some extent, by an exuberant design. Almost every page is decorated with elaborate borders and a miniature version of the famous drawing by Ingrid Schaar that has acquired iconic status in recent years as the archetypal 'whirling dervish'. By standards elsewhere, in fact, the book may be thought overdesigned. Footnotes for one language are printed in black, for another language in blue. The most vexing display is the Table of Contents, which is given the English title 'Contains' and is printed in gold, blue, grey, and white on black and in a font so compressed as to be almost illegible.

The text of the book is divided into two parts. The first offers an introduction to the origins of Mevlevi culture, including sections about Rumi's family, companions such as Shams-i Tabrizi, Selahaddin Zerkoubi, and Husameddin Çelebi, literary works, the rise of the Mevlevi Order, the process of initiation, the contribution of Mevlevi Sufis to various arts, and the significance of the order during the Ottoman Empire. The second part consists of six sections on Mevlevihanes in Istanbul – Galata, Yenikapı,.Kasımpaşa, Beşiktaş, Bahariye, and Üsküdar – with a marked emphasis on famous individuals associated with them.

These latter sections in particular contain fascinating information about shaykhs and their followers or companions at the various Mevlevihanes in Istanbul, most of which is likely to be of considerable interest to any readers of the *Mawlana Rumi Review* who do not know Turkish and who may not have heard of them elsewhere. While Konya is usually admired as the great centre of Mevlevi culture, for obvious reasons, its reputation is not diminished if readers are reminded that Istanbul acquired an enormous significance for the Mevlevi Order after it was captured by Mehmet II in 1453. As the sultan, the court, and the central bureaucracy of the empire were all located in the imperial capital, it could not have been otherwise. By emphasizing the importance of Istanbul and the Mevlevi Sufis who lived and worked there, and by discussing them as part of Ottoman society as a whole, the book offers a valuable corrective to a more romantic view of the order as simply a band of mystics contemplating the infinite and writing poetry in comfortable detachment from the hard facts of life.

Foreign readers, particularly those of a mystical inclination, may find some of the passages curiously nationalistic, and indeed militaristic, especially when attention is drawn to Mevlevi attitudes to war and to what is presented as the treachery of Ottoman subjects during the Balkan campaigns of 1912 and 1913. One might well agree that this more recent history should be a topic of greater interest than it often is to those of us who read Rumi's poetry in the West. Nevertheless, the question that most of us are likely to want explained in a book on Mevlevihanes in Istanbul is not so much the legacy of wars that began in 1912, 1913, or even 1914, as exactly what happened to the Mevlevihanes themselves after 1925. Why was so much damage caused, often by those who were supposedly responsible for them, that restoration or even total reconstruction would become necessary? This tragedy is passed over as if it were a matter of little consequence, or at least of little interest. While such an approach has been common enough in Turkish publications, and it would be unfair to expect the present book by itself to display an unusual or perhaps unique degree of candour, nevertheless the question is likely to become increasingly difficult to ignore.

As a general comment, it might be suggested to Turkish publishers that preparing a book for Turkish readers and then adding an English translation does not necessarily produce a result that is accessible to the foreigners who will try to read it. Their expectations may be very different from those of Turkish readers. On the other hand, the book does offer an excellent opportunity for foreign readers to understand something of the way in which official Turkish circles see the Mevlevi Order and write about the Mevlevi Order. I hasten to add that this is not intended as a cynical remark. The interest of various levels of government in the legacy of the Mevlevi is to be applauded. I agree with the comments made by the mayor of Istanbul in his introduction, and I find them encouraging. The interest of the state is obviously appropriate in historical terms, given the close relations that existed between the Ottoman state and the Mevlevi Order, and the patronage of the state is obviously essential now if Mevlevi culture is to be revived. The devastation of 1925 and later years was the consequence of state decree, and only the state today possesses the authority and the resources to restore and rebuild the Mevlevihanes that have been lost.

The text of the book contains a large number of spelling or type-setting errors. The former are not confined to English, although they are undoubtedly more numerous in English.[2] Even where the text is relatively intact, there are words or passages that can only be understood by referring to the original Turkish.[3] At times, the syntax is only barely recognizable as English:

---

2 A single example from p. 165 will suggest how serious the combination of faulty translation and typesetting can be: 'to practice rites in Mawlawihanes". f For start, irstly they busted occupied Jarrahi takkas and expelled the dervishes thereo.f.'

3 On p. 253, for example, 'MountBlack' is evidently a literal translation of the Turkish *Karadağ*. In English, the recognized form is Montenegro. On p. 323, Neyzen Yusuf Paşa is said in the English version to have held the position of chief of the 'harmonica' forces in the Ottoman military. Fortunately, the translator included the Turkish word *mızıka*, which refers to a military band rather than to a harmonica, but a reader who knew only English would by definition be unlikely to know this.

Legend has it that children at speaking age but could not speak and walking age but could not walk, pass through the rosary they would be able to walk and/or talk immediately.

In some passages, even the Turkish is flawed. In the following clause, which appears on page 151, the first word should obviously be *İşsiz*.

İxxiz kalacakları kaygısıyla matbaa kurulmasını istemeyen hattatlar . . .

There is no index and no bibliography. There are no plans or elevations of the Mevlevihanes. Aside from these problems, the information presented in the English version is at times misleading or simply mistaken. On page 5, for example, in the introduction written by the mayor of Istanbul, the Turkish text refers to the planned restoration of the Bahariye Mevlevihane. The English translation incorrectly states that the restoration has already been completed:

> however, a short time earlier, as part of the projects carried out in association with İstanbul's position as the European Cultural Capital 2010, the Bahariye Mawlawi lodge has been restored and brought back to our city.

On page 66, the English translation incorrectly informs the reader that Ulu Arif Çelebi wrote the *Manaqib al-ʿarifin*. The Turkish original employs the causative participle *yazdıran*, and correctly states that Ulu Arif Çelebi told Aflaki to write the book. The translator has misconstrued the Turkish syntax and produced the following:

> Ulu Aarif was a connoisseur of music. His major literary work is Manaqib'ul Aarifin (The Story of the Sages), where he writes about the lives of some of Mawlana's contemporaries and some others, including the famous astronomer of his own time Shemseddin Ahmad Aflaki.

In addition, little attempt has been made to transcribe Turkish names in a consistent manner, a casual approach that becomes especially obvious in the large number of capitalized subheadings. Although VACİD is rendered as WAJID, for example, KÜÇÜK is simply

KUCUK. For ÇELEBİ, one finds both CHALABI and CELEBI. Similar infelicities could be multiplied almost indefinitely.

The book is therefore not entirely reliable if one is relying solely upon the English text. Furthermore, if one can read Turkish, the information that it contains is readily available, and in greater detail, elsewhere. Nevertheless, there are many things to admire in the book, and the difficulties that affect so many publications produced in Turkey at the moment should not detract from them. There is a real need, it seems to me, for books that contain reliable accounts of Turkish historical subjects, with accurate English translations, and with attractive and relevant illustrations. In other words, one looks forward to seeing Turkish scholarship presented under sound editorial direction to as wide a readership a possible. The history of the Mevlevi Sufi Order in Istanbul, and throughout the Ottoman Empire, is a very different history than one will find in most accounts of Rumi, Shams, and the early decades at Konya. Few scholars elsewhere possess the knowledge of it that Turkish specialists do, and their expertise would be a real contribution to our understanding of the inspiration that has Rumi provided across so many centuries.

Due to the almost complete absence of archival photographs, much of the book consists of illustrations of *sema* held at the Galata Mevlevihane. It can be confusing to read pages about one Mevlevihane, and find oneself gazing in the same chapter at photographs of another. On occasion, the effect is of two distinct books whose pages have somehow been shuffled together. It is also noticeable that the photographs in this book are largely concerned with performance. The impression is that Mevlevilik can be reduced to *sema*, and especially to *sema* for tourists, as if public performance were enough to restore a way of life that has vanished, or almost vanished. So much has been lost, however, and while it is important not to be discouraged, it is also important not to underestimate the scale of the task. Most educated Turks cannot understand a Mevlevi poem written in Turkish during the late nineteenth or early twentieth century, when their parents or grandparents were alive, even if it is transcribed into Latin characters. The words themselves also need to be translated into a more recent form of Turkish with which they are familiar. The substantial amount of Mevlevi poetry written in Persian presents an even greater challenge. While it can therefore be very difficult for foreigners to understand the extent of the dislocation that has occurred in Turkey over the past eight decades, it may also be difficult for many Turks to recognize how much has been lost and to fully appreciate the effort that will be needed to recover even a portion of it. Nevertheless, *İstanbul Mevlevihaneleri* is a valuable record of a particular moment in an attempt to do precisely that. It is therefore difficult not to feel inspired by it, and not to admire it.

The book also suggests that we have entered a new era. No longer do official publications take such obvious pride in what used to be seen as a progressive decision to close the *tekke*s in 1925. Instead, the emphasis is on renewal and indeed on continuity. This is true of other recent books as well, in which a figure such as Abdülbaki Gölpınarlı is presented not simply as a scholar, as he would have been only a few years ago, but as a Mevlevi shaykh standing in a chain of initiatic succession (*silsila*) and with his own *khalifa*. We are still in the early stages of this process. It will be fascinating to see how it develops.

Notes on Contributors

REZA ABBASI graduated with a B.A. in English Translation Studies from Allamah Tabataba'i University, Tehran, and obtained his M.A. in the same major from Islamic Azad University, Tehran. He worked on the literary translation of Rumi's *Mathnawi* by R. A. Nicholson for his M.A. thesis and is currently working on similar projects. He teaches English translation courses at the University of Applied Sciences in Tehran.

MEHDI AMINRAZAVI was born in the city of Mashhad, Iran. He came to the US in 1975 where he attended the University of Washington in Seattle. Having earned his Bachelors degree in Urban Planning and Philosophy and his Masters degree in Philosophy, he continued his graduate work at Temple University in Philadelphia where he received a further Masters degree in Comparative Religion and a Doctorate in Philosophy of Religion. Prof. Aminrazavi's areas of specialization are Islamic Studies, Islamic philosophy and theology, Philosophy of Religion and non-Western philosophical and religious thought. Mehdi Aminrazavi has published eight books and numerous articles. His books include: *Suhrawardi and the School of Illumination* (1996); *The Wine of Wisdom: The Life, Poetry and Philosophy of Omar Khayyam* (2006) and *An Anthology of Philosophy in Persia*, co-edited with S. H. Nasr, three out of five volumes of which have appeared (1999–). He is currently Professor of Philosophy and Religion and the Co-Director of the Leidecker Center for Asian Studies and Director of the Middle Eastern Studies program at the University of Mary Washington in Virginia.

BEHROOZ MAHMOODI BAKHTIARI graduated with a Ph.D. in Linguistics from Allamah Tabataba'i University in Tehran. He is presently Associate Professor of Linguistics and Persian at the University of Tehran and a member of the Faculty of Fine Arts there, where he has taught several courses on Persian language and linguistics. His major fields of interest are teaching Persian as a foreign language, literary translation (with an emphasis on the translation of Persian mythical texts), and discourse analysis of dramatic texts. His published books include *Farsi Biyamuzim* (11 Volumes, 2001), *Tense in Persian* (2002), and *Studies on the Typology of the Iranian Languages* (forthcoming).

WILLIAM C. CHITTICK is a professor in the Department of Comparative Studies at the State University of New York, Stony Brook. Among his publications are *The Sufi Path of Love: The Spiritual Teachings of Rumi* (1983), *The Psalms of Islam* (1988), *The Self-Disclosure of God: Principles of Ibn al-ʿArabi's Cosmology* (1998), *Sufism: A Short Introduction* (2000), *The Heart of Islamic Philosophy: The Quest for Self-Knowledge in the Teachings of Afdal al-Din Kashani* (2001), *The Sufi Doctrine of Rumi: Illustrated Edition* (2005), as well as a translation of Shams al-Din Tabrizi, *Me and Rumi: The Autobiography of Shams-i Tabrizi* (2004). Professor Chittick is one the world's leading translators and interpreters of the mystical poetry of Jalal al-Din Rumi, and a leading authority on the theosophical writings of the Sufi thinker Ibn ʿArabi.

JOHN DECHANT is a graduate student at the Department of Near Eastern Languages and Culture at Indiana University, where he is also pursuing minors in Central Eurasian Studies and Religious Studies. He previously earned a B.A. in History from the State University of New York at Geneseo and an M.A. in Middle Eastern Studies from the University of Chicago. His interests include Sufism, hagiographic literature and saints' cults, Islamization, popular Islam, and Islamic art and architecture, all particularly in the greater Persianate world. Currently he is conducting research for his Ph.D. dissertation, a study of the prominent Khurasanian Sufi family descended from Shaykh Ahmad-i Jam (d. 1141), with an emphasis on the figure of Zayn al-Din-i Taybadi (d. 1389), a non-familial Uvaysi-style disciple of Shaykh Ahmad.

ADEM ESEN graduated in 1984 with a B.A. from the Faculty of Political Sciences at Istanbul University and from the Faculty of Divinity at Marmara University in Istanbul. He studied Arabic at King Saud University in Riyadh, Saudi Arabia, and English at the University of Exeter in England. He later earned an M.A. and a Ph.D. from the Faculty of Economics at Istanbul University. He was Assistant Professor in the Faculty of Law and Associate Professor in the Faculty of Economics and Administrative Sciences at Cumhuriyet University in Sivas, where he also served as

Chairman of the Department of Economics. In 1999, he was elected mayor of the Selçuklu municipality in Konya, whose population of 500,000 makes it one of the largest municipalities in the city. He has also served as a member of the Turkish delegation to the Congress of Local and Regional Authorities at the Council of Europe, and as a member of the Union of Turkish Municipalities. In addition to holding the rank of Professor in the Faculty of Economics and Administrative Sciences at Selçuk University in Konya, where he was appointed Chairman of the Department of Economics and the Centre of Regional Development Application and Research, Prof. Dr Esen is also the founding Rector of Sabahattin Zaim University in Istanbul. Among Prof. Esen's works may be mentioned notably *Mevlana Celaleddin Rumi'nin İktisat Anlayışı* (Mawlana Jalal al-Din Rumi's Understanding of Economics), published at Konya in 2007.

BADIᶜ AL-ZAMAN FURUZANFAR (1903–1970), a professor of Persian literature at the University of Tehran, was the most eminent scholar in the field of Rumi Studies during the last century in Iran. Trained in Persian and Arabic literature, he published twenty-one books and forty-nine articles in Persian, not to mention many poems. His contribution to Rumi Studies in Iran was simply phenomenal. Aside from producing the definitive critical edition of Rumi's *Divan-i Shams* in ten volumes (Tehran 1957–68 with many printings), he also edited and published the first critical text in Persian of Rumi's *Discourses* (*Fihi ma fihi*, Tehran 1951). He published critical editions of the *Discourses* of Baha al-Din Valad (Rumi's father) in two volumes: *Maᶜarif-i Baha Valad* (Tehran 1959), and the *Discourses* of Burhan al-Din Muhaqqiq Tirmidhi (Rumi's first teacher), *Maᶜarif-i Burhan al-Din Muhaqqiq Tirmidhi* (Tehran 1961) in Persian. Prof. Furuzanfar also wrote a book on the sources of the tales, parables, adages and maxims in Rumi's *Mathnawi* (*Ma'khadh-i qasas va tamthilat-i Mathnawi*, Tehran 1954), an annotated bibliography of all the prophetic traditions mentioned in the *Mathnawi* (*Ahadith-i Mathnawi*, Tehran 1955), and the first modern, scholarly biography of Rumi (*Risala dar tahqiq-i awhal va zindiqani-yi Mawlana Jalal al-Din Muhammad*, Tehran 1936), which has served as the cornerstone for several other biographies both in Persian and English. He also composed a commentary on the *Mathnawi,* of which three volumes were completed (covering up to verse 3012 of *daftar* 1) before his death. Prof. Furuzanfar's article presented in this volume of *Mawlana Rumi Review* is the first English translation of his work into English.

RODERICK GRIERSON is currently Menteşezade Research Fellow at the Rumi Institute, Near East University, Nicosia, Cyprus. He was trained in Syriac, Armenian, and Greek at the Oriental Institute, University of Oxford, and after completing the organization of *African Zion: The Sacred Art of Ethiopia*, which opened at The Walters Art Gallery in Baltimore in 1993 with a catalogue of the same title published by Yale University Press, he became a fellow of the DuBois Institute for African and African American Research at Harvard University. He has recently edited and written an introduction to *Deviant Histories: New Perspectives on Turkish Sufism*, a translation of Ahmed Yaşar Ocak's *Türk Sufîliğine Bakışlar*, which has been published by New East University Press. He has also edited and prepared an introduction and bibliography for a revised version of *The City of the Heart*, the first translation into English of the complete text of Yunus Emre's *Divan* according to the edition published in 1961 by Abdülbâki Gölpınarlı, and written a new introduction for a second printing of *The Scholar and the Saint: Studies in Commemoration of Abu'l-Rayhan al-Biruni and Jalal al-Din al-Rumi*. In 2009, he delivered the Süha Faiz Memorial Lectures, which will be published as *The Road to the City of the Heart*. Forthcoming publications in 2011 will also include *Mehmed Fuad Köprülü and the Shamanist Legacy in Turkish Sufism* and the exhibition catalogue: *See What Love Has Done: 175 Years of Printed Books on Yunus Emre*.

ROKUS DE GROOT is a musicologist and composer who specializes in the music of the twentieth and twenty-first centuries, focusing on the systematics and aesthetics of composition, the interaction between different cultural traditions and reconceptualizations of past and present religious ideas in music. Another subject he deals with is polyphony, with its complementary dimensions of counterpoint and mutual attuning, both as a musical practice and as a mode of thought and action. He obtained his M.A. *cum laude* at the University of Amsterdam and his Ph.D. at the University of Utrecht. Since 2000 he has held the Chair of Musicology at the University of Amsterdam, after occupying his own personal chair in 'Music in the Netherlands since 1600', at the University of Utrecht. His guest professorships include those at the American University, Cairo (2009) and Universad Nacional Autónoma de México (1992, 2003). Among his publications may be mentioned his edited collection (with Albert van der Schoot): *Redefining Musical Identities: Reorientations at the Waning of Modernism* (Zwolle 2007); 'Edward Said and Polyphony', in A. Iskandar and H. Rustom (eds.), *Edward Said: A Legacy of Emancipation and Representation* (Berkeley 2010); and 'Music, Religion and Power: Qawwali as Empowering Disempowerment', in M.B. ter Borg and J.W. van Henten (eds.), *Powers, Religion as a Social and Spiritual Force* (New York 2010). He also composes for musical theatre in which singers, musicians and dancers from different traditions cooperate in mutual learning, such as *Song of Songs: The Love of Mirabai* (New Delhi 2005), *Layla and Majnun: A Composition about the Night* (Amsterdam 2006, with texts by Rumi, Nizami and San Juan de la Cruz). Among his compositions on Rumi texts is *Bee bade mast! Drunk without wine!* for a 12-part choir (Amsterdam 2009).

FRANKLIN LEWIS is Associate Professor of Persian in the Department of Near Eastern Languages and Civilizations at the University of Chicago. From 1997 to 2005, Lewis was Assistant, and then Associate Professor of Persian in the Department of Middle Eastern and South Asian Studies at Emory University in Atlanta, Georgia, where he taught Persian language and the literatures and cinemas of the Middle East. His translations from modern Persian literature include *In a Voice of Their Own: A Collection of Stories by Iranian Women written since the Revolution of 1979* (1996). Lewis is also the founder and moderator of *Adabiyat,* an international electronic discussion forum for Persian, Turkish, Arabic and Urdu literature, a book review editor for the *International Journal of Middle East Studies,* and President of the American Institute of Iranian Studies. With Heshmat Moayyad, he has translated and annotated a hagiographical account of a popular Sufi saint of twelfth-century Khurasan, *The Colossal Elephant and His Spiritual Feats: Shaykh Ahmad-e Jām* (2004). In 2001, his book *Rumi: Past and Present, East and West* (2000) received the British-Kuwaiti award for the best work published in the UK in the field of Middle Eastern Studies. His book of literary translations of Rumi's poetry called *Rumi: Swallowing the Sun: Poems Translated from Persian* was published in 2008.

LEONARD LEWISOHN is Senior Lecturer in Persian and Iran Heritage Foundation Fellow in Classical Persian and Sufi Literature at the Institute of Arab and Islamic Studies of the University of Exeter in England where he currently teaches Sufism, history of Iran, as well as courses on Persian texts and Persian poetry in translation. He is the author of *Beyond Faith and Infidelity: The Sufi Poetry and Teachings of Mahmud Shabistari* (1995), and the editor of *The Heritage of Sufism* (1999), vol. 1: *The Legacy of Mediæval Persian Sufism,* vol. 2: *Classical Persian Sufism from its Origins to*

Rumi Classical Persian Sufism from its Origins to Rumi, vol. 3 (with David Morgan): *Late Classical Persianate Sufism: the Safavid and Mughal Period –* covering a millennium of Islamic history. He is editor of (with Christopher Shackle) of *The Art of Spiritual Flight: Farid al-Din ʿAttar and the Persian Sufi Tradition* (2006), co-translator with Robert Bly of *The Angels Knocking on the Tavern Door: Thirty Poems of Hafiz* (2008), and editor of *Hafiz and the Religion of Love in Classical Persian Poetry* (2010). He has contributed articles to the *Encyclopedia of Islam, Encyclopædia of Religion, Encyclopædia of Philosophy, Encyclopædia of Love in World Religions, Encyclopædia Iranica, Iran Nameh, Iranian Studies, African Affairs, Islamic Culture, Journal of the Royal Asiatic Society* and the *Temenos Academy Review.*

PAUL LOSENSKY (Ph.D. University of Chicago, 1993) is an Associate Professor in the Department of Central Eurasian Studies and the Department of Comparative Literature at Indiana University, Bloomington, where he teaches Persian language and literature and translation studies. His research focuses on Persian literary historiography, biographical writing, and the Baroque and Fresh-Style poetry of the sixteenth and seventeenth centuries. His publications include *Welcoming Fighāni: Imitation and Poetic Individuality in the Safavid-Mughal Ghazal* (1998), numerous articles on Persian poetry and literary history, and frequent contributions to *Encyclopedia of Islam* and *Encyclopaedia Iranica.* His translation of *Memorial of God's Friends* by Farid al-Din ʿAttar was published by the Paulist Press in the series Classics of Western Spirituality in 2009. He is currently preparing a translation of selections from the poetry of Amir Khusraw with Sunil Sharma for Penguin Press India.

JAWID MOJADDEDI is Associate Professor of Religion at Rutgers University. Since the publication in 2004 of his verse translation, *The Masnavi: Book One,* as an Oxford World's Classics edition, he has been working towards completing the six books of Rumi's *magnum opus,* and has already published a translation of the second book (2007). He received the Lois Roth Prize for the translation of Persian literature into English in 2005 from the American Institute of Iranian Studies in recognition of this work, after the publication of *The Masnavi: Book One.* His translation of Book Three, from which the passage published here is taken, is due to be published in 2012. In addition to his translations, he has also published several other books, which include *The Biographical Tradition in Sufism* (2001), and, as co-editor and co-translator, *Classical Islam: A Sourcebook of*

Religious Literature (2003), the second edition of which is due to be published in 2012. His forthcoming monograph for the Religion Series of Oxford University Press is tentatively entitled *Beyond Dogma: Rumi's Teachings on Friendship with God and Early Sufi Theories.*

RASOUL SORKHABI, Ph.D., a native of Iran, has lived, studied and worked in India, Japan and the USA over the past three decades. A Research Professor in the field of Energy Geoscience at the University of Utah in Salt Lake City, and a lover of Persian poetry since his teen years, he founded the Rumi Poetry Club (www.rumipoetryclub.com) in 2007 (on the occasion of the 800th anniversary of Rumi's birth) to celebrate and promote spiritual poetry (like that of Rumi) as a way of East–West cross-cultural understanding. He has published dozens of articles and book reviews on Rumi's life, Persian Sufism and poetry in various magazines in the US, Europe and Asia. His most recent articles include 'Henry Corbin and the Renaissance of Persian Sufism' in *Interreligious Insight* (vol. 8, no. 3, pp. 26–37, 2010) and 'Why is Rumi Popular in America?' in *Tiferet: Journal of Spiritual Literature* (Winter 2011, pp. 75–81). He can be contacted at rumipoetryclub@earthlink.net

NAYLA TABBARA is Professor of Islamic Studies and Religious Studies at Saint Joseph University in Beirut. She specializes in the Sufi interpretation of the Qur'an. She is co-founder of Adyan, a Lebanese foundation for Interfaith Studies and spiritual solidarity where she directs a department for education on religious diversity and coexistence in schools. Her publications include: (co-editor), *Christianity and Islam in the Context of Contemporary Culture: Perspectives on Interfaith Dialogue from Russia and the Middle-East* (2009), 'Comparisons between Mystical Experiences in Islam, Christianity and the Vedic Traditions' (in French: 'Demeures, Nafs, Chakras: comparaisons entre expériences mystiques chrétienne, musul-mane et védique') in *L'Orient des dieux*. Vol. VII–IX, (2008–2009), 'The word of God in Qur'anic exegesis: from the particular to the universal' (in French: 'La Parole de Dieu dans l'exégèse coranique: du particulier à l'universel') in *Ecritures et Traditions, Diversité des lectures* (ed. Fadi Daou), (2008), and 'L'itinéraire spirituel d'apres les commentaires soufis du Coran' (forthcoming 2011).

 NEAR EAST UNIVERSITY

Near East University (NEU) was founded in Nicosia, North Cyprus in 1988. NEU is a private institute of higher education with 15 faculties, 4 graduate schools and 4 vocational schools, with 17,000 students from 55 countries, and with a teaching staff from 25 different nations. It has attained international status and has become a major higher education institute in the region.

Near East University is accredited to and fully monitored by the Higher Education Council of Turkey. It is a full member of the International Association of Universities (IAU), European Universities Association (EUA) and the Federation of the Universities of the Islamic World (FUIW). Near East University has membership and accreditation to the International Society for Engineering Education (IGIP) and the Joint Commission International (JCI).

Near East University, Near East Boulevard, Nicosia - TRNC Via Mersin 10 TURKEY Tel: +90 223 64 64 Fax: +90 223 64 61 E-mail:info@neu.edu.tr
w w w . n e u . e d u . t r

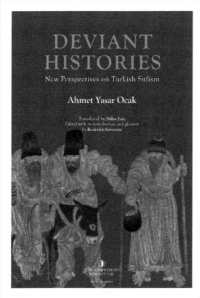

DEVIANT HISTORIES

New Perspectives on Turkish Sufism

Ahmet Yaşar Ocak

Translated by Süha Faiz

Edited with an introduction and glossary by Roderick Grierson

The essays in *Deviant Histories* are a fascinating introduction to the diversity of Sufism among the Turks of Central Asia and Anatolia, but they are also a passionate denunciation of scholarship that Ahmet Yaşar Ocak believes to be deeply flawed. Furthermore, its consequences are not merely academic. The political crises through which Turkey has passed in recent decades, he claims, are the direct result of a failure to understand the significance or even recognize the identity of a mystical heritage that was declared illegal in 1925.

To demonstrate his thesis, Ahmet Yaşar Ocak considers a series of topics of fundamental importance in Turkish cultural history from the twelfth century to the twentieth: Ahmed Yesevi, Mevlana Jalal al-Din Rumi, Yunus Emre, Haji Bektash Veli, the Akhi, and the Alevi and Bektashi traditions.

One of the most remarkable books on the history of Sufism, the original Turkish version entitled *Türkiye'de Tarihin Saptırılması Sürecinde Türk Sûfîliğine Bakışlar* has been reprinted eleven times since its initial publication in 1996 and has never been out of print. For the first time, this classic is now available in English.

'Ahmet Yaşar Ocak, the foremost scholar of Sufi movements in medieval Anatolia . . .' – Karen Barkey, *Empire of Difference*, Cambridge, 2008.

Yakın Doğu Üniversitesi
Rumi Enstitüsü

Near East University
Rumi Institute

Arche
TYPE

www.neu.edu.tr   www.archetypebooks.com

JOURNAL OF
ISLAMIC STUDIES

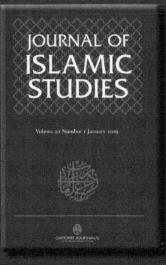

JOURNAL OF
ISLAMIC
STUDIES

Volume 20 Number 1 January 2009

OXFORD JOURNALS

The *Journal of Islamic Studies* is a multi-disciplinary publication dedicated to the scholarly study of all aspects of Islam and of the Islamic world. Particular attention is paid to works dealing with history, geography, political science, economics, anthropology, sociology, law, literature, religion, philosophy, international relations, environmental and developmental issues, as well as ethical questions related to scientific research. The Journal seeks to place Islam and the Islamic tradition as its central focus of academic inquiry and to encourage comprehensive consideration of its many facets; to provide a forum for the study of Islam and Muslim societies in their global context; to encourage interdisciplinary studies of the Islamic world that are crossnational and comparative; to promote the diffusion, exchange and discussion of research findings; and to encourage interaction among academics from various traditions of learning.

For more information check out the *Journal of Islamic Studies* at:

WWW.JIS.OXFORDJOURNALS.ORG

OXFORD JOURNALS
OXFORD UNIVERSITY PRESS

The Middle East in London is a monthly glossy magazine produced by SOAS's London Middle East Institute (LMEI).

Focusing on a different theme each month, *The Middle East in London* covers political, economic, cultural, social and commercial issues related to Middle Eastern Communities in London/UK in addition to providing a comprehensive listing of Middle Eastern events in London and beyond.

Also featuring high-quality photography and artwork, book reviews and profiles, *The Middle East in London* is a leading resource for those interested in the Middle Eastern community in London and London's interaction with the region.

For only £30 (**£20 for students and concessions**), sign up to a year's subscription to *The Middle East in London* at: www.lmei.soas.ac.uk